Chinese Tax Law and International Treaties

Lorenzo Riccardi

Chinese Tax Law and International Treaties

Springer

Lorenzo Riccardi
Bergamo, Italy

ISBN 978-3-319-00274-3 ISBN 978-3-319-00275-0 (eBook)
DOI 10.1007/978-3-319-00275-0
Springer Heidelberg New York Dordrecht London

Library of Congress Control Number: 2013939354

Printed on acid-free paper

Springer is part of Springer Science+Business Media (www.springer.com)

Dedicated to my father
to the colors of his mountains
to the places we traveled together

Contents

Chapter 1
Legislative Background and Tax Reform

The Chinese tax system has recently developed closely to the economic growth of the country. The entry of China into the World Trade Organization (WTO) and the economic boom that has characterized recent years have made clear the necessity of overhauling a regulatory system in order to provide stability in the administration of the country, even in the tax field. The desire of becoming a leader in the Asian region, keeping up with the major world powers, has led China to make numerous amendments to improve the tax system and make it adapt to the rapid expansion of the economy and, at the same time, to attract an increasing number of foreign companies.

As a result, a significant tax system overhaul was achieved on March 16, 2007 with the enactment of the *Enterprise Income Tax Law*, which then came into force on January 1, 2008. The new scheme joined together two systems of corporate income tax that were previously separated, the *Domestic Invested Enterprises* and the *Foreign Invested Enterprises*. The main purpose of the reform was to standardize tax treatments for foreign and local companies, removing privileges for foreign companies and formulating new tax legislation in harmony with Occidental laws.

1.1 Sources of Chinese Tax Law

In China, competent authorities with the power to legislate within the tax field can be listed as in Table 1.1.

1.2 People's Republic of China

The Chinese law system has a hierarchical organization. At the top, there is the *Constitution of the People's Republic of China*, enacted in 1982 and containing the fundamental rights and duties of Chinese citizens and the structure and principles of the government. It states that supreme legislative powers are extended to the

L. Riccardi, *Chinese Tax Law and International Treaties*,

DOI 10.1007/978-3-319-00275-0_1,

Table 1.1 Chinese tax authorities

The *National People's Congress*, which has legislative powers
The *State Council*, which has executive powers
The *People's Congress*, which has legislative powers at local level (provinces, regions, and cities)
The *Ministry of Finance* (MOF) and State Administration of Taxation (SAT), which is responsible for the regulation of financial assets, tax, and currency activities

National People's Congress, which de facto establishes the validity and priority of legal sources, having the last word for enacting and interpreting laws.

1.3 State Council

The State Council is the supreme organ of the executive power controlling ministries and other administrative organizations. It is composed of about 50 members and chaired by the Prime Minister. The National People's Congress delegates most of the legislative powers to the State Council, which promulgates administrative regulations. In addition, these regulations are supplemented with instructions, rules, and precepts in the form of circulars, issued by ministries under the supervision of the State Council. The authorities responsible for fiscal matters are the Ministry of Finance (MOF) and the State Administration of Taxation (SAT).

1.4 Local Tax Bureau

The local Assemblies are authorized to implement local laws and regulations, but these laws and regulations must not be in conflict with the Constitution, laws enacted by National People's Congress, and regulations issued by the State Council.

1.5 Ministry of Finance (MOF) and State Administration of Taxation (SAT)

The State Administration of Taxation (SAT) and Ministry of Finance (MOF) interpret tax laws through the issuance of circulars. The key role in the formulation and coordination of tax policies is played by the SAT, which oversees tax offices' ongoing work at provincial and municipal levels; the MOF provides support to the development of fiscal policies implemented by the SAT. The SAT is put in charge by the State Council of collecting and administrating taxes, which generate revenues for both the central government and local governments. The individual tax offices are responsible for the ordinary resolution of tax matters and for the collection and administration at a local level.

However, the local tax offices must follow the directives of the SAT. For its complexity, the Chinese tax system reflects not only a single national tax law or code but also a system built on several levels that drives individuals and companies' taxation. The MOF and SAT implement, clarify, and supervise the overall tax system by issuing regulations, rulings, and interpretations. In actual fact, laws constituting China's tax code are only general principles, while the mentioned circulars contain detailed provisions regarding tax purposes, taxpayers, and calculation of tax burden. Although circulars do not have the force of law in the sources' hierarchy, those issued by MOF and SAT are guidelines for all taxpayers and courts when addressing tax disputes.

1.6 Tax Classification

See Table 1.2.

1.7 Direct Taxes

Individual Income Tax is governed by the *Individual Income Tax Law* (IITL), which was enacted on January 1, 1994 and amended on June 30, 2011, and related regulations (*Individual Income Tax Implementing Rules—IITIR*) were promulgated on January 28, 1994 and recently amended in July 2011.

1.8 Individual Income Tax

Chinese citizens and foreigners residing in China or having a source of income in the country are subject to taxation (*Individual Income Tax, IIT*) on income earned from employment, self-employment, and other categories of personal income.

The tax liabilities depend on the status of residence in China and on the source of income; salaries and wages are taxed at a rate ranging from 3 % to 45 % in seven brackets.

Table 1.2 Chinese tax categories

a) Direct taxes	*Individual Income Tax* *Company Income Tax*
b) Indirect taxes	*Value Added Tax* *Business Tax* *Consumption Tax*
c) Other taxes	*Stamp Duty* *Deed Tax* *Land VAT* *Real Estate Tax* *Resource Tax, etc.*
d) Customs duties	

1.9 Company Income Tax

The new tax law concerning the Corporate Income Tax (*Enterprise Income Tax Law—EITL*, also known as *Company Income Tax—CIT*), which entered into force on January 1, 2008, was adopted to eliminate the distinction in treatment between local companies and those with foreign participations. A 5-year transition period is guaranteed to those firms that had previously gained advantage from significant tax benefits because the government aims to gradually increase the tax rate by 1–3 % per year until it will reach the new single rate of 25 %.

Taxpayers of the new Company Income Tax are both resident companies for income produced globally (not just within PRC) and nonresident companies that have a permanent establishment in China, limited to the income earned in that territory or effectively connected with it, and nonresident companies without a permanent establishment, limited to the income generated in China in case there is no agreement to avoid double taxation between the countries.

Corporate Income Tax is paid on income from sale of goods, delivery service, and transfer of ownership, as well as on income from dividends, interests, and royalties.

With the reform, the flat tax rate has become 25 % for all companies, dropping to 20 % for small firms (small and thin-profit enterprises) and to a preferential rate of 15 % for firms with high technological investments.

1.10 Indirect Taxes

Turnover taxes can be grouped into three categories:

- Value Added Tax
- Business Tax
- Consumption Tax

1.11 Value Added Tax

The *Provisional Rules on Value Added Tax* were adopted on December 13, 1993 and amended several times till the end of 2008, while the *Provisional Rules on Value-added Tax Implementing Rules* were adopted on December 23, 1993, and amended on October 28, 2011. Deductibility of tangible assets and an introduction of a 3 % VAT single rate for the small-scale taxpayers, which are not required to have the approval of the status of normal taxpayer, were the recent innovations in the area of indirect taxes (small taxpayer).

The VAT is imposed upon entities performing activities such as supply of goods, manufacturing, repair and replacement services, transportation and certain modern services in some regions, and import of goods. The calculation of the VAT is computed by compensation between the VAT paid on purchases (input tax) and on sales (output tax). The relevant period for calculating the VAT is variable and computed by tax authorities according to the amount of tax due. Taxpayers with monthly settlement are required to pay the tax within 15 days after the new month begins.

1.12 Business Tax

Business Tax is levied on services provided by enterprises (not subject to VAT), sales of intangible assets, and real estate transfers in the territory of the People's Republic of China. Business Tax is calculated by multiplying the gross turnover of a single transaction for its tax rate; it is important to remember that costs related to the gross income are deductible only in certain circumstances indicated by MOF (for example, for some forwarding companies under certain conditions).

The rate varies in a range between 3 % and 20 % (the most frequent is 5 %), and the period for the calculation of the tax is variable and is computed by the local tax authorities according to the total tax due. Individuals with monthly settlements are obliged to state and pay the tax within the first 15 days of the following month.

1.13 Consumption Tax

Consumption Tax is paid by producers and importers of certain goods classified by Chinese law as "luxury" or "non-essential," such as alcohol, cosmetics, fireworks jewelry, luxury watches, motorcycles, tobacco, tires, yachts, etc. There are 14 subcategories with different consumption tax rates and different mechanisms for calculating their tax base.

Table 1.3 Other taxes

• *Stamp Duty*: a tax related to contracts, corporate documents, and books
• *Deed Tax*: a tax calculated on the allocation or transfer of ownership rights for land and buildings
• *Land VAT*: a tax calculated on income resulting from allocation or transfer of land use rights, buildings, and associated structures within the Chinese territory
• *Real Estate Tax*: a property or mortgage tax levied on the owner or lender of a property; it is calculated on land value, buildings, and leases
• *Resource Tax*: a tax imposed on entities engaged in an extraction of some mining and natural resources or in a production of salt within the Republic of China

1.14 Other Taxes

See Table 1.3.

1.15 Customs Duties

Customs duties on import/export of goods are calculated on the value of the asset multiplied by the corresponding rate; the value of the property results from the customs declaration. This usually follows a regular check by competent authorities; the single rate is defined from its HS-code (code similar to the INTRASTAT European classification) that identifies the specific product category (Taxable Entities Covered).

1.16 Individual Income Tax Subjects

The National People's Congress enacted the law imposing personal income tax for the first time on September 10, 1980, entering into force on the same day. In the following two decades, there have been numerous amendments made to the original text with the last dated April 25, 2011, when the National People's Congress announced a plan for the amendment of the law subsequently approved on June 30, 2011 and in force since September 1, 2011. The organ carrying out the control and administration of IIT is the State Administration of Taxation, which is also responsible for the collection and distribution of tax revenue, together with local tax offices in provinces and metropolitan cities locally in charge of tax administration. Tax revenue is then divided between the central and local governments.

Individuals regularly residing in China (for family relationships, economic interests, or possession of a home registered under their own name) and those that have spent a period exceeding a year are legally obliged to pay IIT on their income.

An individual is also considered a taxpayer if, despite not having a domicile or being a resident in China for a period exceeding a year, he earns income generated within the Chinese territory. This is its unique IIT tax base.

Regarding the taxable amount of those domiciled and residing in China, the IIT is based on the income globally earned. However, with the approval of the competent tax department, it is usually granted the benefit of paying taxes only on income earned within the Chinese territory to those people living in China for more than a year if they prove they have not been living in China for over 5 years. Once this threshold is passed, the IIT is calculated on the overall income, regardless of their geographical location.

1.17 Company Income Tax Subjects

The new CIT entered into force on January 1, 2008, responding to the demand of an action able to adapt the Wholly Foreign-Owned Enterprises Taxation with Local Firms Taxation. Taxpayers of Company Income Tax are two: resident companies and nonresident companies. The first are established both in China and outside, but their administration and control activities are carried out within the Chinese territory; the latter are companies constituted outside China, whose activities of management and audit are performed outside its boundaries. The resident companies are subject to CIT on income earned inside and outside PRC territory, while the nonresident enterprises pay taxes on income earned either in the territory of the PRC or outside but connected with a permanent establishment located in China.

Eventually, the CIT is collected in the form of withholding tax for nonresidents without a permanent establishment in the country but with a source of income situated therein, as well as for companies having a permanent establishment in China and also generating income not connected with the Chinese territory. All companies subject to the CIT must be registered with the competent tax authorities within 30 days after receiving the business license. The CIT is collected on an annual basis, but the taxpayer on a monthly or quarterly basis must submit periodic financial statements and tax returns to the competent tax office within 15 days by the end of the reporting period as an advance payment of the annual settlement.

Chapter 2
Individual Income Tax Law

The draft amendment of the law concerning personal income tax announced on April 25, 2011 by the National People's Congress was approved on June 30, 2011 and was entered into force on September 1, 2011.

The tax reform has introduced an increase of the monthly standard deduction, an extension of the deadline for paying taxes, and a modification of income brackets and tax rates for employment income.

2.1 Taxation Criteria

Chinese citizens and foreigners residing in China or deriving income in the country are subject to IIT on income earned from employment, self-employment, or other categories of personal income.

The tax liability depends both on the status of residence in China and on the source of income; salaries and wages are taxed at a rate ranging from 3 % to 45 % in seven progressive bands. There are two key factors that determine who are subject to IIT:

- Residence
- Length of stay

2.2 Residence and Length of Stay

Article 2 of the Individual Income Tax Implementing Rules provides that to be considered residents of the PRC, individuals shall have a permanent registered address, family or economic interest in the country. The liability to pay IIT depends also on the length of stay; for instance, if a nonresident or domiciled individual exceeds a certain threshold of time spent in the PRC, he is considered "taxable" for

L. Riccardi, *Chinese Tax Law and International Treaties*,

DOI 10.1007/978-3-319-00275-0_2,

IIT by tax authorities. Therefore, the days spent within Chinese boundaries (as well as the domicile) implicate the taxability of personal income.

The fiscal year follows the calendar year, which begins on January 1 and ends on December 31, and for each session there is an independent current liability. To calculate the length of stay, the entry and exit days are counted as days entirely spent in China. However, if an individual enters and leaves during the same day, it is counted only as a single day. Another fundamental aspect is how to consider absences from the PRC.

An individual's absence can be instrumental to the calculation of IIT. In case an absence goes over a certain threshold, the individual can even be excluded completely from taxation. In particular, absences cannot be deducted from the total days spent in China during a single tax year if they represent less than 30 consecutive or 90 cumulative days. On the other hand, a single absence of more than 30 consecutive or many exceeding 90 cumulative days entails subtracting the days exceeding the threshold (30 or 90) from the total of those spent in the People's Republic.

2.3 Worldwide Taxation

If an individual lives in China for five consecutive years without ever leaving the country for more than 30 consecutive or 90 cumulative days, he is subject to IIT on a global basis from the sixth year. To avoid Worldwide Income Taxation, an individual shall exit the country during a fiscal year and leave it for over 30 consecutive or 90 cumulative days before a 5-year period deadline. After the fifth year, it is sufficient to stay in China for a period not exceeding 90 or 183 days (in case there exists an agreement on double taxation between China and the country of origin).

2.4 Taxpayers and Tax Liability

Residence and length of stay identify three taxpayers' categories: residents, nonresidents, and "expatriates."

2.5 Resident Status

Tax residents are people who have a registered residence, family or economic interest in China; it implies that they are subject to IIT on their worldwide income.

2.6 Temporary Visitor

Indicated by law with the name *temporary visitors*, nonresidents are individuals who neither have domicile in China nor have spent a period exceeding 90 or 183 days therein (in case there exists an agreement on double taxation between China and the country of origin).

In order to calculate the total length of stay, Circular No 97 Guoshuifa art. 1, 2004 establishes that both entry and exit days from China are days of presence in the territory of the PRC. *Temporary visitors* are subject to tax only on income earned from domestic firms or representative offices located in China and are not subject on income from a non-Chinese company established in another country. However, this special treatment is not indiscriminately the same across the country. Some local authorities can consider subjecting to IIT individuals who, although have not exceeded 90 days or 183 days of stay, work at a branch of a foreign company in China. Therefore, it is recommended to check the real scenario and the existence of this benefit with the local tax authorities.

2.7 Nonresident Status

The days that can be spent by an individual in the PRC without running into the IIT and in order to be considered as *temporary visitors* vary from 90 to 183, depending on the existence of any agreement against double taxation between China and the other country.

For example, the agreement signed by Italy has allowed Italian citizens who are not receiving any payment from local organizations to stay in China up to a maximum of 183 days before becoming taxable. To understand the functioning of this calculation, we can compare an Italian citizen (whose country signed such agreement) and a Taiwanese citizen (whose country does not have such an agreement). The Italian citizen becomes taxable when he exceeds the 183-day-stay limit in the PRC, while the other is subject to taxation as soon as he exceeds the 90-day limit.

2.8 Chief Representative

In charge of a representative office of a non-Chinese company located in China, the Chief Representative is excluded from the benefits mentioned before and is always subject to IIT without any consideration about the limit of 90/183 days.

2.9 "Expatriates"

The category named by law as "expatriates" includes three different types of distinct subject: "expatriates" living in China for more than 5 years, "expatriates" having spent more than one but less than 5 years therein, and "expatriates" with less than 1 year but more than 90 or 183 days spent in the country.

The first type of "expatriates" are people who have continuously lived in China for five fiscal years without leaving the country for a period exceeding 30 consecutive or 90 cumulative days during a single fiscal year. They are subject to IIT on worldwide income anywhere generated and produced from the sixth year onwards. Only an absence of more than 30 consecutive or 90 cumulative days, starting from the sixth year, allows them to be subject to IIT only on income generated inside the country.

Characterized by spending a full year in China, this category has not been allowed to take off any days spent away from the Republic from the total amount. With the approval of the competent tax authorities, the taxable income of these individuals is limited to the part produced in the PRC if a Chinese individual or company does not earn it. After the fifth consecutive year of stay, the tax benefit is not granted anymore and the total income is subject to IIT.

Individuals belonging to this category have been living in China for more than 90 or 183 days (according to country's agreement) but less than 1 year. They are required to pay taxes on income generated within the territory of PRC, regardless of the place where the income is earned, for example in Italy. This is due to the fact that the income related to provision of services held in China on behalf of a foreign company with no permanent establishment is thought of as generated in China, despite payments that may come from other countries. For example, if an Italian person held consultant services for Italian companies in China, he will be subject to IIT only if his stay will exceed 183 days, without any issue about payments. As a result, the nonresident who resides in China for less than 90 or 183 days, previously named *temporary visitor*, is not subject to IIT.

2.10 Tax Summary Table

See Table 2.1.

2.11 Income Classification Group

Income categories, regardless of payment method, either in cash or in kind, can be classified into the following four groups:

Table 2.1 Taxable income for expatriates

Length of stay	Taxable income
More than 5 years	Worldwide income from the sixth year of stay
Less than 5 consecutive years	Income produced in China
More than 1 year	Income produced in China, only if paid by individuals or companies residing in China
Less than 1 year	Income produced in China, anywhere earned
More than 90 or 183 days in a year	Income produced and earned in China
Less than 90 or 183 days in a year	Income not taxable
Temporary visitors	
Chief representative	Income produced in China, anywhere earned

- Employment income
- Individual personal income
- Royalties, interest, and dividends
- Rents and revenues from sales of goods

2.11.1 Employment Income

This category consists of income from employment performed under the others' direction and dependencies. This includes wages and salaries, bonuses, per diems, expense contributions, stock options, severance payments, payments in kind, and donations related to the employment contract. The tax rate ranges in a progressive band from 3 % to 45 %. Nevertheless, not all the income received by employees is subject to IIT: there are some benefits for expatriates. For instance, Caishuizi "No 20" of 1994 and Guoshuifa "No 54" of 1997 have declared some payments in kind not subject to IIT applicable only to foreigners: the housing rent, meal, and laundry allowances received as vouchers or through reimbursement (for which a supporting documentation of receipts and invoices may be required by the tax authorities as evidence); reimbursements for travel expenses and travel allowances for entry to/exit from the country and trips back home, so long as they are reasonable in the opinion of tax authorities; education allowances and foreign language courses, insurance and social security benefits (so long as the premium has not been already deducted for the calculation of the Enterprise Income Tax). The circular Caishui No 10 of 2006 identifies some benefits: pension and health insurance premiums and unemployment benefits paid by an employer or employee in accordance with government obligations. Regarding the severance indemnity, as specified in Caishui No 157, 2001, it is subject to IIT only if it is triple the monthly salary received from the subject, which can amortize the payment by the number of working years accrued. Finally, the year-end bonus received in the form of a lump sum must be taxed separately from the monthly salary of the taxpayer, which can now receive a favorable tax treatment.

2.11.2 Income from Self-Employment

This category includes income from arts and professions gained from the regular exercise of self-employment activities. The Chinese Legislature, as well as the Italian Legislature, identifies a wide range of activities considered as self-employment, so that the distinction from the above-mentioned categories becomes of great importance. It shall be noted that administrators' fees are taxed and included in this category. Article 8, paragraph 4 of the *Individual Income Tax Implementing Rules* lists the types of services the Legislature has classified as self-employed activities. Among these we can find legal and tax services, journalism, painting, calligraphy, translating and interpreting, sculpture, decoration, design, advertising, etc. Although the rate for these type of activities varies from 20 % to 40 %, compared with the range from 3 % to 45 % of income from employment, each self-employment activity, followed by emission of invoices, is subject also to business tax or value added tax, whose rate is typically of 5 % or 3 %.

2.11.3 Income from Royalties, Interest, and Dividends

Income from royalties, interest, and dividends are respectively accrued following the granting of the right to use trademarks, patents, copyrights, scientific know-how (royalties), loans of money (interest), and holding of investment securities (dividends). Usually, the payer acts as a withholding agent, deducting at source part of the compensation that he has to pay to the Chinese authority in place of the beneficiary.

2.11.4 Rents and Income from Lease and Transfer of Property

This category includes income from rental of machinery and equipment, property, ships and vehicles, etc. Income accrued from disposal of securities (stocks, bonds, etc.), real estate, vehicles and vessels, machinery, and equipment are considered as proceeds from sale of goods.

2.12 Tax Deductions

The IIT in China, as well as in Italy, consists of a progressive tax rate determined in relation to different income brackets. Various deductions are granted for each IIT category, as well as a fixed deduction for each bracket (quick deduction).

2.13 Employment Tax Standard Deduction

Deductions for employment income amount to CNY 3,500 for local workers and CNY 4,800 for foreign workers. These amounts represent a lump sum to be deducted from the employee's monthly salary. Even basic medical expenses and unemployment compensation can be deducted in calculating taxable income. The no-tax area for local workers has been increased from CNY 2,000 to CNY 3,500 from the draft amendment of the Individual Income Tax Law approved on June 30, 2011 and entered into force on 1 September 2011.

2.14 Self-Employment Tax Standard Deduction

Self-Employment Tax Standard Deductions are at a 20 % of each compensation if the compensation is not less than CNY 4,000; if it is lower, a lump sum of CNY 800 applies. For deductions on employment income, self-employment tax standard deductions are calculated in proportion to the volume of business turnover (and not to the tax period).

2.15 After-Tax Deduction (Tax Credit)

The tax allowance for the calculation of net IIT depends on the category and income bracket referred to. For employment income, the minimum deduction is CNY 105 for salaries between CNY 1,501 and CNY 4,500 up to a maximum of CNY 13,505 for those higher than CNY 80,000.

2.16 Tax Liabilities Computation

In order to comprehend the calculation of the IIT, the Legislature provides specific reference tables (Tables 2.2, 2.3, 2.4, 2.5), along with some useful examples to study and learn the regulation and become familiar with its principles.

Table 2.2 New parameters and tax rates

New brackets and rates for calculating the Individual Income Tax on net monthly income (Effective September 1, 2011)		
(A) Gross		
Gross monthly income (CNY)	Rate	Deductions (quick deduction) (CNY)
0 to 1,500	3 %	0
1,501 to 4,500	10 %	105
4,501 to 9,000	20 %	555
9,001 to 35,000	25 %	1,005
35,001 to 55,000	30 %	2,755
55,001 to 80,000	35 %	5,505
> 80,000	45 %	13,505
(B) Net		
Net monthly income (CNY)	Rate	Deductions (quick deduction) (CNY)
0 to 1,455	3 %	0
1,456 to 4,155	10 %	105
4,156 to 7,755	20 %	555
7,756 to 27,255	25 %	1,005
27,256 to 41,255	30 %	2,755
41,256 to 57,505	35 %	5,505
> 57,505	45 %	13,505

Table 2.3 IIT self-employment rates

Taxable income for work performance (CNY)	Rate	Deductions (quick deduction) (CNY)
0 to 20,000	20 %	0
20,001 to 50,000	30 %	2,000
>50,000	40 %	7,000

2.17 Employment Income

In the past, a different manner of calculating employment income tax was used, referred to in the table below, shown in the official English translation. Now it was revised by a draft amendment approved on June 30, 2011 by the National People's Congress and entered into force on 1 September, 2011.

The draft amendment added the following new features: an increase of the standard monthly deduction from CNY 2,000 to CNY 3,500 for local workers, with no mention of expatriate's deductions. In addition, it extended the time limit for paying tax on personal income, from the previous seven to 15 days after the current month, and it introduced a change in tax rates, which can now vary from 3 % to 45 % according to seven different income brackets.

As shown in Table 2.2A, seven income brackets replaced the nine progressive bands. The tax is calculated by multiplying the taxable income by the corresponding rate in the brackets. To calculate the taxable income, it is necessary to subtract from the monthly gross income the deductions granted by the bureau

Table 2.4 IIT different rates for individual business owners, sole proprietors, investors/partners of partnership enterprises

Gross annual income (CNY)	Rate	(Quick deduction) (CNY)
0 to 15,000	5 %	0
15,001 to 30,000	10 %	750
30,001 to 60,000	20 %	3,75
60,001 to 100,000	30 %	9,75
> 100,000	35 %	14,75

Table 2.5 National social contributions (varies by city)

Contributions	Paid by the employer	Paid by the employee
Pension insurance	12 %	8 %
Medical insurance	8 %	2 %
Unemployment insurance	2 %	1 %
Work injury insurance	0.2 %	–
Housing funds	5–12 %	12–15 %

plus the no-tax area (CNY 3,500 for local workers, CNY 4,800 for foreign workers).

For the last step, the gross tax must be reduced by a quick deduction, as indicated in the table. The formula of IIT is shown below:

$$\text{Net monthly tax} = [(\text{Gross monthly income} - \text{Deductions}) \times \text{Tax rate}] \\ - \text{Quick deduction}.$$

If the compensation received is net, the employer acts as a withholding agent and the formula becomes this:

$$\text{Taxable income} = (\text{Net monthly income} - \text{Deduction on a monthly basis} \\ -\text{Quick deduction})/(1 - \text{Tax rate}).$$

The table below includes progressive tax rates and deductions for net payments provided under new IIT rules in force since September 1, 2011.

2.18 Annual Bonus

The rules for calculating the IIT on annual bonuses were amended by Circular Guoshuifa No. 9, 2005, which introduced a different treatment than the usual taxation on salaries. The bonus is divided by 12, which is the number of months necessary to receive the annual bonus; hence, the quick deduction is applied, thus arriving at the taxable amount, in which the appropriate rate is applied).

The formula for calculating the amount of tax and annual bonus is shown below:

$$\begin{aligned}\text{Annual bonus}/12 &= \text{Parameter to identify the income tax rate net tax}\\ &= \text{Bonus} \times \text{Tax rate} - \text{Quick deduction.}\end{aligned}$$

2.19 Calculation of IIT on Self-Employment Income

Self-employment income tax is calculated on the value of a single compensation for each performance carried out. The calculation, with the related deductions, shall be done on each invoice (The rate is 20 % for amounts not exceeding CNY 20,000).

Table and formulas may vary according to the reform of the IIT in force since September 1, 2011. As is shown in Table 2.3, the progressive income brackets are only three and not seven as in IIT calculated on employment income and deductions are about 20 % of the remuneration received if the amount of the invoice is not less than CNY 4,000. If it is lower, it consists in a flat amount of CNY 800. The net tax result is then achieved by subtracting the standard deductions from the payment stated in the invoice, which is the taxable amount, and then multiplying this by the related rate; eventually, to find the net tax due, the standard tax allowance is subtracted.

2.20 IIT on Income from Royalties, Interest, and Dividends

A deduction of 20 % is allowed on income from *royalties* if the amount received is equal or higher than CNY 4,000. If it is lower, a lump sum of CNY 800 with a flat rate of 20 % is charged.

Here is the formula on income from royalties:

$$\text{Net tax} = (\text{Income from royalties} - \text{Deduction}) \times 20\,\%.$$

The same rate of 20 % is levied on income from interest and dividends. Although a directive concerning a reduction of 50 % of the rate for income earned by companies listed on China stock markets (Shanghai and Shenzhen) have been issued, the duration of this benefit has not yet been arranged.

2.21 Production and Business Operation Income Earned by Individual Business Owners, Sole Proprietors, and Investors/Partners of Partnership Enterprises

The *Individual Income Tax* reform has also changed the progressive band on which to calculate taxes on an individual's income, defined as *production and business operation, income earned by individual business owners, proprietors only, and investors/partners of partnerships enterprises.*

2.22 Director Fees

Fees paid to directors are taxed as income from self-employment if the director does not have employment relationship with the company. If the administrator is also an employee of the company, the compensation is taxed in the same way as income from employment.

2.23 National Social Contributions

All employers must do a special registration with the local authorities. The legislation allows local governments to confirm their welfare and social security contribution rates, which vary according to their city and are calculated on the basis of minimum and maximum remuneration for workers approved on an annual basis.

2.24 Social Insurance Law Reform

The new *PRC Social Insurance Law* promulgated on 28 October 2010 and producing effects by 2011 has introduced significant changes in relation to social security contributions for foreign workers in China. Before the reform, foreign workers were not subject to pay any social insurance in the PRC. Now, with the new *Social Insurance Law*, it is made clear that foreign workers must pay social security contributions. At the time of this writing, the authorities have not clarified the method of calculation and reimbursement for expatriate workers. Currently, only Germany and South Korea have signed an agreement on welfare with China (Tables 2.6, 2.7, 2.8, 2.9, 2.10, 2.11, 2.12).

Table 2.6 Shanghai Social Insurance Index 2012

Category	Base	Employer rate	Employee rate
Pension	2599–12993	22 %	8 %
Medical	2599–12993	12 %	2 %
Unemployment (not available for expat)	2599–12993	2 %	1 %
Injury	2599–12993	0.5 %	–
Maternity (not available for expat)	2599–12993	0.5 %	–

Source: Fesco-Adecco 2012

Table 2.7 Beijing Social Insurance Index 2012

Category	Base	Employer Rate	Employee Rate
Pension	1869–14016	20 %	8 %
Medical	2803–14016	10 %	2 % + 3
Unemployment	1869–14016	1 %	0.2 %
Injury	2803–14016	0.3 % (Floating rate)	–
Maternity	2803–14016	0.8 %	–

Source: Fesco-Adecco 2012

Table 2.8 Calculation of the maximum monthly contribution burden for foreigners in Beijing (2012–2013). This calculation is based on the monthly remuneration of a foreigner in Beijing above the maximum basis (12,603 CNY)

Insurance item	Employer		Employee	
Pension	20 %	CNY 2,520.6	8 %	CNY 1,008.24
Medical	10 %	CNY 1,260.3	2 % + 3 CNY	CNY 255.06
Work-related	0.3 %	CNY 37.81	0 %	–
Unemployment	1 %	CNY 126.03	0.2 %	CNY 25.206
Maternity	0.8 %	CNY 100.824	0 %	–
Total	32.1 %	CNY 4,045.56	10.2 % + 3 CNY	CNY 1,288.5

Source: L. Riccardi, New Social Welfare Law for expats, China–Italy Chamber of Commerce, 28 June 2012, Shanghai, P.R. China (materials from the seminar)

Table 2.9 Calculation of the maximum monthly contribution burden for foreigners in Shanghai. This calculation is based on the monthly remuneration of a foreigner in Shanghai above the maximum basis (11,688 CNY)

Insurance item	Employer		Employee	
Pension	22 %	CNY 2,571	8 %	CNY 935
Medical	12 %	CNY 1,403	2 %	CNY 234
Work-related	0.5 %	CNY 58	0 %	–
Unemployment	1.7 %	CNY 199	1 %	CNY 116
Maternity	0.8 %	CNY 95	0 %	–
Total	37 %	CNY 4,325	11 %	CNY 1,286

Source: L. Riccardi, New Social Welfare Law for expats, China–Italy Chamber of Commerce, 28 June 2012, Shanghai, P.R. China (materials from the seminar)

Table 2.10 Calculation of the maximum monthly contribution burden for foreigners in Suzhou. This calculation is based on the monthly remuneration of a foreigner in Suzhou above the maximum basis (11,392 CNY)

Insurance item	Employer		Employee	
Pension	20 %	CNY 2,278	8 %	CNY 911
Medical	9 %	CNY 1,025	2 %	CNY 228
Work-related	1 %	CNY 114	0 %	–
Unemployment	2 %	CNY 228	1 %	CNY 114
Maternity	1 %	CNY 114	0 %	–
Total	33 %	CNY 3,759	11 %	CNY 1,253

Source: L. Riccardi, New Social Welfare Law for expats, China–Italy Chamber of Commerce, 28 June 2012, Shanghai, P.R. China (materials from the seminar)

Table 2.11 Calculation of the maximum monthly contribution burden for foreigners in the different cities

City	Employer (in CNY)	Employee (in CNY)
Beijing	4,045	1,289
Shanghai	4,325	1,286
Suzhou	3,760	1,253
Guangzhou	4,250–4,479	1,499
Shenzhen	4,016–4,142	1,262

Source: L. Riccardi, New Social Welfare Law for expats, China–Italy Chamber of Commerce, 28 June 2012, Shanghai, P.R. China (materials from the seminar)

Table 2.12 Calculation of the maximum monthly contribution burden for foreigners in Shanghai who enjoy full exemption under a bilateral social insurance agreement

Insurance item	Employer		Employee	
Medical	12 %	CNY 1,403	2 %	CNY 234
Work-related	0.5 %	CNY 58	0 %	–
Maternity	0.8 %	CNY 95	0 %	–
Total	12.5 %	CNY 1,555	2 %	CNY 234

Source: L. Riccardi, New Social Welfare Law for expats, China–Italy Chamber of Commerce, 28 June 2012, Shanghai, P.R. China (materials from the seminar)

Chapter 3
Company Income Tax

3.1 The Innovations Introduced by the New EITL

The *Enterprise Income Tax Law*—EITL, also known as *Company Income Tax*—CIT, has entered into force on January 1, 2008, eliminating the distinction between local companies and foreign companies by ensuring a 5-year transition period to whoever has previously enjoyed significant tax benefit and gradually increasing the tax rate of 1–3 % per year until the new flat rate of 25 %.

3.2 Taxable Entities

Taxable entities include resident companies for income produced worldwide (inside and outside the territory of the PRC), nonresident enterprises that have a permanent establishment in China on income earned within the territory of the PRC or effectively connected with a permanent establishment, nonresident companies without a permanent establishment on income produced in China, reserving the respect of any agreements for the avoidance of double taxation.

The following are entities subject to corporate income tax:

- Resident companies in China
- *Representative offices* (RO)
- Permanent establishments of nonresidents
- Nonresident companies without permanent establishment in the Republic

3.3 Resident Company

Resident companies in China are established under China tax law and have their management placed in the country; examples are domestic firms, including state enterprises, private companies, cooperatives, corporations, and firms with foreign

L. Riccardi, *Chinese Tax Law and International Treaties*,
DOI 10.1007/978-3-319-00275-0_3, © Springer International Publishing Switzerland 2013

capital investments, including wholly foreign-owned enterprises (WFOE), equity joint ventures, cooperative joint ventures, and Chinese holding companies. Residents are subject to pay the Company Income Tax on income earned both inside and outside the territory of the Republic of China.

3.4 The Wholly Foreign-Owned Enterprise

The WFOE represents the most common approach being adopted among foreign traders for investing in China. The WFOE may be identified as a *limited liability company* established by foreigners, whose capital is completely owned by one or more foreign investors.

3.5 Representative Offices

Representative offices are not set with an independent legal personality because their business is restricted to the exercise of coordination between parent and local partners and activities of market research. Apart from exceptions (representative offices of financial institutions, law firms, accounting consulting firms, etc.), they cannot take on any business activities generating profit or commercial contracts with third parties or directly selling products or services/activities of brokerage and agency for sale of such products/services. The representative offices are registered with the competent Chinese authorities, with the appointment of a *Chief Representative*, and they have specific limitations on the permitted activities, restricted to those of *Liaison* between the company and customers or parent and Chinese suppliers. The *Representative Office* has a specific method to calculate *Company Income Tax*, and it is subject only on income generated within the territory of the Republic of China and on foreign income effectively connected with the office itself.

3.6 Permanent Establishments of Nonresidents

Article 5 of the *Implementation Regulations of the Corporate Income Tax Law of the People's Republic of China* considers as permanent establishments the following legal entities:

- Management or business offices
- Workshops, farms, or places of extraction of raw materials
- Locations where are provided work activities
- Locations developing projects like construction, installation, assembly, repair, and exploration activity
- Nonindependent agents

Therefore, a foreign resident that does not have a permanent establishment in China is subject to *Company Income Tax* on income generated inside the territory of the PRC and income connected with the organization but generated outside the territory of the PRC.

3.7 Nonresident Companies Without a Permanent Establishment in the PRC

Nonresident companies without a *permanent establishment* are subject to *Company Income Tax* on the portion of income earned within the boundaries, such as dividends, interest, *royalties*, *capital gains*, etc.

The collection of tax on corporate income tax is withheld at source (withholding tax).

3.8 Categories of Taxable Income

The categories of the corporate income being taxed are listed in Art. 6 of the Enterprise Income Tax Law and grouped as follows:

- Revenues from sale of goods, provision of services and transfer of goods, and related rights
- Dividends, interest, rents, *royalties,* donations, and other nonoperating income
- Any exchange of goods (tangible or intangible, or services) sold by way of donation, reparation, *sponsorship,* advertising, sampling, transfer or for any other reason

3.9 The Sources of Income

A relevant issue is to identify the origin of the profits of a company, as to whether they come from inside or outside China. As mentioned before, only resident companies are subject to worldwide income taxation, while nonresident enterprises, having a permanent establishment in China, are subject to tax only on the portion of income generated within the Republic. To identify the source of income are followed principles defined by the Chinese Legislator (Art. 7 of EITIR). In particular, it is necessary to know these information:

- The place where the company carries out sale of goods
- The place where services are provided, for the part of income coming from the provision of services

- The place where the property is located or in which the company has its head office, for income generated from transfer of real property or shareholding of the company
- The place where the company is situated, for income from distribution of dividends
- The place where the company or the permanent establishment is sited, the place where the income is paid, or the domicile of the person paying the income, for income from interest, rents, and *royalties*

The *State Administration of Taxation* and the *Ministry of Finance* decide on the origin of other types of income.

3.10 Tax Liabilities and Computation

Taxable income is determined by starting from a gross income that includes revenues from sale of goods, provision of services, transfer of goods, and related rights, adding dividends, interests, rents and *royalties,* donations, and other nonoperating income. The allowable deductions are related to costs that have been incurred during the course of business, including expenses, losses on disposal of assets, currency speculation, and certain taxes. Depreciation and old losses are also deductible but not the following negative components of income:

- Dividends or other equity investment proceeds paid to investors
- Payments relating to *Company Income Tax*
- Tax penalty
- Penalties or losses incurred during seizure of property
- Not qualified donations
- Costs of sponsorship
- Unverified provisions

It is permitted to carry forward tax losses for five tax periods.

3.11 Deduction of Mortgage Interest

Interest on loans, being signed during ordinary business activity, are fully deductible as well as interest granted by nonfinancial institutions but only for the same maximum percentage, mortgage, and period, while interest paid for acquisition or construction of tangible or intangible assets, because of their estimated long life, must be capitalized, increasing the value of the assets itself, and so deducted, according to the depreciation criteria stated in the implementing rules.

Table 3.1 CIT deductions

Costs (Art. 29 EITIR)	• Sales costs • Cost of goods sold • Business expenditures • Other consumable expenditures
Expenses (Art. 30 EITIR)	• Sales expenses • Administrative expenses • Financial expenses
Taxes (Art. 31 EITIR)	• Various taxes apart from CIT and value added tax • Surtaxes incurred
Losses (Art. 32 EITIR)	• Shortfall loss • Damage loss • Loss from scrapping of fixed assets and inventories • Loss on property transfers • Loss on doubtful accounts • Loss on bad debts • Loss resulting from force majeure

3.12 Business Entertainment and Sponsorship Expenses

Among the negative income components there are entertainment expenses, which are deductible within the limit of 60 % of the total amount incurred and up to 0.5 % of revenue of a fiscal year. Advertising and promotion expenses can be deducted from the total income up to a maximum amount of 15 % of revenues from sale of goods. The excess can be recovered in subsequent years.

3.13 Company Income Tax Deduction Tables

Table 3.1 shows the corporate income tax deductions as read from the official English translation of the *Enterprise Income Tax Law* and *Enterprise Income Tax Law Implementing Rules*.

3.14 Depreciation

3.14.1 Depreciation Policy

The method used to calculate depreciation is the *straight-line method*, which consists in subtracting the *salvage value* of the asset from its *purchase price* and dividing it by the time period during which the asset will be used in the business.

The purchase value is the original, historical price of the asset at the time of purchasing, and the depreciation period begins a month following the one in which the asset has been used by the company.

Table 3.2 Depreciable assets (Art. 57 EITIR)

Buildings
Structures
Machinery
Mechanisms
Means of transport
Other equipment, appliances and tools, etc. that are relevant to the ITS production and business operations

Table 3.3 Amortizable assets (Art. 65 EITIR)

Patent
Trademark
Copyright
Land use right
Know-how
Goodwill
Other amortizable assets

In addition, according to Art. 13 EITL and Arts 68 and 69 EITIR, the alteration, improvement, and overhaul costs incurred for assets shall be capitalized and depreciated within the remaining useful lives of the assets.

3.14.2 Depreciation Period

Reestimating the useful life every year in proportion to the use of the asset, it is possible to reconsider an acceleration or a reduction of its depreciation period upon the competent tax authority's approval.

In order to consider that, one of the two following legal requirements is needed: a) the asset has to be subject to obsolescence for progresses reached in the area of business to which it belongs, and b) it has to be in regular exposure to elements that can affect its nature. It is not possible in any way to reduce a depreciation period over 60 % of the minimum period of amortization.

3.14.3 Depreciation of Intangible Assets

Intangible assets are characterized by a depreciation period greater than 10 years.

Not all the possessions of a company can be depreciated, such as self-produced intangible assets when costs of production have been fully deducted on tax purpose, intangible assets not relevant to the activities of the company, etc.

3.14.4 Tables

Tables 3.2, 3.3, 3.4, 3.5, and 3.6 below illustrate which are the depreciable assets, as reported from the official English translation of the *Enterprise Income Tax Law* and *Enterprise Income Tax Law Implementing Rules*.

Table 3.4 Minimum period of depreciation (Art. 60 EITIR)

Buildings and structures	20 years
Aircraft, trains, vessels, machinery, mechanics, and other production equipment	10 years
Appliances, tools, furniture, etc. that are related to production and business operations	5 years
Means of transport other than aircraft, trains, and vessels	4 years
Electronic equipment	3 years

Table 3.5 Biological assets (Art. 62 EITIR)

Economic forest
Firewood forest
Livestock kept for breeding
Livestock for labor

Table 3.6 Minimum period of amortization of intangible biological assets

Art. 64 EITIR	
Production-biological nature of forestry assets in the nature	10 years
Production-biological natures assets in the nature of livestock	3 years

3.15 Withholding Tax

Nonresident companies without a permanent establishment in China are subject to *Company Income Tax*, which is withheld at source on income earned within the PRC's territory. The taxable income may consist of earnings from dividends, *royalties,* interest, rental, and *capital gains.* To determine the origin of a source of income, it is recommended to consult Art. 7 of EITIR, where the Chinese Legislator has laid down principles to verify the provenance of sources and their possible liability to corporate income tax.

The withholding tax on income from nonresident companies without a *permanent establishment* in China is equal to 10 % unless otherwise stated (Table 3.7).

3.16 Income from Dividends

When a company allocates dividends to its shareholders coming out of the leftover equity, those dividends are subject to withholding tax for a final 10 % of the amount paid.

Agreements on double taxation may likely determine ways to recuperate taxes paid abroad or privileged rates different from the home rate of 10 % (Table 3.8).

3.17 The Withholding Agent

In China, withholding tax is levied on nonresident companies providing services to China-based business. The income tax payable on such income derived by nonresident enterprises shall be withheld at source, and the client, becoming a withholding

Table 3.7 Treaty withholding tax rates on dividends derived by nonqualifying companies and individuals

Country	Status	Dividends (%)
Albania	Effective January 1, 2006	10
Algeria	Effective January 1, 2008	10
Armenia	Effective January 1, 1997	10
Australia	Effective January 1, 1991	10
Austria	Effective January 1, 1993	10
Azerbaijan	Effective January 1, 2006	10
Bahrain	Effective January 1, 2003	5
Bangladesh	Effective January 1, 1998	10
Barbados	Effective January 1, 2001 Protocol effective January 1, 2011	10
Belarus	Effective January 1, 1997	10
Belgium	Effective January 1, 1988 Protocol effective January 1, 2001 New treaty signed October 7, 2009	10
Bosnia and Herzegovina	Effective January 1, 1998	5
Botswana	Signed April 11, 2012	Not yet confirmed
Brazil	Effective January 1, 1994	10
Brunei	Effective January 1, 2007	5
Bulgaria	Effective January 1, 1991	10
Canada	Effective January 1, 1987	10
Croatia	Effective January 1, 2002	5
Cuba	Effective January 1, 2004	10
Cyprus	Effective January 1, 1992	10
Czech Republic	Effective January 1, 2012	10
Denmark	Effective January 1, 1987 New treaty signed June 16, 2012	10
Ecuador	Signed January 21, 2013	Not yet confirmed
Egypt	Effective January 1, 2000	8
Estonia	Effective January 1, 2000	10
Ethiopia	Effective January 1, 2013	5
Finland	Effective January 1, 2011	10
France	Effective January 1, 1986	10
Georgia	Effective January 1, 2006	10
Germany	Effective January 1, 1985	10
Greece	Effective January 1, 2006	10
Hong Kong	Effective January 1, 2007	10
Hungary	Effective January 1, 1995	10
Iceland	Effective January 1, 1998	10
India	Effective January 1, 1995	10
Indonesia	Effective January 1, 2004	10
Iran	Effective January 1, 2004	10
Ireland	Effective January 1, 2001	10
Israel	Effective January 1, 1996	10
Italy	Effective January 1, 1991	10
Jamaica	Effective January 1, 1998	5

(continued)

Table 3.7 (continued)

Country	Status	Dividends (%)
Japan	Effective January 1, 1985	10
Kazakhstan	Effective January 1, 2004	10
Korea (Republic of)	Effective January 1, 1995	10
Kuwait	Effective January 1, 1989	5
Kyrgyzstan	Effective January 1, 2004	10
Laos	Effective January 1, 2000	5
Latvia	Effective January 1, 1998	10
	Protocol effective January 1, 2013	
Lithuania	Effective January 1, 1997	10
Luxembourg	Effective January 1, 1996	10
Macau	Effective January 1, 2004	10
	Protocol effective January 1, 2011	
Macedonia	Effective January 1, 1998	5
Malaysia	Effective January 1, 1987	10
Malta	Effective January 1, 2012	10
Mauritius	Effective January 1, 1996	5
Mexico	Effective January 1, 2007	5
Moldova	Effective January 1, 2002	10
Mongolia	Effective January 1, 1993	5
Montenegro	Effective January 1, 1998	5
Morocco	Effective January 1, 2007	10
Nepal	Effective January 1, 2011	10
Netherlands	Effective January 1, 1989	10
New Zealand	Effective January 1, 1987	10
Nigeria	Effective January 1, 2010	7.5
Norway	Effective January 1, 1987	10
Oman	Effective January 1, 2003	5
Pakistan	Effective July 1, 1990	10
Papua New Guinea	Effective January 1, 1996	10
Philippines	Effective January 1, 2002	10
Poland	Effective January 1, 1990	10
Portugal	Effective January 1, 2001	10
Qatar	Effective January 1, 2009	10
Romania	Effective January 1, 1993	10
Russia	Effective January 1, 1998	10
Saudi Arabia	Effective January 1, 2007	5
Serbia	Effective January 1, 1998	5
Seychelles	Effective January 1, 2000	5
Singapore	Effective January 1, 2008	10
Slovakia	Effective January 1, 1988	10
Slovenia	Effective January 1, 1996	5
South Africa	Effective January 1, 2001	5
Spain	Effective January 1, 1993	10
Sri Lanka	Effective January 1, 2006	10
Sudan	Effective January 1, 2000	5

(continued)

Table 3.7 (continued)

Country	Status	Dividends (%)
Sweden	Effective January 1, 1987	10
	Protocol effective January 1, 1997	
Switzerland	Effective January 1, 1990	10
Syria	Effective January 1, 2012	10
Tajikistan	Effective January 1, 2010	10
Thailand	Effective January 1, 1987	10
Trinidad and Tobago	Effective July 1, 2005	10
Tunisia	Effective January 1, 2004	8
Turkey	Effective January 1, 1997	10
Turkmenistan	Effective January 1, 2011	10
Ukraine	Effective January 1, 1997	10
United Arab Emirates	Effective January 1, 1995	7
United Kingdom	Effective January 1, 1985	10
	New treaty signed June 27, 2011	
United States	Effective January 1, 1987	10
Uzbekistan	Effective January 1, 1997	10
Venezuela	Effective January 1, 2005	10
Vietnam	Effective January 1, 1997	10
Zambia	Effective January 1, 2012	5

agent, has the responsibility to transfer this amount to the *State Treasury* in the name and on behalf of the tax bureau. The process ends with a tax return delivered within 7 days after the payment (Tables 3.9 and 3.10).

3.18 Tax Computation and Tax Return

3.18.1 Tax Formula

Corporate Income Tax is calculated by multiplying the tax base by its proportional rate and then subtracting tax credits previously accrued, thanks to preferential treatments and taxes already paid abroad. The annual statement must be released within 5 months after the closing of the fiscal year, which always coincides with the calendar year as stated in the *Company Income Tax Law*. Advance payments are finally required based on quarterly interim financial statements released every 3 months and followed by a net balance adjustment sum paid to the tax authorities after the submission of the annual statement.

Table 3.8 Treaty withholding tax rates on dividends derived by qualifying companies

Country	Status	Dividends derived by qualifying companies (%)
Albania	Effective January 1, 2006	10
Algeria	Effective January 1, 2008	5
Armenia	Effective January 1, 1997	5
Australia	Effective January 1, 1991	10
Austria	Effective January 1, 1993	7
Azerbaijan	Effective January 1, 2006	10
Bahrain	Effective January 1, 2003	5
Bangladesh	Effective January 1, 1998	10
Barbados	Effective January 1, 2001 Protocol effective January 1, 2011	5
Belarus	Effective January 1, 1997	10
Belgium	Effective January 1, 1988 Protocol effective January 1, 2001 New treaty signed October 7, 2009	5
Bosnia and Herzegovina	Effective January 1, 1998	5
Botswana	Signed April 11, 2012	
Brazil	Effective January 1, 1994	10
Brunei	Effective January 1, 2007	5
Bulgaria	Effective January 1, 1991	10
Canada	Effective January 1, 1987	10
Croatia	Effective January 1, 2002	5
Cuba	Effective January 1, 2004	5
Cyprus	Effective January 1, 1992	10
Czech Republic	Effective January 1, 2012	5
Denmark	Effective January 1, 1987 New treaty signed June 16, 2012	5
Ecuador	Signed January 21, 2013	
Egypt	Effective January 1, 2000	8
Estonia	Effective January 1, 2000	5
Ethiopia	Effective January 1, 2013	5
Finland	Effective January 1, 2011	5
France	Effective January 1, 1986	10
Georgia	Effective January 1, 2006	0/5
Germany	Effective January 1, 1985	10
Greece	Effective January 1, 2006	5
Hong Kong	Effective January 1, 2007	5
Hungary	Effective January 1, 1995	10
Iceland	Effective January 1, 1998	5
India	Effective January 1, 1995	10
Indonesia	Effective January 1, 2004	10
Iran	Effective January 1, 2004	10
Ireland	Effective January 1, 2001	5
Israel	Effective January 1, 1996	10
Italy	Effective January 1, 1991	10
Jamaica	Effective January 1, 1998	5

(continued)

Table 3.8 (continued)

Country	Status	Dividends derived by qualifying companies (%)
Japan	Effective January 1, 1985	10
Kazakhstan	Effective January 1, 2004	10
Korea (Republic of)	Effective January 1, 1995	5
Kuwait	Effective January 1, 1989	0
Kyrgyzstan	Effective January 1, 2004	10
Laos	Effective January 1, 2000	5
Latvia	Effective January 1, 1998	5
	Protocol effective January 1, 2013	
Lithuania	Effective January 1, 1997	5
Luxembourg	Effective January 1, 1996	5
Macau	Effective January 1, 2004	5
	Protocol effective January 1, 2011	
Macedonia	Effective January 1, 1998	5
Malaysia	Effective January 1, 1987	10
Malta	Effective January 1, 2012	5
Mauritius	Effective January 1, 1996	5
Mexico	Effective January 1, 2007	5
Moldova	Effective January 1, 2002	5
Mongolia	Effective January 1, 1993	5
Montenegro	Effective January 1, 1998	5
Morocco	Effective January 1, 2007	10
Nepal	Effective January 1, 2011	10
Netherlands	Effective January 1, 1989	10
New Zealand	Effective January 1, 1987	10
Nigeria	Effective January 1, 2010	7.5
Norway	Effective January 1, 1987	10
Oman	Effective January 1, 2003	5
Pakistan	Effective July 1, 1990	10
Papua New Guinea	Effective January 1, 1996	10
Philippines	Effective January 1, 2002	10
Poland	Effective January 1, 1990	10
Portugal	Effective January 1, 2001	10
Qatar	Effective January 1, 2009	10
Romania	Effective January 1, 1993	10
Russia	Effective January 1, 1998	10
Saudi Arabia	Effective January 1, 2007	5
Serbia	Effective January 1, 1998	5
Seychelles	Effective January 1, 2000	5
Singapore	Effective January 1, 2008	5
Slovakia	Effective January 1, 1988	10
Slovenia	Effective January 1, 1996	5
South Africa	Effective January 1, 2001	5
Spain	Effective January 1, 1993	10
Sri Lanka	Effective January 1, 2006	10
Sudan	Effective January 1, 2000	5

(continued)

Table 3.8 (continued)

Country	Status	Dividends derived by qualifying companies (%)
Sweden	Effective January 1, 1987 Protocol effective January 1, 1997	5
Switzerland	Effective January 1, 1990	10
Syria	Effective January 1, 2012	5
Tajikistan	Effective January 1, 2010	5
Thailand	Effective January 1, 1987	10
Trinidad and Tobago	Effective July 1, 2005	5
Tunisia	Effective January 1, 2004	8
Turkey	Effective January 1, 1997	10
Turkmenistan	Effective January 1, 2011	5
Ukraine	Effective January 1, 1997	5
United Arab Emirates	Effective January 1, 1995	7
United Kingdom	Effective January 1, 1985 New treaty signed June 27, 2011	5
United States	Effective January 1, 1987	10
Uzbekistan	Effective January 1, 1997	10
Venezuela	Effective January 1, 2005	5
Vietnam	Effective January 1, 1997	10
Zambia	Effective January 1, 2012	5

3.18.2 Tax Rate

Company Income Tax is configured as a proportional tax on the income of the company. From January 1, 2008, with the entry into force of a tax reform, the ordinary tax rate has been 25 % of the taxable income, identical for all companies.

For small companies with:

(a) Annual taxable income of less than CNY 300,000,
(b) Number of employees limited to less than 100 (or 80 for nonindustrial companies),
(c) Total asset of less than CNY 30 million (or CNY 10 million for nonindustrial companies),

it is granted a tax rate reduced to 20 %.

However, a lower tax rate of 15 % has been determined for firms with high-technology investments. Finally, for nonresident companies without a permanent establishment in the PRC, the tax rate is about 10 % of the invoices issued, paid as a *withholding* tax.

Table 3.9 Treaty withholding tax rates on interest

Country	Status	Interest (%)
Albania	Effective January 1, 2006	10
Algeria	Effective January 1, 2008	7
Armenia	Effective January 1, 1997	10
Australia	Effective January 1, 1991	10
Austria	Effective January 1, 1993	10
Azerbaijan	Effective January 1, 2006	10
Bahrain	Effective January 1, 2003	5
Bangladesh	Effective January 1, 1998	10
Barbados	Effective January 1, 2001	10
	Protocol effective January 1, 2011	
Belarus	Effective January 1, 1997	10
Belgium	Effective January 1, 1988	10
	Protocol effective January 1, 2001	
	New treaty signed October 7, 2009	
Bosnia and Herzegovina	Effective January 1, 1998	5
Botswana	Signed April 11, 2012	Not yet confirmed
Brazil	Effective January 1, 1994	10
Brunei	Effective January 1, 2007	10
Bulgaria	Effective January 1, 1991	10
Canada	Effective January 1, 1987	10
Croatia	Effective January 1, 2002	10
Cuba	Effective January 1, 2004	7.5
Cyprus	Effective January 1, 1992	10
Czech Republic	Effective January 1, 2012	7.5
Denmark	Effective January 1, 1987	10
	New treaty signed June 16, 2012	
Ecuador	Signed January 21, 2013	Not yet confirmed
Egypt	Effective January 1, 2000	10
Estonia	Effective January 1, 2000	10
Ethiopia	Effective January 1, 2013	7
Finland	Effective January 1, 2011	10
France	Effective January 1, 1986	10
Georgia	Effective January 1, 2006	10
Germany	Effective January 1, 1985	10
Greece	Effective January 1, 2006	10
Hong Kong	Effective January 1, 2007	7
Hungary	Effective January 1, 1995	10
Iceland	Effective January 1, 1998	10
India	Effective January 1, 1995	10
Indonesia	Effective January 1, 2004	10
Iran	Effective January 1, 2004	10
Ireland	Effective January 1, 2001	10
Israel	Effective January 1, 1996	10-Jul
Italy	Effective January 1, 1991	10
Jamaica	Effective January 1, 1998	7.5
Japan	Effective January 1, 1985	10

(continued)

Table 3.9 (continued)

Country	Status	Interest (%)
Kazakhstan	Effective January 1, 2004	10
Korea (Republic of)	Effective January 1, 1995	10
Kuwait	Effective January 1, 1989	5
Kyrgyzstan	Effective January 1, 2004	10
Laos	Effective January 1, 2000	10
Latvia	Effective January 1, 1998	10
	Protocol effective January 1, 2013	
Lithuania	Effective January 1, 1997	10
Luxembourg	Effective January 1, 1996	10
Macau	Effective January 1, 2004	7
	Protocol effective January 1, 2011	
Macedonia	Effective January 1, 1998	10
Malaysia	Effective January 1, 1987	10
Malta	Effective January 1, 2012	10
Mauritius	Effective January 1, 1996	10
Mexico	Effective January 1, 2007	10
Moldova	Effective January 1, 2002	10
Mongolia	Effective January 1, 1993	10
Montenegro	Effective January 1, 1998	10
Morocco	Effective January 1, 2007	10
Nepal	Effective January 1, 2011	10
Netherlands	Effective January 1, 1989	10
New Zealand	Effective January 1, 1987	10
Nigeria	Effective January 1, 2010	7.5
Norway	Effective January 1, 1987	10
Oman	Effective January 1, 2003	10
Pakistan	Effective July 1, 1990	10
Papua New Guinea	Effective January 1, 1996	10
Philippines	Effective January 1, 2002	10
Poland	Effective January 1, 1990	10
Portugal	Effective January 1, 2001	10
Qatar	Effective January 1, 2009	10
Romania	Effective January 1, 1993	10
Russia	Effective January 1, 1998	10
Saudi Arabia	Effective January 1, 2007	10
Serbia	Effective January 1, 1998	10
Seychelles	Effective January 1, 2000	10
Singapore	Effective January 1, 2008	10
Slovakia	Effective January 1, 1988	10
Slovenia	Effective January 1, 1996	10
South Africa	Effective January 1, 2001	10
Spain	Effective January 1, 1993	10
Sri Lanka	Effective January 1, 2006	10
Sudan	Effective January 1, 2000	10
Sweden	Effective January 1, 1987	10
	Protocol effective January 1, 1997	

(continued)

Table 3.9 (continued)

Country	Status	Interest (%)
Switzerland	Effective January 1, 1990	10
Syria	Effective January 1, 2012	10
Tajikistan	Effective January 1, 2010	8
Thailand	Effective January 1, 1987	10
Trinidad and Tobago	Effective July 1, 2005	10
Tunisia	Effective January 1, 2004	10
Turkey	Effective January 1, 1997	10
Turkmenistan	Effective January 1, 2011	10
Ukraine	Effective January 1, 1997	10
United Arab Emirates	Effective January 1, 1995	7
United Kingdom	Effective January 1, 1985	10
	New treaty signed June 27, 2011	
United States	Effective January 1, 1987	10
Uzbekistan	Effective January 1, 1997	10
Venezuela	Effective January 1, 2005	10
Vietnam	Effective January 1, 1997	10
Zambia	Effective January 1, 2012	10

3.18.3 Reform

For companies that had a preferential tax treatment until the entry into force of the new *Company Income Tax*, they have been granted a 5-year transition period aimed to gradually increase the tax rate by 1–3% per year to get to a 25 % flat rate. In particular, companies that enjoyed a privileged tax rate equal to 15 % in the past before January 1, 2008 have been seeing increasing their rate as follows: in FY 2008, the tax rate first rose to 18 %, followed by FY 2009 of 20 %; in FY 2010, the tax rate was a 22 %; in FY 2011, it rose to 24 % to end up to 25 % in 2012. Companies that instead enjoyed a 2-year period of tax exemption followed by a further 3 years subjecting to half tax rate (tax holiday) from the first year of registering profits are obliged to start the *tax holiday period* from 2008 without any further delay due to operating losses. A company that is subject to corporation tax in a country other than the PRC obtains a tax credit when paying it to the Chinese tax authorities. The maximum credit is established every year, and any excess may be carried forward up to five subsequent years.

3.18.4 Specific Procedure to Calculate Representative Office's Taxable Income

Regarding the assessment of Corporate Income Tax for a representative office, there are three alternative systems to determine the amount of taxable income: a) actual revenue method, b) deemed income method, and c) *cost-plus method.*

Table 3.10 Treaty withholding tax rates on royalties

Country	Status	Royalties (%)
Albania	Effective January 1, 2006	10
Algeria	Effective January 1, 2008	10
Armenia	Effective January 1, 1997	10
Australia	Effective January 1, 1991	10
Austria	Effective January 1, 1993	10
Azerbaijan	Effective January 1, 2006	10
Bahrain	Effective January 1, 2003	10
Bangladesh	Effective January 1, 1998	10
Barbados	Effective January 1, 2001	10
	Protocol effective January 1, 2011	
Belarus	Effective January 1, 1997	10
Belgium	Effective January 1, 1988	10
	Protocol effective January 1, 2001	
	New treaty signed October 7, 2009	
Bosnia and Herzegovina	Effective January 1, 1998	5
Botswana	Signed April 11, 2012	Not yet confirmed
Brazil	Effective January 1, 1994	10
Brunei	Effective January 1, 2007	10
Bulgaria	Effective January 1, 1991	10
Canada	Effective January 1, 1987	10
Croatia	Effective January 1, 2002	10
Cuba	Effective January 1, 2004	5
Cyprus	Effective January 1, 1992	10
Czech Republic	Effective January 1, 2012	10
Denmark	Effective January 1, 1987	10
	New treaty signed June 16, 2012	
Ecuador	Signed January 21, 2013	Not yet confirmed
Egypt	Effective January 1, 2000	8
Estonia	Effective January 1, 2000	10
Ethiopia	Effective January 1, 2013	5
Finland	Effective January 1, 2011	10
France	Effective January 1, 1986	10
Georgia	Effective January 1, 2006	5
Germany	Effective January 1, 1985	10
Greece	Effective January 1, 2006	10
Hong Kong	Effective January 1, 2007	7
Hungary	Effective January 1, 1995	10
Iceland	Effective January 1, 1998	10
India	Effective January 1, 1995	10
Indonesia	Effective January 1, 2004	10
Iran	Effective January 1, 2004	10
Ireland	Effective January 1, 2001	10
Israel	Effective January 1, 1996	10
Italy	Effective January 1, 1991	10
Jamaica	Effective January 1, 1998	10
Japan	Effective January 1, 1985	10

(continued)

Table 3.10 (continued)

Country	Status	Royalties (%)
Kazakhstan	Effective January 1, 2004	10
Korea (Republic of)	Effective January 1, 1995	10
Kuwait	Effective January 1, 1989	10 %
Kyrgyzstan	Effective January 1, 2004	10
Laos	Effective January 1, 2000	10
Latvia	Effective January 1, 1998 Protocol effective January 1, 2013	7
Lithuania	Effective January 1, 1997	10
Luxembourg	Effective January 1, 1996	10
Macau	Effective January 1, 2004 Protocol effective January 1, 2011	7
Macedonia	Effective January 1, 1998	10
Malaysia	Effective January 1, 1987	10
Malta	Effective January 1, 2012	10
Mauritius	Effective January 1, 1996	10
Mexico	Effective January 1, 2007	10
Moldova	Effective January 1, 2002	10
Mongolia	Effective January 1, 1993	10
Montenegro	Effective January 1, 1998	10
Morocco	Effective January 1, 2007	10
Nepal	Effective January 1, 2011	15
Netherlands	Effective January 1, 1989	10
New Zealand	Effective January 1, 1987	10
Nigeria	Effective January 1, 2010	7.5
Norway	Effective January 1, 1987	10
Oman	Effective January 1, 2003	10
Pakistan	Effective July 1, 1990	10
Papua New Guinea	Effective January 1, 1996	10
Philippines	Effective January 1, 2002	10
Poland	Effective January 1, 1990	10
Portugal	Effective January 1, 2001	10
Qatar	Effective January 1, 2009	10
Romania	Effective January 1, 1993	7
Russia	Effective January 1, 1998	10
Saudi Arabia	Effective January 1, 2007	10
Serbia	Effective January 1, 1998	10
Seychelles	Effective January 1, 2000	10
Singapore	Effective January 1, 2008	10
Slovakia	Effective January 1, 1988	10
Slovenia	Effective January 1, 1996	10
South Africa	Effective January 1, 2001	10
Spain	Effective January 1, 1993	10
Sri Lanka	Effective January 1, 2006	10
Sudan	Effective January 1, 2000	10
Sweden	Effective January 1, 1987 Protocol effective January 1, 1997	10

(continued)

Table 3.10 (continued)

Country	Status	Royalties (%)
Switzerland	Effective January 1, 1990	10
Syria	Effective January 1, 2012	10
Tajikistan	Effective January 1, 2010	8
Thailand	Effective January 1, 1987	10
Trinidad and Tobago	Effective July 1, 2005	10
Tunisia	Effective January 1, 2004	10
Turkey	Effective January 1, 1997	10
Turkmenistan	Effective January 1, 2011	10
Ukraine	Effective January 1, 1997	10
United Arab Emirates	Effective January 1, 1995	10
United Kingdom	Effective January 1, 1985	6/7/10
	New treaty signed June 27, 2011	
United States	Effective January 1, 1987	10
Uzbekistan	Effective January 1, 1997	10
Venezuela	Effective January 1, 2005	10
Vietnam	Effective January 1, 1997	10
Zambia	Effective January 1, 2012	5

3.18.5 Actual Revenue Method

The actual revenue method is the most simple and instantaneous way to calculate the tax base of a *representative office* as the amount of taxable income results by subtracting costs from revenue. The formula is shown in Table 3.11.

This technique is used only by *representative offices* usually practicing economic activities and issuing invoices *(representative offices* of law firms, financial institutions, and others).

3.18.6 Deemed Income Method

This second technique determines the tax base, estimating the income in proportion to revenues generated by the parent company in China (Table 3.12).

The rate has a minimum of 15 %, and the value of the total revenue is estimated based on the revenues of the parent on the Chinese territory.

3.18.7 Cost-Plus Method

The *cost-plus* method is based on costs incurred by the office and revenue and income estimated by launching a benchmarking scheme, as in Table 3.13 below.

Table 3.11 How to calculate the tax base of a representative office: method of actual revenues

Method of actual revenues
Taxable income = Revenue − Costs
Company income tax = Taxable income × 25 %
Business tax = 5 % × Total revenues

Table 3.12 Deemed income method

(a) Taxable income = Total revenues × Deemed income rate
(b) Company income tax = Taxable income × 25 %
(c) Business tax = 5 % × Total revenues

Table 3.13 Cost-plus method

(a) Total revenue = Expenses / (1 − Estimated income rate − 5 % BT)
(b) Company income tax revenue = Total × Estimated income rate × 25 %
(c) Business tax = 5 % × Total revenues

3.19 Anti-Avoidance Rules

3.19.1 Enterprise Income Tax Law Reform

The new *Enterprise Income Tax Law*, in force since January 1, 2008, has introduced a series of anti-avoidance rules aimed at designing a general framework in line with the principles adopted in the legal systems of Western countries.

In particular were introduced the following anti-avoidance rules:

- Standard on transfer prices between related parties
- Standard on *controlled foreign companies*
- Standard on *Advance Pricing Agreement* between a firm and tax authority about transaction prices between related parties
- Standard on *Cost Sharing Agreement* that involves the deductibility of common costs charged to intragroup companies
- Legal obligation to document ongoing transactions between the entity and its affiliated companies ("Related Party Transaction Annual Report")

3.19.2 General Anti-Avoidance Clause

Tax authorities have also introduced a general anti-avoidance clause that enables local officials to make adjustments in a wide range of cases:

> In case an enterprise makes any reasonable commercial arrangement not for purpose, which effectively decrease the causes of its taxable income or revenue, the tax organ may, through reasonable method, make an adjustment.

Table 3.14 Appropriate methods for the calculation of transfer pricing

Transfer pricing methods	*Comparable uncontrolled price method* *Resale price method* *Cost-plus method* *Net profit method* *Profit split method* *Other methods justified*

Table 3.15 Exemption for transfer pricing documentation

There is no obligation to keep an ongoing transfer pricing documentation between the company and its related parties if:	The value of transactions in trade of goods is less than CNY 200 million The value of transactions in services is less than CNY 40 million Transaction values are arranged by an advance pricing agreement between the company and the tax authorities The company has foreign investors for a market share below 50 % and transactions regard only domestic associated enterprises

3.19.3 Thin Capitalization

The backing of a company with a large credit coming from affiliated company lead to the risk of nondeductibility of interest expenses, in contrast to the "thin capitalization" of a society. Indeed, the Chinese Legislature has introduced measures to penalize under-capitalized companies: if the loan, guaranteed by shareholders of related organizations, exceeds five times the amount of their own share of capital (or twice for company not operating in the financial sector), the interests connected to that excess become nondeductible and non-recoverable in the future, and such interests are reclassified as dividends and subject to income tax.

3.19.4 Controlled Foreign Companies

With the entry into force of the reform of the *Enterprise Income Tax Law,* since January 1, 2008, all the Chinese companies are obliged to include part of revenues generated by their foreign subsidiaries in case they are based in countries with a privileged income tax rate of less than 50 % compared with the standard rate of 25 % and in case foreign subsidiaries do not distribute dividends without a valid economic reason.

3.20 Transfer Pricing

In accordance with transfer pricing, companies must engage with associated companies economic transactions at market values. Local authorities have the right to make adjustments where such transactions are performed at different values causing a reduction in tax revenue for the Chinese administration. The *Enterprise Income Tax Law Implementing Rules* show a number of criteria to help determine the degree of control between companies in order to confirm when they might be considered associated for tax purposes. In case of an examination, the authorities can make adjustments in relation to the type, nature, and purpose of the inspection. In Table 3.14 below are quoted the methods for the calculation of transfer prices on the basis of which adjustments can be made.

Companies have the ongoing obligation to document the transactions with related parties within June 1 of the year following the transaction, and the documentation must be kept for 10 years. It might be possible to be exempt from the documentation on *transfer pricing* in case the limits discussed in Table 3.15 are not exceeded.

Chapter 4
Turnover Taxes

4.1 Type of Taxes

The category of turnover taxes is composed of the following:

- *Business Tax* (BT)
- *Value Added Tax* (VAT)
- *Consumption Tax* (CT)

4.2 Business Tax

Business Tax is a turnover tax promulgated by Decree No 136 of the *State Council* of December 13, 1993, subsequently amended on November 5, 2008 with the *Interim Regulations on Business Tax of the People's Republic of China* (IRBT) that finally entered into force on January 1, 2009. The State Administration of Taxation and local tax authorities administer it, while revenues are divided between the central and local governments.

4.3 Taxpayers and Activities Subject to Business Tax

According to article 1 of the *Interim Regulations on Business Tax of the People's Republic of China*, *Business Tax* is levied on services (not subject to VAT), performance of work, transfer of intangible property, sale of real property or rights on real estate whether in return for payment or free of charge. Article 6 of the *Provisional Regulations on Business Tax Implementing Rules* has introduced the concept of business "mixed" sales. When a taxpayer, who sells goods, engages in services not subject to VAT, the activity resulting from this combination is identified by the Legislature with the epithet of "mixed" sales activity and is subject

L. Riccardi, *Chinese Tax Law and International Treaties*,

DOI 10.1007/978-3-319-00275-0_4, © Springer International Publishing Switzerland 2013

to *Business Tax* or *Value Added Tax*, depending on the operation type of the taxpayer. For these subjects referred to in article 6 of the *Provisional Regulations on Business Tax Implementing Rules*, it is necessary to separate the accounts for activities subject respectively to *Value Added Tax* and *Business Tax*. If this is not the case, the competent tax authority determines a taxable amount for each tax.

4.4 The Tax Base

The tax base for *business tax* is the volume of business of the subject. Turnover means the sum of all revenues in addition to the costs incurred in that particular activity, such as service charges, management fees, etc. Costs are not normally deductible with the exception of those incurred by forwarding and construction companies, for which is granted the deductibility of expenses related to activities carried out by *subcontractors*. For a complete list of allowed deductions, refer to the prospectus at the end of paragraph. It has to be borne in mind that if a company's turnover is unjustifiably low, tax authorities may consider modifying that value, raising it to the average price the taxpayer has practiced during the same period for the provision of similar services.

4.5 Determination of the Business Tax

To determine *business tax*, it is sufficient to multiply the value of the business turnover by its tax rate. The formula is the following:

$$\text{Business tax} = \text{Turnover} \times \text{Tax rate}.$$

It is also necessary to emphasize which currency is accepted by the authorities for tax payment. In fact, if the turnover of a taxpayer is in a foreign currency other than CNY, the taxpayer is required to convert the amount in the Chinese currency with the most favorable exchange rate between one of the days on which the income was produced and one on the first day of the month of income production. The tax rate ranges between 3 % (construction, sports and culture, etc.) and 20 % (entertainment business), but it is generally applied a 5 % rate. For a comprehensive list of tax rates, see the table at the end of paragraph.

4.6 Business Tax Tables

See Tables 4.1 and 4.2.

Table 4.1 Business tax subjects

Business tax subjects (art.1 IRBT & art.9 PRBTIR)
Enterprises
Administrative units
Institutions
Military units
Individual industrial
Commercial households
Other units
Other individuals

Table 4.2 Business tax rates

Activities subject to business tax	Rate
Communications & transportation	3 %
Construction	3 %
Finance & insurance	5 %
Posts & telecommunications	3 %
Cultural and sports industry	3 %
General services	5 %
Transfer of intangible assets and immovable property	5 %
Entertainment	5–20 %

4.7 Business Tax Reform

Since 2012, the PRC has undergone a significant turnover tax reform ("Reform") to gradually transit Business Tax to Value Added Tax. Pursuant to Circular Caishui no. 110, no. 111, and no.131, 2011; Caishui no. 71, 2012; and SAT Announcement no. 38, no. 42, and no. 43, 2012, the Reform was first piloted in Shanghai from January 1, 2012, later followed by other eight provinces and municipalities from the third and fourth quarter of 2012.

The scope of this Reform includes transportation and certain modern services, which were previously subject to Business Tax and would be liable to Value Added Tax after the relevant effective dates set out in the aforementioned circulars. Transportation service shall be subject to 11 % VAT, and the other certain modern services shall be subject to 6 % VAT (except that leasing is subject to a 17 % rate). Certain modern services shall refer to R&D and technology services, information technology services, culture and creativity services, logistics supporting services, lease of tangible and movable assets, and assurance and advisory services.

At the time of writing, the regions applicable to the Reform are Shanghai (from January 1, 2012), Beijing (from September 1, 2012), Jiangsu Province and Anhui Province (from October 1, 2012), Fujian Province and Guangdong Province (from November 1, 2012), Tianjin, Zhejiang Province and Hubei Province (from December 1, 2012). The Reform is expected to further enlarge its effectiveness to more regions and categories of services in the near future.

4.8 Value Added Tax

The *Provisional Rules on Value added Tax* were adopted on December 13, 1993 and amended several times, until the end of 2008, while the *Provisional Rules on Value-added Tax Implementing Rules* were adopted on December 23, 1993 and last amended on October 28, 2011. The latest innovations in indirect taxes field have introduced a deductibility of fixed assets and a single VAT rate of 3 % for start-up companies that have not applied for obtaining the status of *normal taxpayer* (so-called small-scale taxpayer). *Value Added Tax* is applicable to all entities performing activities such as sale of goods, services, manufacturing (processing), repairing or replacement services, and import of goods. In addition, owing to the Business Tax Reform, transportation and certain modern services in pilot regions are subject to Value Added Tax.

The calculation of the VAT due is determined by compensation between VAT receivable on purchases (input tax) and VAT on sales (output tax).

Value Added Tax is ruled by the *State Administration of Taxation*, and the related revenues, which are among the most profitable revenues for the Chinese government, are shared out between the central and local governments.

4.9 Taxable Subjects

VAT taxpayers are individuals, state enterprises, domestic and foreign enterprises, institutions, military units, social communities, etc. engaged in activities subject to *Value Added Tax*. Therefore, unlike business companies, not all the individuals are required to pay the VAT but only those that exceed certain thresholds of income in carrying out taxable transactions. These thresholds are not precisely stated by the central government, which instead suggests a *range* containing the maximum limit, but are differently determined by regional and provincial tax authorities. Therefore, pursuant to paragraph 1 of Article 37 IRVATIR, individuals, either Chinese or foreigners, who have a business of less than CNY 5,000 per month referring to goods supplier or less than CNY 5,000 for services provision and yet less than CNY 300 for a total daily value of transactions are not subject to *Value Added Tax*.

4.10 Small-Scale and Normal Taxpayers

Taxpayers who are not individuals, however, are divided into two categories: *small-scale* and *normal taxpayers*. The distinction is primarily based on the turnover value of the taxpayer and its financial management system.

The *small-scale taxpayers* have an unsophisticated internal accounting and inadequate managing system of VAT. A firm operating in the territory of the

PRC requires an annual turnover not over CNY 500,000 for manufacturing companies and less than CNY 800,000 for commercial companies.

The major benefit for *small-scale taxpayers* is represented by a low tax rate of 3 % on issued invoices, but they cannot offset the VAT on purchases with the VAT on sales and the invoices must be issued through the tax office of jurisdiction.

The *normal taxpayer* owns an internal accounting system capable of managing the *Value Added Tax*, and its annual revenue generally exceeds the thresholds established for *small-scale taxpayers*. Hence, the Legislature considers as *normal taxpayers* those manufacturing enterprises with an annual turnover of more than CNY 500,000 and commercial companies with more than CNY 800,000. Unlike *small-scale taxpayers*, *normal taxpayers* issue invoices subject to a tax rate generally equal to 17 % and can deduct the VAT on purchases by the VAT on sales (since January 1, 2009 also on purchases of machinery). The *general taxpayers* may also request a VAT refund on export volume, which varies depending on the Customs Code of the specific category product. Finally, the *taxpayers* generally have their own billing system set on a 17 % VAT rate without any connection with the *tax bureau* as it is for *small-scale taxpayers*.

4.11 Activities Subject to Value Added Tax

Value Added Tax is levied on taxable transactions carried out in the territory of the PRC. These transactions include the following:

- Supply of goods against payment transferring the ownership of assets
- Services of processing (*processing*), repairing or replacement upon payment
- Transportation services in pilot regions of Business Tax Reform
- Certain modern services in pilot regions of Business Tax Reform
- Imports of goods
- Other similar operations

The performance of services other than those listed above is generally subject to *Business Tax*.

4.12 Goods and Services Exempt from Value Added Tax

Not all goods and services are indiscriminately subject to *Value Added Tax*. *In fact*, some are exempted from it. They are numerous and varied and are indicated by the Legislature in Article 15 of the IRVAT and Article 35 of IRVATIR. Among those products there are agricultural commodities; contraceptive drugs and devices in medicine; ancient books; goods imported to be used in scientific research, experiments, and education; goods imported by foreign governments for humanitarian purposes; secondhand goods; etc.

4.13 Calculation of Value Added Tax

Taxpayers adopting monthly or quarterly terms payment shall pay within 15 days after that term passed, while taxpayers who have opted for a shorter period of liquidation, by the fifth. In its tax return statement, the general taxpayer compares the active operations carried out, which constitute the turnover, and passive activities, purchases of goods and services received, during the same period. The difference between taxes on the first active operations and on the second passive activities is the tax that must be paid to the Treasury of China. The calculation formula of the *Value Added Tax* due is shown below:

$$\text{VAT payable} = \text{VAT on sales} - \text{VAT on purchases.}$$

If the VAT on sales is not sufficient to compensate the VAT on purchases, the excess can be deducted in the following tax periods. The calculation of the VAT for *small-scale taxpayers* is simplified. It is granted a reduced tax rate (3 %), and they cannot deduct VAT on purchases.

Generally, *normal taxpayers* are taxed at a rate of 17 %, with *small-scale taxpayers* at 3 %. However, there is also a tax rate of 13 %, for example cereals and edible vegetable oils, books, newspapers, magazines, liquefied petroleum gas (LPG), natural gas, methane, feed, chemical fertilizers, agricultural chemicals, agricultural machinery, etc. Further reductions and special rates can be confirmed by the SAT and specific circulars.

VAT does not affect exports unless stated by the *State Council* for goods, whose export is discouraged. Finally, companies that provide services of *processing*, repair, or replacement shall only be subject to a VAT rate of 17 %.

4.14 VAT Refund on Exports

A partial refund of the VAT is guaranteed in relation to imported and exported goods by manufacturing and commercial companies with a license for import/export.

The rates of refund are different according to the type of product and can be equal to 17 %, 16 %, 15 %, 14 %, 13 %, 11 %, 9 %, and 5 %. That refund rate depends on the HS-code of the specific product category.

There are two methods to calculate the export VAT refund, which vary according to the performance of the export. Production companies utilize the "exemption, deduction and refund method," while commercial companies adopt the "exemption and refund method."

In order to obtain a VAT refund on exports, a company must submit the appropriate application within 90 days from the export, providing a supportive documentation filed together with the client shipping receipt.

Table 4.3 Entities subject to VAT (art. 1 IRVAT and art. 9 IRVATIR)

• Enterprises
• Administrative units
• Institutions
• Military units
• Individual industrial and commercial households
• Other units
• Other individuals

4.15 VAT Subjects and Rates Tables

Taxable goods and activities subject to VAT are illustrated in Tables 4.3, 4.4, and 4.5 below, extracted from the official English translation of the *Interim Regulations of the People's Republic of China on Value Added Tax* and the *Detailed Rules for Implementing the Interim Regulations of the People's Republic of China on Value Added Tax*, respectively promulgated by the *State Council* on November 5, 2008 and October 28, 2011, and taking effect since January 1, 2009.

4.16 Consumption Tax

Consumption Tax is a tax payable by producers and importers of certain goods classified by Chinese law as a "luxury" or "non-essential," such as tobacco, liquor, cosmetics, jewelry, fireworks, tires, motorcycles, *yachts*, luxury watches, etc.

It was promulgated by the *State Council* on December 13, 1993 and entered into force on January 1, 1994. It was finally amended on November 5, 2008, and the final version the *Interim Regulations on Consumption Tax of the People's Republic of China* (IRCT) was entered into force on January 1, 2009. The *Consumption Tax* is administered by the SAT and is an important source of revenue for the central government.

4.17 Taxpayers

Taxpayers of *Consumption Tax* are entities and individuals that import, produce, or commission goods and sell jewelry at retail stage. There are 14 categories to classify the goods subject to *Consumption Tax*. They are quite different and listed under the title of "luxury goods" as stated by the Chinese law. Therefore, goods subject to *Consumption Tax* are tobacco, liquor, cosmetics, jewelry, precious stones, fireworks, petroleum products (such as gasoline, diesel, fuel oil, kerosene), tires, motorcycles, cars, balls and equipment for the game of golf, luxury watches, *yachts*, disposable wooden chopsticks for food, and slatted wooden floor (parquet). However, in Article 11 of the IRCT are exempted from *Consumption Tax* those

Table 4.4 Activities subject to VAT (art. 1 IRVAT and art. 1 Caishui no. 111, 2011), detail of activities subject to VAT (art. 2 IRVATIR) and exempted goods

• Sales of goods	
• Provision of processing, repair, and replacement services	
• Importation of goods	
• Transportation services in pilot regions of Business Tax Reform	
• Certain modern services in pilot regions of Business Tax Reform	
Specifics of activities subject to Value Added Tax (art. 2 IRVATIR and Caishui no. 111, 2011)	
"Goods"	Tangible movables, including electric power, thermal power, and gas
"Processing"	A business where the entrusted party produces goods with the raw materials and principal materials provided by the entrusting party according to the requirements of the entrusting party and receives processing fees
"Repair and replacement"	A businesses carrying out the restoration of damaged or malfunctioning goods to their original conditions and functions
"Transportation"	Business involved in the delivery of goods or passengers to their destination through the use of any means of transportation, including land transportation, waterway transportation, air transportation, and pipeline transmission
"Certain modern services"	Business carried on to provide technical or intellectual services surrounding the manufacturing, cultural, modern logistics, etc. industries, including R&D and technology services, information technology services, culture and creativity services, logistics supporting services, leasing of tangible and movable assets, and assurance and advisory services
***Value Added Tax* exempted goods (art. 15 IRVAT and art. 35 IRVATIR)**	
Self-produced agricultural products sold by agricultural producers (plant production, livestock breeding, forestry, animal husbandry, and aquatic products industry)	
Contraceptive medicines and devices	
Antique books (ancient and used books)	
Importation of instruments and equipment directly used in scientific research, experiment, and education	
Importation of materials and equipment from foreign governments and international organizations as assistance free of charge	
Articles imported directly by the organizations of the disabled for special use by the disabled	
Sale of goods that have been used by the sellers	

goods targeted for export, unless stated differently by the *State Council*. Goods used for the production of other consumer goods are exempted from Consumption Tax.

4.18 Tax Period

The obligation of paying *Consumption Tax* arises every time a luxury item or, in general, an asset subject to CT is produced or imported. The payment of the CT must be due at the *tax bureau* where the taxpayer (individual or company) is a resident, unless otherwise ordered by the *State Council*. Regarding goods produced on commission, unless demanded by an individual, the payment must be done in the place of residence of the client and for imported goods, at the office where the

Table 4.5 Rates of VAT (art. 2 IRVAT and art. 12 Caishui no. 111, 2011)

For taxpayers selling or importing goods		17 %
For taxpayer providing processing, repairs, and replacement services		17 %
For taxpayers selling or importing the following goods:	Edible vegetable oils	13 %
	Tap water	
	Heating gas	
	Cooling gas	
	Hot water	
	Coal gas	
	Liquefied petroleum gas	
	Natural gas	
	Methane gas	
	Coal/charcoal products	
	For household use	
	Books	
	Newspapers	
	Magazines	
	Feeds	
	Chemical fertilizers	
	Agricultural chemicals	
	Agricultural machinery	
	Plastic film for farming	
	Other goods as specified by the State Council	
Transportation services		11 %
Leasing of tangible and movable assets		17 %
Certain modern services		6 %
For taxpayers exporting goods		0 %

customs declaration is made. The payment terms limits are normally settled by the competent tax authority according to the amount due and consist in a day, 3 days, 5 days, 10 days, 15 days, or 1 month. Taxpayers who adopt settlement terms of 1 or 3 months are required to pay within 15 days after the end of that period, while *taxpayers* who opt for a shorter period are required to pay within 5 days from that.

4.19 Tables

Here below is reported Table 4.6 with the categories of goods subject to *Consumption Tax* extracted from the official English translation of the *Interim Regulations on Consumption Tax of the People's Republic of China*, promulgated by the *State Council* on November 5, 2008, and entered into force on January 1, 2009.

Table 4.6 Goods subject to Consumption Tax, revised in Caishui no. 84, 2009

Goods subject to *Consumption Tax*	Tax rate
I. Tobacco (in production stage)	
1. Cigarettes	
(1) Cigarettes, category A	56 % plus 0.003 CNY/piece
(2) Cigarettes, category B	36 % plus 0.003 CNY/piece
2. Cigars	36 %
3. Cut tobacco	30 %
Cigarettes (in wholesale stage)	5 %
II. Alcoholic drinks and alcohol	
1. Distilled spirits	20 % plus 0.5 CNY/500 g (or 500 mL)
2. Rice wine	240 CNY/ton
3. Beer	
(1) Beer, category A	250 CNY/ton
(2) Beer, category B	220 CNY/ton
4. Other alcoholic drinks	10 %
5. Alcohol	5 %
III. Cosmetics	30 %
IV. Jewelry and precious stones	
1. Gold & silver jewelry, platinum jewelry, and diamond & diamond jewelry	5 %
2. Other precious jewelry and precious stone	10 %
V. Firecrackers and fireworks	15 %
VI. Product oil	
1. Petrol	
(1) Leaded petrol	0.28 CNY/L
(2) Unleaded petrol	0.20 CNY/L
2. Diesel oil	0.10 CNY/L
3. Aviation kerosene	0.10 CNY/L
4. Naphtha	0.20 CNY/L
5. Solvent oil	0.20 CNY/L
6. Lubricating oil	0.20 CNY/L
7. Fuel oil	0.10 CNY/L
VII. Motor vehicle tires	3 %
VIII. Motorcycles	
1. Cylinder capacity (displacement, the same below) lower than 250 mL (including 250 mL)	3 %
2. Cylinder capacity higher than 250 mL	10 %
IX. Motor cars	
1. Passenger vehicle	
(1) Cylinder capacity (displacement, the same below) lower than 1.0 L (including 1.0 L)	1 %
(2) Cylinder capacity of 1.0 L–1.5 L (including 1.5 L)	3 %
(3) Cylinder capacity of 1.5 L–2.0 L (including 2.0 L)	5 %
(4) Cylinder capacity of 2.0 L–2.5 L (including 2.5 L)	9 %

(continued)

Table 4.6 (continued)

Goods subject to *Consumption Tax*	Tax rate
(5) Cylinder capacity of 2.5 L–3.0 L (including 3.0 L)	12 %
(6) Cylinder capacity of 3.0 L–4.0 L (including 4.0 L)	25 %
(7) Cylinder capacity higher than 4.0 L	40 %
2. Medium and light commercial buses	5 %
X. Golf ball and its equipment	10 %
XI. High-grade wrist watch	20 %
XII. Yacht	10 %
XIII. Disposable wooden chopsticks	5 %
XIV. Wooden floor boards	5 %

Chapter 5
Profiles of International Tax

5.1 Agreements Against Double Taxation

China has signed tax agreements with the major countries in the world. Table 5.1 is a summary of withholding taxes covered by the agreements against double taxation signed between the Republic of China and foreign countries. Since January 1, 2008 income and dividends distributed to countries without these agreements are subject to a standard tax rate of 10%.

L. Riccardi, *Chinese Tax Law and International Treaties*,
DOI 10.1007/978-3-319-00275-0_5,

Table 5.1 Anti-double taxation Chinese agreements

Country	Status	Dividends (%)	Dividends—qualifying companies (%)	Interest (%)	Royalties (%)
Albania	Effective January 1, 2006	10	10	10	10
Algeria	Effective January 1, 2008	10	5	7	10
Armenia	Effective January 1, 1997	10	5	10	10
Australia	Effective January 1, 1991	10	10	10	10
Austria	Effective January 1, 1993	10	7	10	10
Azerbaijan	Effective January 1, 2006	10	10	10	10
Bahrain	Effective January 1, 2003	5	5	5	10
Bangladesh	Effective January 1, 1998	10	10	10	10
Barbados	Effective January 1, 2001 Protocol effective January 1, 2011	10	5	10	10
Belarus	Effective January 1, 1997	10	10	10	10
Belgium	Effective January 1, 1988 Protocol effective January 1, 2001 New treaty signed October 7, 2009	10	5	10	10

(continued)

Table 5.1 (continued)

Country	Status	Dividends (%)	Dividends—qualifying companies (%)	Interest (%)	Royalties (%)
Bosnia and Herzegovina	Effective January 1, 1998	5	5	5	5
Botswana	Signed April 11, 2012	Not yet confirmed		Not yet confirmed	Not yet confirmed
Brazil	Effective January 1, 1994	10	10	10	10
Brunei	Effective January 1, 2007	5	5	10	10
Bulgaria	Effective January 1, 1991	10	10	10	10
Canada	Effective January 1, 1987	10	10	10	10
Croatia	Effective January 1, 2002	5	5	10	10
Cuba	Effective January 1, 2004	10	5	7.5	5
Cyprus	Effective January 1, 1992	10	10	10	10
Czech Republic	Effective January 1, 2012	10	5	7.5	10
Denmark	Effective January 1, 1987 New treaty signed June 16, 2012	10	5	10	10
Ecuador	Signed January 21, 2013	Not yet confirmed		Not yet confirmed	Not yet confirmed
Egypt	Effective January 1, 2000	8	8	10	8
Estonia	Effective January 1, 2000	10	5	10	10
Ethiopia	Effective January 1, 2013	5	5	7	5

(continued)

Table 5.1 (continued)

Country	Status	Dividends (%)	Dividends—qualifying companies (%)	Interest (%)	Royalties (%)
Finland	Effective January 1, 2011	10	5	10	10
France	Effective January 1, 1986	10	10	10	10
Georgia	Effective January 1, 2006	10	0/5	10	5
Germany	Effective January 1, 1985	10	10	10	10
Greece	Effective January 1, 2006	10	5	10	10
Hong Kong	Effective January 1, 2007	10	5	7	7
Hungary	Effective January 1, 1995	10	10	10	10
Iceland	Effective January 1, 1998	10	5	10	10
India	Effective January 1, 1995	10	10	10	10
Indonesia	Effective January 1, 2004	10	10	10	10
Iran	Effective January 1, 2004	10	10	10	10
Ireland	Effective January 1, 2001	10	5	10	10
Israel	Effective January 1, 1996	10	10	10-Jul	10
Italy	Effective January 1, 1991	10	10	10	10
Jamaica	Effective January 1, 1998	5	5	7.5	10

(continued)

Table 5.1 (continued)

Country	Status	Dividends (%)	Dividends—qualifying companies (%)	Interest (%)	Royalties (%)
Japan	Effective January 1, 1985	10	10	10	10
Kazakhstan	Effective January 1, 2004	10	10	10	10
Korea (Republic of)	Effective January 1, 1995	10	5	10	10
Kuwait	Effective January 1, 1989	5	0	5	10%
Kyrgyzstan	Effective January 1, 2004	10	10	10	10
Laos	Effective January 1, 2000	5	5	10	10
Latvia	Effective January 1, 1998 Protocol effective January 1, 2013	10	5	10	7
Lithuania	Effective January 1, 1997	10	5	10	10
Luxembourg	Effective January 1, 1996	10	5	10	10
Macau	Effective January 1, 2004 Protocol effective January 1, 2011	10	5	7	7
Macedonia	Effective January 1, 1998	5	5	10	10
Malaysia	Effective January 1, 1987	10	10	10	10
Malta	Effective January 1, 2012	10	5	10	10

(continued)

Table 5.1 (continued)

Country	Status	Dividends (%)	Dividends—qualifying companies (%)	Interest (%)	Royalties (%)
Mauritius	Effective January 1, 1996	5	5	10	10
Mexico	Effective January 1, 2007	5	5	10	10
Moldova	Effective January 1, 2002	10	5	10	10
Mongolia	Effective January 1, 1993	5	5	10	10
Montenegro	Effective January 1, 1998	5	5	10	10
Morocco	Effective January 1, 2007	10	10	10	10
Nepal	Effective January 1, 2011	10	10	10	15
Netherlands	Effective January 1, 1989	10	10	10	10
New Zealand	Effective January 1, 1987	10	10	10	10
Nigeria	Effective January 1, 2010	7.5	7.5	7.5	7.5
Norway	Effective January 1, 1987	10	10	10	10
Oman	Effective January 1, 2003	5	5	10	10
Pakistan	Effective July 1, 1990	10	10	10	10
Papua New Guinea	Effective January 1, 1996	10	10	10	10
Philippines	Effective January 1, 2002	10	10	10	10
Poland	Effective January 1, 1990	10	10	10	10

(continued)

Table 5.1 (continued)

Country	Status	Dividends (%)	Dividends—qualifying companies (%)	Interest (%)	Royalties (%)
Portugal	Effective January 1, 2001	10	10	10	10
Qatar	Effective January 1, 2009	10	10	10	10
Romania	Effective January 1, 1993	10	10	10	7
Russia	Effective January 1, 1998	10	10	10	10
Saudi Arabia	Effective January 1, 2007	5	5	10	10
Serbia	Effective January 1, 1998	5	5	10	10
Seychelles	Effective January 1, 2000	5	5	10	10
Singapore	Effective January 1, 2008	10	5	10	10
Slovakia	Effective January 1, 1988	10	10	10	10
Slovenia	Effective January 1, 1996	5	5	10	10
South Africa	Effective January 1, 2001	5	5	10	10
Spain	Effective January 1, 1993	10	10	10	10
Sri Lanka	Effective January 1, 2006	10	10	10	10
Sudan	Effective January 1, 2000	5	5	10	10

(continued)

Table 5.1 (continued)

Country	Status	Dividends (%)	Dividends—qualifying companies (%)	Interest (%)	Royalties (%)
Sweden	Effective January 1, 1987 Protocol effective January 1, 1997	10	5	10	10
Switzerland	Effective January 1, 1990	10	10	10	10
Syria	Effective January 1, 2012	10	5	10	10
Tajikistan	Effective January 1, 2010	10	5	8	8
Thailand	Effective January 1, 1987	10	10	10	10
Trinidad and Tobago	Effective July 1, 2005	10	5	10	10
Tunisia	Effective January 1, 2004	8	8	10	10
Turkey	Effective January 1, 1997	10	10	10	10
Turkmenistan	Effective January 1, 2011	10	5	10	10
Ukraine	Effective January 1, 1997	10	5	10	10
United Arab Emirates	Effective January 1, 1995	7	7	7	10
United Kingdom	Effective January 1, 1985 New treaty signed June 27, 2011	10	5	10	6/7/10
United States	Effective January 1, 1987	10	10	10	10

(continued)

Table 5.1 (continued)

Country	Status	Dividends (%)	Dividends—qualifying companies (%)	Interest (%)	Royalties (%)
Uzbekistan	Effective January 1, 1997	10	10	10	10
Venezuela	Effective January 1, 2005	10	5	10	10
Vietnam	Effective January 1, 1997	10	10	10	10
Zambia	Effective January 1, 2012	5	5	10	5

Chapter 6
Introduction to International Taxation

6.1 Defining International Taxation

The returns on trade and investment within national borders are naturally subject to income taxation. The way in which those incomes are taxed is based upon a country's domestic tax policy. The same principle also applies to international trades and investments. As technology and capital markets have developed over time, people have moved around more and more, often living in different countries over long periods of time and/or generating income in different countries concurrently. As a country's trade and commerce become increasingly internationalized, the taxation of international transactions becomes ever more important. Once an entity extends its arm beyond its national borders, it is most likely to fall within the ambit of the tax laws of another country. The way in which that country's tax laws impact the entity will have consequences for the manner in which the entity is taxed domestically. Thus, the tax regimes of each country become interrelated.

This phenomenon is called "international tax" and can be regarded as a subset of the broader notion of "international law." This perspective is particularly relevant in the context of double tax treaties. However, there is no definitive, overarching international tax law applicable to countries that choose to comply with it. In fact, international tax law is more correctly referred to as the international aspect of the income tax laws of individual countries. With minor exceptions, tax laws are not "international." They are creations of sovereign states. A country at its federal, national, state, or local government level can impose those laws. Most often the tax burden on international transactions is imposed at the national level. However, there are international bodies such as the United Nations (UN) and the Organization for Economic Cooperation and Development (OECD) that attempt to organize and harmonize the tax systems of various nations.

International tax is best regarded as the body of laws of different countries that covers the tax aspects of cross-border transactions. It encompasses all tax issues arising under a country's income tax laws that include some foreign elements. Although income tax aspects of cross-border trade in goods and services represent

L. Riccardi, *Chinese Tax Law and International Treaties*,

DOI 10.1007/978-3-319-00275-0_6,

one important category, international taxation may also include estate taxes, gift taxes, inheritance taxes, general wealth taxes, sales taxes, customs duties, and a variety of special levies.

The international aspects of estate and gift taxes are particularly important. For example, such wealth transfer taxes have important international implications when a resident receives a bequest or gift from a nonresident or non-domiciled individual or when a person dies owning property in a foreign county. Other issues include cross-border manufacturing by a multinational enterprise, cross-border investment by individuals or by investment funds, and taxation of individuals who work or do business outside the country where they usually reside. An activity falling within one of these categories usually presents an international tax issue under the tax laws of at least two countries.

Tax treaties are probably the most obvious international element of a nation's income tax system. Most developed countries have entered into tax treaties with their major trading partners as well. Many developing countries also have extensive treaty networks. These treaties impose significant limitations on the taxation powers of the treaty partners. Tax treaties, however, do not generally impose tax. In fact, in most countries, they are exclusively relieving the tax burden. Although tax treaties are binding agreements between sovereign states, they generally do not have any effects on taxpayers unless they are specifically incorporated into a country's tax law by domestic statute.

International tax situations vary in their complexity. Some international tax laws must be applied to extremely complex situations. One example would be the reorganization of a multinational corporation with foreign subsidiaries in several countries. On the other hand, other situations may be quite simple. For example, an international tax issue would arise under the tax laws of most countries if a resident individual attempts to claim a deduction for the support of a dependent spouse or child residing in a foreign country.

Different countries have addressed the issue of who is liable to tax (the "taxable subject") in an international transaction or economic event (which produces a "taxable object," usually income or capital) in different ways over time for various political, cultural, and historical reasons. However, despite the methodology adopted, if a government wishes to tax transactions and economic events that occur across its borders, it needs to have some underlying policy rationale to substantiate its impost. That justification is based on its "international tax policy."

The generally accepted convention under international law is that while a country is free to levy tax however it chooses, it cannot enforce its tax claims on the territory of another country. In other words, it cannot extend its taxing power on taxable objects that arise in another country. For example, France cannot levy its tax on Germans who derive all of their income from Germany. Therefore, typically a country's tax jurisdictions are confined to taxable subjects and objects that have some sort of connection with the country. Those tax laws normally cover two kinds of activities: (1) the activities of a resident of that country in foreign countries and (2) the activities of a nonresident in that country.

Tax analysts often refer to a transaction involving the export of capital or other resources from a country as an outward-bound or "outbound" transaction.

Conversely, the term inward-bound or "inbound" transaction is commonly used to refer to a transaction involving the import of capital or other resources from a foreign country. A transaction that a country considers to be an outward-bound transaction typically involves its rules for taxing the foreign income of resident taxpayers. Inward-bound transactions, in contrast, typically imply a country's rules for taxing nonresidents on domestic income. In some circumstances, a single transaction may have consequences under both sets of rules. An example is the liquidation of a foreign affiliate into a domestic parent corporation.

6.2 Determining International Tax Policy

The international tax policy adopted by a country will be driven by its economic and social objectives, ultimately, of course, because any country decisions about international tax policies are political ones dictated by those broader economic and social imperatives. However, in order that a conscious decision is taken, proper considerations of different and often conflicting international tax policies are essential. There are generally four major objectives underlying a country's incorporation of international tax rules into its own tax legislation: revenues, investment appeal, import capital neutrality, and/or export capital neutrality.

6.2.1 Revenues

A major goal of a country involved with international tax rules is to provide itself with its fair share of the tax revenues resulting from income generated by transnational activities of domestic and foreign taxpayers. Since the way international transactions are taxed ultimately determines the allocation of the tax imposed between the two (or more) states involved in the international transaction(s), the attempt to maximize national wealth requires that a country maximize its share of that impost. This encompasses both the private return that is obtained by an investor that invests abroad and the tax revenue that the investor's government collects from that investor in respect of the foreign investment. Furthermore, a country must protect its domestic tax base. That is, it must develop good domestic tax rules and avoid entering into tax treaties that inappropriately limit its right to tax its domestic-source income.

6.2.2 Investment Appeal

Each country wants to avoid tax measures that could undermine its competitive position in the global economy. In the international context, removing those provisions of the tax law that lead to a capital flight and a brain drain best enhances a country's competitiveness or that discourages the import of capital and workers. In the medium and long run, however, a country's competitiveness is not enhanced by tax incentives and other beggar-thy-neighbor policies that invite a retaliatory response by foreign governments. Such policies simply erode the ability of all governments to impose fair and effective taxes on income from movable capital.

Moreover, the economic competitiveness of a country's domestic economy would be more stable if taxation does not drive a wedge into optimal investment decision-making. This means that since investors will make investment decisions capable of generating the maximum return, the tax impost on the pretax return on an investment should not distort the after-tax return on the investment and thereby create a bias in the investor's decision-making process. In order to achieve an unbiased outcome, the imposition of tax must be neutral among the array of different domestic and foreign investment options that an investor faces.

6.2.3 Import/Export Capital Neutrality

The principle of capital export neutrality suggests that a country should design its international tax rules so as to neither encourage nor discourage outflows of capital. In practice, policymakers typically treat capital export neutrality as a secondary goal. In virtually every country of the world, capital inflows generally are considered desirable and are encouraged through tax and other economic policies. Conversely, capital outflows are generally thought to diminish national wealth.

In reality, many countries adopt measures designed to discourage capital outflows although they might also have provisions of their tax laws that have the unintended effect of encouraging outflows. Prudent policymakers exercise caution in discouraging outflows because limitations on capital outflows might discourage capital inflows. For example, a country that imposes excessively high withholding taxes on dividends, interest, and royalties paid to nonresidents is likely to discourage nonresidents from investing in that country.

According to the principle of capital export neutrality, a country should avoid international tax rules that might cause its multinational companies to bear a higher effective tax burden in foreign markets than the multinational companies of other countries. To implement this principle fully, residence countries would need to exempt all foreign-source income from domestic tax.

Although no consensus has been reached among tax analysts on the proper balance between these principles in the design of international tax rules, most countries have adopted international tax rules that contain some features consistent with capital export neutrality. For example, most countries tax resident individuals on their worldwide income. Nevertheless, other features are consistent with capital import neutrality. For example, most countries do not tax foreign-source income earned by foreign corporations controlled by residents except in special circumstances.

Generally, it is unwise for small capital-importing countries to adhere strictly to a policy of capital export neutrality to achieve the most efficient worldwide allocation of resources when that country has a negligible impact on global capital markets, while other countries adopt a more relaxed international tax policy position. In setting its international tax policies, a country must take account of the policies adopted by other countries, particularly its major trading partners, and (especially if it is a capital-importing country) the countries competing for the capital investment that it seeks. Therefore, the objectives of international tax policy may well conflict, in which case, a government must decide which objectives shall be predominant in the light of the broader social and economic aims that it is trying to achieve for its citizens.

However, some countries may not have this freedom as the European Union imposes directives upon its 27 individual Member States, which govern, inter alia, how certain transactions between taxable subjects of one Member State and taxable subjects of another Member State have to be treated for tax purposes. For example, the Sixth Directive establishes rules about the imposition of value added tax on cross-border transactions between Member States. Similarly, the Parent-Subsidiary Directive and the Savings Directive specify rules about the imposition (or non-imposition) of income tax on cross-border transactions (of the types addressed in the directives) between Member States.

6.2.4 Other Considerations

As far as the planning of domestic tax policy is concerned, the above international tax policy objectives are formulated within the context of attempting to minimize compliance and administrative costs. In other words, a government that wishes to adopt sound international tax policies will try to ensure that taxpayer's compliance and the tax authority's administrative costs are minimized once the policy is operational. Compliance costs represent a dead-weight loss (costs to the economy arising from the imposition of a tax). Different international tax policies will have different levels of dead-weight loss. For example, international taxation of foreign-sourced income on an accrual basis, which distinguishes between black, white, and gray list countries, will impose greater compliance costs and administrative costs than a policy that does not require such differentiation or a simpler policy that merely exempts foreign-sourced income from the tax base of an investor's country.

In addition, it is generally desirable for a country's international tax policies to be compatible with those of other countries. In a globalized world, where capital freely flows between most countries, a sensible government would not want to impose significantly harsher international tax policies on people investing in its country than those implemented by other countries, which would most likely result in an outflow of resources from that country. Furthermore, where a country's international tax policies are not compatible with those of other countries, arbitrage opportunities are created whereby tax planners can arrange international transactions to take advantage of the asymmetric international tax regimes to the detriment of the tax base of at least one of the countries through which the transactions take place.

6.3 Double Taxation

Some countries tax their citizens or residents on their worldwide income. Others tax only income sourced in their own state. Furthermore, others use a combination of these approaches. As a result, it is quite possible (and, in fact, it is rather common) that taxpayers engaging in cross-border transactions are taxed more than once (usually twice) on the same amount of income. This phenomenon is known as "double taxation." Double taxation can take different forms, but regardless of the form it inhibits economic activity. Therefore, international tax policymakers have designed ways to try to ensure that income derived by a taxpayer is ultimately taxed only once.

Technically, "international double taxation" has been defined as the imposition of comparable income taxes by two or more sovereign countries on the same item of income (including capital gains) in the hands of the same taxable person and for the same taxable period. The juridical or legal definition of international double taxation is a very narrow one, excluding from its scope much of what commentators frequently refer to as double taxation. It identifies what many commentators consider to be the necessary ingredients of international double taxation. Even so, it is not always easy to determine whether double taxation exists under this definition in a particular case. For example, questions may arise as to whether the taxes levied by the two countries are comparable or whether the items of income subject to tax are the same.

International double taxation should be distinguished from internal or domestic double taxation. Domestic double taxation may arise, for example, with respect to income earned by a corporation and distributed to its domestic shareholders under the so-called classical method of corporate taxation. It may also arise when tax is imposed on the income of a person by both the central government of a country and one or more of its political subdivisions. Double taxation by national and subnational governments is not necessarily objectionable. Indeed, when the levels of taxation are properly regulated to avoid excessive tax burdens, such double taxation may be an inevitable feature of fiscal federalism.

Furthermore, the legal definition of international double taxation should be distinguished from the broader economic concept of double taxation. Under the latter definition, double taxation occurs whenever there is multiple taxation of the same item of economic income. Under the legal definition, taxation of a subsidiary company by one country and the taxation of the parent company on a dividend from that subsidiary by another country is not international double taxation because the two companies are separate legal entities. In the economic sense, however, the parent and the subsidiary constitute a single enterprise. Economic but not legal double taxation also may arise when income is taxed to a partnership and to the partners or when it is taxed to a trust and to the beneficiaries of the trust.

The methods for relieving international double taxation use both the legal and the economic definition of double taxation. Double taxation relief sometimes extends to taxes paid by foreign subsidiaries and other foreign affiliates, as dictated by the economic definition. In most other contexts, however, the legal definition predominates. The reason is that the economic definition is exceedingly broad and difficult to specify with the precision needed for the tax laws purpose(s). For example, some economic double taxation occurs when income is taxed as earned and again as consumed. Yet no country is prepared to extend double taxation relief to sales taxes or other consumption taxes. Similarly, countries are not prepared to grant relief from the economic double taxation resulting from the imposition of both an income tax and an estate or wealth tax.

6.4 Sources of Conflict

Most countries tax on the basis of both the residence status of the taxpayer and the source of income. Consequently, both the country of source and the country of residence absent relief provisions designed to prevent double taxation may tax foreign-source income earned by a resident of a country. If income tax rates are low, as they were in the early years of the twentieth century, the inefficiencies and unfairness caused by double taxation are modest enough to be bearable. However, when tax rates reach the levels currently prevailing, double-tax burdens can become onerous and interfere substantially with international commerce. Therefore, the necessity for relief is clear on grounds of equity and economic policy.

6.4.1 Tax Jurisdictions

Before exploring the different types of double taxation, it will first be necessary to examine the types of tax jurisdictions that can become entangled. In the context of taxation of cross-border economic activity, a government is broadly concerned about two things: (a) the activities of residents of other countries in its country and (b) the activities of its residents in foreign countries. These two aspects give rise to the two fundamental platforms of a country's international tax law, commonly known as the (a) *source jurisdiction of taxation* and (b) *residence jurisdiction of taxation.*

6.4.2 Source Jurisdiction

The source jurisdiction of taxation means that a country taxes nonresident individuals and corporations on income generated domestically. In principle, this system of taxation captures income derived by the nonresidents from the sale or use of goods, services, capital, or other resources in the country where these business activities are being undertaken.

Simply put, the reason behind taxation of an income that has a source in a particular country stems from the benefit theory of taxation. A country taxes income of which it is the source because of an evident nexus between it and the income-generating activities. There is an identifiable and tangible connection between the country and the income-earning activity. In other words, the country will tax income arising or having a source within its jurisdiction if it has provided public goods (e.g., roads and other infrastructure, police and military protection, the form and administration of the legal system, etc.) for the benefit of the nonresident taxpayers to enable the taxpayer to undertake its economic activity, which generated the income. In this respect, the tax imposed can be regarded as a contribution towards the cost of those public goods.

Therefore, the benefit theory's rationale behind the source basis of taxation implies that the nonresident taxpayer needs to have some sort of presence in the country of business activities in order to be able to take advantage of the public goods and services offered by the government. This logic explains why, in principle, DTAs require a nonresident business taxpayer to have a "permanent establishment" in such a country before it may impose tax on the nonresident's business income derived in that country. It hence follows that a nonresident merely exporting goods or services from overseas to that country is not liable to be taxed there on income from those export sales (notwithstanding that the income is derived from that country) because the simple exporting of goods or services by a nonresident to that country does not involve any presence there of the nonresident exporter. Thus, as the foreign exporter obtains no benefit of that country's public goods and services, no contribution to the cost of its public goods and services issues.

A similar conclusion can be reached by reference to the "doctrine of economic allegiance," which considers that in an international development "...a part of the total sum paid according to the ability of a person ought to reach the competing authorities according to his economic interest under each authority." One element of the doctrine of allegiance then is to look to where the income or wealth is produced in a physical or economic sense, in other words, to ascertain the origin of the income or wealth produced.

6.4.3 *Residence Jurisdiction*

The residence jurisdiction involves the taxation of a country's resident individuals and corporations on income arising in foreign countries (and also in the country itself), i.e. on the taxpayer's worldwide income. This encompasses income derived by the resident from the sale or use of goods, services, capital, or other resources to, or in, other countries. Again, applying the benefit theory of taxation, income is taxed because of a nexus between a country and the person (not the activity) that earns the income. The resident taxpayer is taxed on his worldwide income because (a) the taxpayer draws the benefit of the government's public goods and services to facilitate the economic activity that produces his income from all sources (both within and outside the country of residence) and (b) the resident taxpayer typically obtains a greater level of public goods and services from the government than a nonresident taxpayer does, e.g. public education and social welfare benefits. Over a longer term, at least some of those public goods and services have put the resident (natural person) taxpayer in a position to earn his or her worldwide income, and therefore it seems reasonable to provide a greater contribution towards the government's costs.

6.5 Types of Double Taxation

International double taxation can arise from a variety of causes. The following three types of double taxation arise from conflicts over tax jurisdiction.

6.5.1 *Source–Source Conflicts*

Two or more countries assert the right to tax the same income of a taxpayer because they all claim the income was sourced in their country.

6.5.2 *Residence–Residence Conflicts*

Two or more countries assert the right to tax the same income of a taxpayer because they claim the taxpayer is a resident of their country. A taxpayer that is a resident of two countries is commonly referred to as a "dual-resident taxpayer."

6.5.3 Residence–Source Conflicts

One country asserts the right to tax foreign-source income of a taxpayer because the taxpayer is a resident of that country, and another country asserts the right to tax the same income because the source of the income is in that country.

International double taxation can also occur due to differences in the way countries define income and in the timing and tax accounting rules they adopt. International double taxation also may occur due to disputes among countries over how to set a proper arm's-length price on cross-border transactions between related parties. Other rules adopted to curtail tax avoidance can also produce double taxation. For example, if one country denies the deduction of interest paid by a resident corporation to a shareholder in another country pursuant to thin capitalization rules, the amount may be taxable in both countries.

Tax treaties typically provide relief from the three major types of international double taxation and from some of the other types as well. Double taxation resulting from source–source conflicts is addressed by seeking some uniformity in source rules. For example, Article 11 (5) of the OECD Model Treaty provides rules concerning the source of interest income. However, most tax treaties do not contain extensive source rules. Instances of the source–source type of double taxation that are not resolved by the specific provisions of a treaty may be resolved through consultation between tax officials of the two treaty countries (the "competent authorities") under the treaty's mutual agreement procedures. Resolution of such issues is not easy, however, because the competent authorities of most countries are reluctant to bargain away their country's source jurisdiction.

Individual taxpayers almost always obtain relief from international double taxation resulting from residence–residence conflicts through tax treaties. Many residence–residence conflicts involving legal entities are also resolved by treaty. Article 4 (2) of the OECD Model Treaty provides a series of "tie-breaker" rules to resolve cases in which an individual is a resident in both countries. The question of dual residence of a legal entity is resolved under the OECD Model Treaty by deeming the entity to be a resident in the country where the place of effective management is located. Countries using the place-of-incorporation test for determining the residence of a corporation usually modify this tiebreaker rule. The mutual agreement procedure is sometimes used to deal with dual-residence cases that are not resolved explicitly in the treaty.

Of these three types of international double taxation, residence–source conflicts are the most likely to occur if measures to relieve double taxation are not put into force. Residence–source conflicts are very difficult for a taxpayer to avoid through tax planning. To some degree, taxpayers can minimize their exposure to the other types of double taxation through careful tax planning. Most of the attempts of the international tax community to deal with international double taxation have focused on the elimination of residence–source conflicts. The residence country ordinarily grants relief from double taxation resulting from the imposition of tax by a residence country and a source country on the same income. In other words, the source country's right to tax has priority over the residence country's right.

6.6 Tax Treaty Models

Countries, as developed by international organizations, generally use double tax treaty models as a basis for negotiations of their bilateral tax treaties. The two models most widely recognized as part of the continuing international efforts aimed at eliminating double taxation are (1) the United Nations Model: Double Taxation Convention between Developed and Developing Countries and (2) the OECD Model: Tax Convention on Income and on Capital. These models formed the basis for most of the several thousand tax treaties currently in force, thus providing a profound influence on international tax treaty practice. The similarities between these two leading models reflect the importance of achieving consistency where possible. On the other hand, the divergences between them reflect the different membership and priorities of the two organizations. The key differences relate, in particular, to the issue as to what extent a country should forego, under bilateral tax treaties, taxing rights, which would be otherwise available to it under domestic law, with a view to avoiding double taxation and encouraging investments.

In general terms, the UN Model tends to preserve a greater share of taxing rights for the source country, which is the country where investment or other activity takes place. The OECD Model, on the other hand, favors retention of a greater share of taxing rights by the residence country, which is the country of the investor or trader. Thus, the UN Model would normally allow developing countries more taxing rights on income generated by foreign investments in these countries. This has long been regarded as an issue of particular importance for developing countries in view of their development goals. Nevertheless, it is also a position that some developed countries seek in their bilateral tax treaties.

6.6.1 The Organization for Economic Cooperation and Development (OECD) Model

The Organization for Economic Cooperation and Development (OECD) is an international economic organization of 34 countries founded in 1961 to stimulate economic progress and world trade. It is a forum of countries committed to democracy and the market economy, providing a platform to compare policy experiences, seeking answers to common problems, identifying good practices, and coordinating domestic and international policies of its members.

The OECD defines itself as a "forum of countries committed to democracy and the market economy; providing a setting to compare policy experiences, seek answers to common problems, identify good practices, and coordinate domestic and international policies." Its mandate covers economic, environmental, and social issues. It acts by peer pressure to improve policy and implement "soft law"—nonbinding instruments that can occasionally lead to binding treaties. In this work, the OECD cooperates with businesses, trade unions, and other representatives of civil society. Collaboration at the OECD regarding taxation, for example, has fostered the growth of a global web of bilateral tax treaties.

The OECD published and updates a model tax convention that serves as a template for bilateral negotiations regarding tax coordination and cooperation. This model is accompanied by a set of commentaries that reflect OECD level interpretation of the content of the model convention provisions. In general, this model allocates the primary right to tax to the country from which capital investment originates (i.e., the home or resident country) rather than the country in which the investment is made (the host or source country). As a result, it is most effective as between two countries with reciprocal investment flows, such as among the OECD member countries, but can be very unbalanced when one of the signatory countries is economically weaker than the other (such as between OECD and non-OECD parties).

Since 1998, the OECD has led a charge against harmful tax practices, mainly targeting the activities of tax havens (while principally accepting the policies of its member countries, which would tend to encourage tax competition). These efforts have been met with mixed reactions: the primary objection is the consideration of tax policy as a matter of sovereign entitlement. The OECD maintains a "blacklist" of countries it considers uncooperative in the drive for transparency of tax affairs and the effective exchange of information, officially called "The List of Uncooperative Tax Havens." In May 2009, all remaining countries were removed from the list.

In an OECD meeting in Paris (October 22, 2008), 17 countries led by France and Germany decided to draw up a new blacklist of tax havens. The OECD has been asked to investigate around 40 new tax havens in the world where undeclared revenue is hidden and that host many of the nonregulated hedge funds that have come under fire during the 2008 financial crisis. Germany, France, and other countries called on the OECD to specifically add Switzerland to a blacklist of countries that encourage tax fraud. China treaties generally follow the OECD model.

6.6.2 The United Nations (UN) Model

The UN Model aims at both encouraging investments and increasing public revenues for sustainable development. To this end, it seeks a compromise between the so-called source taxation (i.e., taxation in the host country of the investment) and the so-called residence taxation (i.e., taxation in the home country of the investor). However, compared to other leading international double tax treaty models, the UN Model gives more weight to source taxation, thus protecting the specific interest of developing countries to retain a greater share of taxing rights over the income sourced in those countries so that the proceeds can be used to meet development needs. However, the provisions of the UN Model take into consideration the fact that taxation in the source country should not be too high in order not to discourage investment and recognize the appropriateness of the sharing of revenue with the country providing the capital. For instance, unlike other leading international tax treaty models that allocate taxing rights over royalties only to the country of residence of the recipient, the UN Model provides that royalties may also be taxed in the country where they originate to a maximum percentage negotiated in the bilateral tax treaty. The country of residence of the recipient is also allowed to tax the royalties but needs to deduct the amount already paid in the other country. There is an obligation in the UN Model that the country of residence of the recipient grant double taxation relief for taxes paid in the country where the royalties originate.

Tax treaties based on the UN Model, therefore, play a key role in preventing double taxation over cross-border income, thus promoting international investments, trade, and transfer of technology. By the same token, they also retain appropriate shares of taxing rights over income sourced in developing countries in support of achieving their development goals.

Recently reaching a milestone in its ongoing efforts to enhance international tax cooperation, the United Nations encourages international investments for development. An updated version of the United Nations Model: Double Taxation Convention between Developed and Developing Countries was adopted in 2011. It culminates the work carried out by the UN Committee of Experts on International Cooperation in Tax Matters for over more than a decade since the last revision of the UN Model in 1999 (which was published in 2001). The main objective of this revision of the UN Model has been to take into account recent developments in the area of international tax policies of both developing and developed countries. Moreover, the updated UN Model further clarifies and improves the operation of its provisions aimed to prevent double taxation over income from cross-border investments and activities and also offers improved explanations to help countries make their own decisions on these important issues of tax policy and practice.

Chapter 7
Transfer Pricing Policies in China

7.1 Definitions and Application in China

Transfer pricing is the common term for the pricing charged on intra-firm, cross-border transactions of associated enterprises established in different tax jurisdictions. Rapid advances in technology, communication, and transportation have given rise to a large number of multinational enterprises that have integrated global operations. The fact is that a significant volume of global trade nowadays consists of international transfer of large quantities of goods and services among operating subsidiaries in different countries, as well as capital and intangibles.

The pricing system for such intragroup and cross-border transactions entails extensive tax and managerial troubles due to its direct effects on the profits of the parties and the taxable revenue of the countries involved in the transactions. The structure of these international transactions is a combination of market and group conditions, which can be driven by the common interests of the parties of the group. In such cases, tax authorities need to protect their revenue base and control "on an arm's length basis" (ALP) the runaway transactions between companies.

This principle refers to (article 9) of the Organization for Economic Cooperation and Development (OECD) Model Tax Convention, which ensures that the transfer prices between multinational enterprises are established on a market value basis. The OECD Transfer Pricing Guidelines required a comparison between what the taxpayer has done and what an independent party would have done under similar circumstances. The arm's-length principle (ALP) is applied by comparing controlled transactions with transaction between independent enterprises. The prices of transactions should be the same as they would have been if the parties were not related. If the prices of transaction are different, the tax authority can make adjustments to eliminate their effect. This principle uses the comparison with independent parties as a guide to determinate the allocation of income and expenses between related parties. The aim of transfer prices is to calculate the income of the parties of the group involved in the cross-border transaction. In this scenario, there are three parties: the multinational group and the taxing authorities of the two

L. Riccardi, *Chinese Tax Law and International Treaties*,

DOI 10.1007/978-3-319-00275-0_7,

Table 7.1 Chinese transfer pricing legislation

1991	Income Tax Law of the People's Republic of China for Foreign Invested Enterprises and Foreign Enterprises—art. 13	Reasonable adjustments if transactions were not carried out at arm's length
1998	Tax Administration Rules and Procedures for Transactions between Related Parties—SAT Circular No. 59	Standardized transfer pricing examination and audit procedures
2004	Implementation Rules for Advance Pricing Agreements for Transactions between Related Parties—Guo Shui Fa [2004] No. 118	Guidelines on Advance Pricing Agreement (APA) procedures
2007	2007 Guo Shui Han [2007]	SAT guidelines considering the profitability of the FIEs and foreign enterprises in China that undertake the sole function of manufacturing for their overseas parent companies
2007	Corporate Income Tax Law of the People's Republic of China—State Council Order No. 63 of People's Republic of China	New CIT Law repealing the 1991 Income Tax Law for FIEs and FEs and including a range of measures designed to strengthen transfer pricing compliance and enforcement in China
2007	Implementation Rules of the Corporate Income Tax Law in People's Republic of China	Implemented regulation
2007	Guo Shui Han [2007] No. 363	Documentation to be submitted for the audit
2008	Draft Administrative Regulations of Special Tax Adjustment (Trial)	Signed the opening of a period of discussions and feedbacks about the final form of the Regulations
2008	Guo Shui Fa [2008] No. 114	Related party disclosure forms that will be required to be submitted by all taxpayers with any related party transactions
2009	Implementation Measures of Special Tax Adjustments—Guo Shui Fa [2009] No. 2	Definitive Transfer Pricing Regulation

countries involved in the transaction. The increasing prominence in the international economy and, in particular, the phenomenal spread of foreign-invested enterprises have made China's tax system more rigorous in transferring prices issued. In particular, in 2008, with enforcement in 2009 and in 2010, new regulation came into effect. This means that the detailed transfer pricing documentation is required and that the companies have to disclose related party information on tax returns, as well as consider a possible audit.

The EITL, which came into effect on January 1, 2008, included the following article(s) regarding transfer pricing regulations:

> *For business transactions between an enterprise and a related party which do not comply with the arm's length principle thus resulting in reduced taxable revenue or taxable income for the enterprise or its related enterprise, tax bureau has the right to make adjustments based on reasonable methods. Costs associated with the joint development or transfer of intangible assets, or with the provision or receipt of labour services shall be allocated based on the arm's length principle when computing taxable income.*

The State Administration of Taxation (SAT) published the Implementation Regulation for Special Tax Adjustments, which provides a detailed guidance on which enforced tax adjustments, in particular, are connected with transfer pricing. The issuance of the SAT Rules is a landmark in the history of Chinese transfer pricing rules, which is now closer to the international transfer pricing standards (Table 7.1).

7.2 OECD Guidelines

Chinese authorities do not formally endorse the OECD Transfer Pricing Guidelines for Multinational Enterprises and Tax Administrations (OECD guidelines). The new Chinese Regulations, however, are generally consistent with the OECD guidelines. This chapter describes the OECD criteria that are followed by the Chinese legislation. Paragraph 1 of Article 9 of the Model Tax convention defines the statement of the arm's-length principle:

> *[Where] conditions are made or imposed between the two [associated] enterprises in their commercial or financial relations which differ from those which would be made between independent enterprises, then profits which would, but for those conditions, have accrued to one of the enterprises, but, by reason of those conditions, have not so accrued, may be included in the profits of that enterprise and taxed accordingly.*

The arm's-length principle expresses the approach of treating the members of a cross-border group as separate entities and not as independent. The reason of the adoption of this principle is to avoid the creation of tax advantages or disadvantages between same entity enterprises. The focus of this principle is promoting the growth of international trade and investment. The practical difficulty connected with the application of the arm's-length principle is that it is not always easy to make a comparison between the companies. Sometimes members of the same group face different commercial circumstances that independent enterprises would not undertake. Guidelines of the transfer pricing are summed up in the glossary of the OECD transfer pricing guidelines for multinational enterprises and tax administration as follows.

7.2.1 *Advance Pricing Arrangement ("APA")*

> *An arrangement that determines, in advance of controlled transactions, an appropriate set of criteria (e.g. method, comparable and appropriate adjustments thereto, critical assumptions as to future events) for the determination of the transfer pricing for those transactions over a fixed period of time. An advance pricing arrangement may be unilateral involving one tax administration and a taxpayer or multilateral involving the agreement of two or more tax administrations.*

7.2.2 Arm's-Length Principle

The international standard that OECD member countries have agreed should be used for determining transfer prices for tax purposes. It is set forth in Article 9 of the OECD Model Tax Convention as follows: where "conditions are made or imposed between the two enterprises in their commercial or financial relations which differ from those which would be made between independent enterprises, then any profits which would, but for those conditions, have accrued to one of the enterprises, but, by reason of those conditions, have not so accrued, may be included in the profits of that enterprise and taxed accordingly".

7.2.3 Arm's-Length Range

A range of figures that are acceptable for establishing whether the conditions of a controlled transaction are arm's length and that are derived either from applying the same transfer pricing method to multiple comparable data or from applying different transfer pricing methods

7.2.4 Associated Enterprises

Two enterprises are associated enterprises with respect to each other if one of the enterprises meets the conditions of Article 9, sub-paragraphs 1a) or 1b) of the OECD Model Tax Convention with respect to the other enterprise.

7.2.5 Balancing Payment

A payment, normally from one or more participants to another, to adjust participants' proportionate shares of contributions, that increases the value of the contributions of the payer and decreases the value of the contributions of the payee by the amount of the payment.

7.2.6 Buy-In Payment

A payment made by a new entrant to an already active CCA for obtaining an interest in any results of prior CCA activity.

7.2.7 Buy-Out Payment

Compensation that a participant who withdraws from an already active CCA may receive from the remaining participants for an effective transfer of its interests in the results of past CCA activities.

7.2.8 Commercial Intangible

An intangible that is used in commercial activities such as the production of a good or the provision of a service, as well as an intangible right that is itself a business asset transferred to customers or used in the operation of business.

7.2.9 Comparability Analysis

A comparison of a controlled transaction with an uncontrolled transaction or transactions. Controlled and uncontrolled transactions are comparable if none of the differences between the transactions could materially affect the factor being examined in the methodology (e.g. price or margin), or if reasonably accurate adjustments can be made to eliminate the material effects of any such differences.

7.2.10 Comparable Uncontrolled Transaction

A comparable uncontrolled transaction is a transaction between two independent parties that is comparable to the controlled transaction under examination. It can be either a comparable transaction between one party to the controlled transaction and an independent party ("internal comparable") or between two independent parties, neither of which is a party to the controlled transaction ("external comparable").

7.2.11 Comparable Uncontrolled Price (CUP) Method

A transfer pricing method that compares the price for property or services transferred in a controlled transaction to the price charged for property or services transferred in a comparable uncontrolled transaction in comparable circumstances.

7.2.12 Compensating Adjustment

An adjustment in which the taxpayer reports a transfer price for tax purposes that is, in the taxpayer's opinion, an arm's length price for a controlled transaction, even though this price differs from the amount actually charged between the associated enterprises. This adjustment would be made before the tax return is filed.

7.2.13 Contribution Analysis

An analysis used in the profit split method under which the combined profits from controlled transactions are divided between the associated enterprises based upon the relative value of the functions performed (taking into account assets used and risks assumed) by each of the associated enterprises participating in those transactions, supplemented as much as possible by external market data that indicate how independent enterprises would have divided profits in similar circumstances.

7.2.14 Controlled Transactions

Transactions between two enterprises that are associated enterprises with respect to each other.

7.2.15 Corresponding Adjustment

An adjustment to the tax liability of the associated enterprise in a second tax jurisdiction made by the tax administration of that jurisdiction, corresponding to a primary adjustment made by the tax administration in a first tax jurisdiction, so that the allocation of profits by the two jurisdictions is consistent.

7.2.16 Cost Contribution Arrangement ("CCA")

A CCA is a framework agreed among enterprises to share the costs and risks of developing, producing, or obtaining assets, services, or rights, and to determine the nature and extent of the interests of each participant in the results of the activity of developing, producing, or obtaining those assets, services, or rights.

7.2.17 Cost-Plus Markup

A mark up that is measured by reference to margins computed after the direct and indirect costs incurred by a supplier of property or services in a transaction.

7.2.18 Cost-Plus Method

A transfer pricing method using the costs incurred by the supplier of property (or services) in a controlled transaction. An appropriate cost plus mark up is added to this cost, to make an appropriate profit in light of the functions performed (taking into account assets used and risks assumed) and the market conditions. What is arrived at after adding the cost plus mark up to the above costs may be regarded as an arm's length price of the original controlled transaction.

7.2.19 Direct Charge Method

A method of charging directly for specific intra-group services on a clearly identified basis.

7.2.20 Direct Costs

Costs that are incurred specifically for producing a product or rendering service, such as the cost of raw materials.

7.2.21 Functional Analysis

An analysis of the functions performed (taking into account assets used and risks assumed) by associated enterprises in controlled transactions and by independent enterprises in comparable uncontrolled transactions.

7.2.22 Global Formulary Apportionment

An approach to allocate the global profits of an MNE group on a consolidated basis among the associated enterprises in different countries on the basis of a predetermined formula.

7.2.23 Gross Profits

The gross profits from a business transaction are the amount computed by deducting from the gross receipts of the transaction the allocable purchases or production costs of sales, with due adjustment for increases or decreases in inventory or stock-in-trade, but without taking account of other expenses.

7.2.24 Independent Enterprises

Two enterprises are independent enterprises with respect to each other if they are not associated enterprises with respect to each other.

7.2.25 Indirect Charge Method

A method of charging for intra-group services based upon cost allocation and apportionment methods.

7.2.26 Indirect Costs

Costs of producing a product or service which, although closely related to the production process, may be common to several products or services (for example, the costs of a repair department that services equipment used to produce different products).

7.2.27 Intragroup Service

An activity (e.g. administrative, technical, financial, commercial, etc.) for which an independent enterprise would have been willing to pay or perform for itself.

7.2.28 Intentional Setoff

A benefit provided by one associated enterprise to another associated enterprise within the group that is deliberately balanced to some degree by different benefits received from that enterprise in return.

7.2.29 Marketing Intangible

An intangible that is concerned with marketing activities, which aids in the commercial exploitation of a product or service and/or has an important promotional value for the product concerned.

7.2.30 Multinational Enterprise Group (MNE Group)

A group of associated companies with business establishments in two or more countries.

7.2.31 Multinational Enterprise (MNE)

A company that is part of an MNE group.

7.2.32 Mutual Agreement Procedure

A means through which tax administrations consult to resolve disputes regarding the application of double tax conventions. This procedure, described and authorized by Article 25 of the OECD Model Tax Convention, can be used to eliminate double taxation that could arise from a transfer pricing adjustment.

7.2.33 Net Profit Indicator

The ratio of net profit to an appropriate base (e.g. costs, sales, assets).

The transactional net margin method relies on a comparison of an appropriate net profit indicator for the controlled transaction with the same net profit indicator in comparable uncontrolled transactions.

7.2.34 "On Call" Services

Services provided by a parent company or a group service center, which are available at any time for members of an MNE group.

7.2.35 Primary Adjustment

An adjustment that a tax administration in a first jurisdiction makes to a company's taxable profits as a result of applying the arm's length principle to transactions involving an associated enterprise in a second tax jurisdiction.

7.2.36 Profit Potential

The expected future profits. In some cases it may encompass losses. The notion of "profit potential" is often used for valuation purposes, in the determination of an arm's length compensation for a transfer of intangibles or of an ongoing concern, or in the determination of an arm's length indemnification for the termination or substantial renegotiation of existing arrangements, once it is found that such compensation or indemnification would have taken place between independent parties in comparable circumstances.

7.2.37 Profit Split Method

A transactional profit method that identifies the combined profit to be split for the associated enterprises from a controlled transaction (or controlled transactions that it is appropriate to aggregate under the principles of Chapter III) and then splits those profits between the associated enterprises based upon an economically valid basis that approximates the division of profits that would have been anticipated and reflected in an agreement made at arm's length.

7.2.38 Resale Price Margin

A margin representing the amount out of which a reseller would seek to cover its selling and other operating expenses and, in the light of the functions performed (taking into account assets used and risks assumed), make an appropriate profit.

7.2.39 Resale Price Method

A transfer pricing method based on the price at which a product that has been purchased from an associated enterprise is resold to an independent enterprise. The resale price is reduced by the resale price margin. What is left after subtracting the resale price margin can be regarded, after adjustment for other costs associated with the purchase of the product (e.g. custom duties), as an arm's length price of the original transfer of property between the associated enterprises.

7.2.40 Residual Analysis

An analysis used in the profit split method which divides the combined profit from the controlled transactions under examination in two stages. In the first stage, each participant is allocated sufficient profit to provide it with a basic return appropriate for the type of transactions in which it is engaged.

Ordinarily this basic return would be determined by reference to the market returns achieved for similar types of transactions by independent enterprises.

Thus, the basic return would generally not account for the return that would be generated by any unique and valuable assets possessed by the participants. In the second stage, any residual profit (or loss) remaining after the first stage division would be allocated among the parties based on an analysis of the facts and circumstances that might indicate how this residual would have been divided between independent enterprises.

7.2.41 Secondary Adjustment

An adjustment that arises from imposing tax on a secondary transaction.

7.2.42 Secondary Transaction

A constructive transaction that some countries will assert under their domestic legislation after having proposed a primary adjustment in order to make the actual allocation of profits consistent with the primary adjustment.

Secondary transactions may take the form of constructive dividends, constructive equity contributions, or constructive loans.

7.2.43 Shareholder Activity

An activity which is performed by a member of an MNE group (usually the parent company or a regional holding company) solely because of its ownership interest in one or more other group members, i.e. in its capacity as shareholder.

7.2.44 Simultaneous Tax Examinations

A simultaneous tax examination, as defined in Part A of the OECD Model Agreement for the Undertaking of Simultaneous Tax Examinations, means an "arrangement between two or more parties to examine simultaneously and independently, each on its own territory, the tax affairs of (a) taxpayer(s) in which they have a common or related interest with a view to exchanging any relevant information which they so obtain."

7.3 Transfer Pricing In China

The SAT is very motivated to enforce transfer pricing, especially since the introduction of a unified corporate income tax rate (25 %) has increased the tax burden imposed on many multinationals in China, as well as a range of other factors. Transfer pricing audits will focus on these enterprises:

1. Those that have various types of related party transactions;
2. Those that have been in long-term consecutive losses, low profitability, or fluctuating profit;
3. Those whose profit levels are lower than those in the same industry;
4. Those showing an obvious mismatch between their profit levels and their functional and risk profile;
5. Those that have business dealings with related parties in tax havens;
6. Those that have not complied with the reporting of their related party transactions or preparation of contemporaneous documentation; and
7. Those obviously violating the arm's-length principle.

Furthermore, the SAT has intensified its investigation on industries and on group-oriented enterprise. During 2011, the pharmaceutical and automotive industries have been a primary target for transfer pricing investigations.

7.4 Related Party Transactions

China's local and national tax authorities can adjust taxpayers' transfer prices to an arm's-length level. Taxpayers are obliged to support with prepared evidence that their transfer prices are at arm's length. The China Transfer Pricing regulations have application to all the corporations that fall within the definition of "related parties."

The China Transfer Prising regulations consider in Circular 2 the term "related parties" as follows[3]:

1. One party directly or indirectly holds a total of 25 % or more of another party's shares, or a third party holds, directly or indirectly, 25 % or more of the shares of both parties. Where one party holds the shares of another party through an intermediary, if the party holds 25 % or more of the shares of the intermediary, that party's shareholding percentage of the other party will be considered the same as the intermediary's. Shares held by the intermediate party shall be applied to calculate the percentage of the other party's share held by that party.

2. Debts owed by one party to another party (except to an independent financial institution) exceed 50 % of the party's actual received capital, or 10 % or above of the total debts owed by one party is guaranteed by another party (except by an independent financial institution).
3. More than half of one party's senior management personnel (including the members of the board of directors and managers), or at least one senior member of the board of directors who is able to exert control over the board of directors, is appointed by another party or two parties with more than half of their senior management personnel (including the members of the board of directors and managers), or more than one senior member of the board of directors who is able to exert control over the board of directors, is appointed by the same third party.
4. More than half of one party's senior management personnel (including the members of the board of directors and managers) concurrently holds senior management positions (including the members of the board of directors and managers) of another party or at least one senior member of the board of directors who is able to exert control over the board of directors concurrently holds the position of senior member of the board of directors of another party.
5. One party's normal production and operational activities are dependent on intangibles licensed from another party (including industrial property rights or know-how).
6. The purchase or sales activities are primarily controlled by another party.
7. One party's provision or receipt of services is primarily controlled by another party.
8. One party has substantial control over another party's production, operation, and transactions or has other relationships on interests (including the relationship where one party shares basically the same interests with major shareholders of another party even though the shareholding percentage requirement of (1) is not satisfied, as well as family relationships).

7.5 Documentation and Disclosure Requirements

Circulars Guoshuifa no. 114, 2008 and Guoshuifa no. 2, 2009 state that enterprises are required to prepare a precise documentation and disclosure requirement during the tax filling from 2008 and 2009. In particular, there are nine related party disclosure forms that need to be completed and submitted by taxpayers along with their annual tax return on or before 31 May of the following year.

The nine forms required are as follows:

1. Annual Reporting of Related Party Transactions—Associated Parties
2. Annual Reporting of Related Party Transactions—Transaction Summary
3. Annual Reporting of Related Party Transactions—Sales and Purchases
4. Annual Reporting of Related Party Transactions—Services
5. Annual Reporting of Related Party Transactions—Transfer of Intangible Assets

Table 7.2 Documentation requirements

Organizational structure and specific information	**– Organizational structure** **– Information of related parties and relationship** **– Preferential tax treatment of related parties** **– Effective tax rates of related party**
Business operation	– Overview of principal business operations – Market position and environment – Consolidated financial statement – Assets, functions and risks profile
Related party transactions	– Descriptions of the related party transactions – Copy of relevant contracts – Factor influencing pricing
Comparability analysis	– Description of comparable transaction – Comparable analysis – Adjustments
Selection and application of TP methods	– Pricing methods selected – Result of comparability analysis – Other assumptions and judgments

6. Annual Reporting of Related Party Transactions—Transfer of Fixed Assets
7. Annual Reporting of Related Party Transactions—Financing
8. Annual Reporting of Related Party Transactions—Outbound Investments
9. Annual Reporting of Related Party Transactions—Outbound Payments

These forms require all taxpayers with related party transactions to provide considerably detailed information regarding those transactions to the SAT on a yearly basis. The SAT Rules specify that contemporaneous documentation should include the following details:

(a) Organizational structure
(b) Summary of business operations
(c) Information about the related party transactions
(d) Comparability analysis
(e) Selection and application of transfer pricing methods

However, there are three exemptions for contemporaneous documentation requirements:

(a) Annual amount of related party purchases and sales is lower than Chinese Yuan Renminbi (CNY) 200 million, and other related party transactions total less than CNY 40 million;
(b) An Advance Pricing Arrangement (APA) is in place;
(c) A company's foreign-owned shares account for less than 50 % of the total, and related party transactions are with domestic related parties only.

Taxpayers should submit their contemporaneous transfer pricing documentation within 20 days of the date of request by the tax bureau. The documentation needs to

Table 7.3 Disclosure forms

Related parties	**– Background information of relationship** **– Type of association** **– Information about the parties**
Summary of RP transactions	– Type and amount of related party transaction, domestic and cross border
Purchase and sales	– Financial information about sales between the related parties and third parties – Name and location of the parties
Services	– Service revenue and expenses from transactions with cross-border and domestic related parties
Intangible assets	– Information on acquisition and disposal of intangible assets between the parties
Tangible assets	– Information on acquisition and disposal of tangible assets between the parties
Financing	– Information on debt financing of the parties
Foreign investment	– Information of investment in foreign enterprises – Financial information on the invested company – Profit and dividend distribution, shareholding, and income tax status
Foreign payments	– Information about outbound payments – Any beneficial treatment under tax

be completed by May 31 of the year following the tax year, e.g. for the tax year ended December 31, 2010, the due date is May 31, 2011. All documents, including those originally in a foreign language, must be submitted to the tax bureau in Chinese language and must be retained for 10 years from June 1 following the relevant tax year. Such documentation is the only accepted method of giving the tax authorities a clear understanding of the transfer pricing model and commercial realities of the business of a taxpayer. Most significantly, it is the best means of presenting the company's case to the local tax bureau's staff in a favorable light, with a view to avoiding a lengthy and costly transfer pricing audit (Tables 7.2 and 7.3).

7.6 Penalties

In China, if the taxpayer under investigation refuses to provide documents, fails to provide the required documents, or provides false/incomplete information, tax authorities may order them to rectify the situation within a certain time limit and impose a fine of up to RM 50,000. Furthermore, the tax bureau is authorized to adjust the taxpayer's taxable income in accordance with "reasonable" deemed methods. Anyway, even if taxpayers are not required to prepare transfer pricing documentation, it is recommended to do so in the following circumstances:

Table 7.4 Interest and penalty

Interest and penalty	**Cash penalty:** **RMB 10,000–50,000 for any enterprise that refuses to provide contemporaneous documentation and other relevant information on related party transaction or provides false or incomplete information. Deemed profit adjustment; additional interest: the interest will be levied on a daily basis. The interest rate is the contemporaneous basic RMB lending rate plus 5 % as surcharge. If the audited entity can provide contemporaneous documentation as requested by tax authority, the 5 % surcharge could be waived.**

- The taxpayer has characteristics that render it at high risk of transfer pricing audit and investigation, such as being a loss-making manufacturer or a distributor achieving net margins lower than the industry norm;
- The taxpayer operates in a high-risk industry or is part of a large multinational group that is at high-risk of a transfer pricing audit;
- The taxpayer discloses unusual or suspicious related party transactions or transfer pricing methods when completing the obligatory related party disclosure forms (Table 7.4).

7.7 Transfer Pricing Methods

The following TP methods have been prescribed in Chinese tax laws and regulations for the determination of whether a related party transaction is conducted following the arm's-length principle:

- Comparable uncontrolled price method ("CUP")
- Resale price method ("RPM")
- Cost-plus method ("CPM")
- Transactional net margin method ("TNMM")
- Profit split method ("TNMM")
- Other appropriate methods that comply with the arm's-length principle

The methods prescribed in the China Transfer Pricing Regulations coincides with the method described by the OECD guidelines. There are no specific methods required in the Chinese regulations because the selection of the right method should be based on the particular facts and circumstances of a transaction and results in a reliable determination of the arm's-length price. However, the Chinese tax authorities typically focus on the method that focuses on the net margin (e.g., TNMM).

This tends towards arguing for a (residual) profit split, especially when the taxpayer has a profitable supply chain and the sales are made to the Chinese market. CUPs are not commonly used in the Chinese context.

A comparable analysis should primarily consider the following five aspects when selecting a reasonable transfer pricing method:

(1) Characteristics of the transacted assets or services, mainly including: the physical characteristics, quality, and quantity of the tangible properties; the nature and scope of the services; the types, the transaction forms, the duration and scope, and the expected returns of the intangible properties;
(2) Functions performed and risks assumed by all parties to the transactions. Functions mainly include: R&D, design, purchasing, processing, assembling, manufacturing, inventory management, distribution, after-sale services, advertising, transportation, storage, financing, finance, accounting, legal and human resource management, etc. When comparing functions, close attention should be paid to the similarity of assets employed by the enterprises to perform these functions. Risks mainly include: R&D risks, purchase risks, production risks, distribution risks, marketing risks, management and financial risks, etc.;
(3) Contractual terms, mainly including: the subject of the transaction, the quantity and prices of the transactions, the forms and terms of payment; the terms of delivery; the scope and terms of the after-sale services; the agreement of the provision of additional services; the rights related to modifying and amending the content of the contract; the validity duration of the contract; and the termination and extension rights of the contract;
(4) Economic environment, mainly including: industry overview, geographical region, market scale, market level, market share, degree of market competition, consumer purchasing power, substitutability of the goods and services, prices of the production factors, cost of transportation, governmental regulations, etc.;
(5) Business strategy, mainly including: innovation and R&D strategies, business diversification strategies, risks avoidance strategies, market penetration strategies, etc.

7.7.1 Comparable Uncontrolled Price Method (Cup)

The CUP method could be applied to all types of related party transactions, and it provides the best benchmark of an arm's-length price for a related party transactions.

It may be possible to reliably adjust CUPs where services, goods, or property are identical but the sales terms are different.

7.7.2 Resale Price Method

This method is more used in service transactions than in transactions involving goods.

The arm's-length price is determined by deducting gross profit of an uncontrolled transaction from the resale price to nonrelated party for goods purchased.

Table 7.5 Main transfer pricing method formula

Resale price method	**Arm's-length purchased price = resale price to nonrelated parties × (1 − gross margin of comparable uncontrolled transaction)**
Cost plus method	Arm's-length price = reasonable cost × (1 + cost plus margin of comparable uncontrolled transaction)

7.7.3 Cost Plus Method

This method is usually applied to the related party transaction of manufactories.

In this case, the arm's-length price is the full cost of the good or service plus a gross profit markup.

7.7.4 Transactional Net Margin Method

This method is normally used in related party transactions of sales, transfer and usage of goods, labor service, and transfer of intangible assets.

It refers to the use of net profit margins from market transaction compared with the use thereof from related party transaction.

7.7.5 Profit Split Method

This method is usually applied when the related party transaction is highly integrated. The methods are two: (a) general profit split method; (b) residual profit split method.

In general, it refers to the methodology where the total profit of a transaction is allocated to each enterprise according to their respective contributions (Table 7.5).

7.8 Transfer Pricing Audit and Adjustments

Potential audit targets include taxpayers that

- Have large amounts of related party transactions or multiple types of related party transactions;
- Have long-term losses, marginal or fluctuating profits;
- Have profit levels lower than the industry;
- Have profit levels that do not match with the functions they perform and the risks they assume;
- Have transactions with related parties registered in tax havens;

- Fail to submit annual related party transaction disclosure forms or fail to prepare contemporaneous transfer pricing documentation;
- Do not comply with the arm's-length principle.

When an entity has been selected for TP audit, the tax authorities can request any relevant information about the pricing of related party transactions.

The documents required could be the enterprise's foundation approval documents, including articles of association, business and tax registration certificates, investment and operational contracts, feasibility studies, annual financial statements, internal audit reports, account books and vouchers, commercial contracts and other relevant documents, financial information, including profits/losses on sales of assets, rates of return on investments, sales revenues, cost of sales and operating expenses, interest rates, and prices paid for the acquisition or use of tangible and intangible property.

Once this information is reviewed, the tax officer will determine if it will be necessary to require more documents. Audit enterprises will have a limited amount of time to submit the required information to tax bureaus upon request. The deadline is 20 days upon request, and other required information must be submitted within the time frame specified by the tax bureau in charge. All transfer pricing audit settlement determinations must be approved by the SAT. *The China Transfer Pricing Regulation* defines the following rules for the field audit:

1. A field investigation team must comprise at least two persons.
2. Field investigators shall produce a "Tax Inspection Permit" and issue a "Tax Inspection Notice" when conducting field investigations.
3. In accordance with relevant legal proceedings, field investigators may raise inquiries, request accounting records, and conduct on-site verifications.
4. Field investigators raising inquiries shall prepare a "Record of Inquiries (Investigation)" and inform the enterprises under investigation of their legal obligations if they fail to truthfully provide the information required. The "Record of Inquiries (Investigation)" shall be verified and confirmed with the enterprises under investigation.
5. Field investigators requesting accounting records shall, in accordance with Article 86 of the Tax Collection Regulations, prepare a "Notice for Requesting Accounting Records" and a "List of Requested Accounting Records" and follow the relevant legal proceedings. The requested information, including book of accounts and vouchers, should be kept properly and returned to the enterprises within the legal time frame.
6. Issues identified and information obtained during field investigation shall be described in the "Record of Inquiries (Investigation)" by investigators. The "Record of Inquiries (Investigation)" shall be signed by at least two investigators and verified and confirmed with the enterprise under investigation where necessary, or if the enterprise under investigation refuses to verify and confirm, the "Investigation Record" can be signed and filed for record by at least two investigators.

7. Notes, tape recordings, videos, photographs, and copies of original documents or information can be taken when requesting relevant information associated with the case. However, sources and original record keepers must be quoted. The notes, tape recordings, videos, photographs, and copies obtained shall be sealed or stamped and labeled with "checked against original documents" by the original record keepers or providers.
8. Witnesses, if needed, shall be informed of their legal obligations if they do not truthfully provide the information requested. Testimony and information provided shall be signed or sealed by the witnesses.

Furthermore, authorities can request relevant information from the enterprise under investigation, its related parties, and other enterprises relevant to the investigation. In such cases, it will issue a "Tax Investigation Notice." This means that any company considered comparable is required to provide any information requested by tax authorities. When information on overseas entities and transactions are required, the tax authorities may request this through the exchange of information provisions in the respective tax treaties, which may need to be notarized by the taxpayer.

During the audit, the "Form of Enterprises Comparability Factor Analysis" can be required to be filled from the tax authorities while they will complete the "Related Party Relationships Assessment Form," the "Related Party Transactions Assessment Form," and "Enterprise's Comparability Factors Analysis Assessment Form." With the release of Circular 363, many companies in a number of provinces and municipalities such as Beijing and Tianjin have received inquiries from local SAT regarding transfer pricing matters.

Furthermore, the Beijing State Tax Bureau has recently issued notices requesting detailed information on related party transactions to over 400 foreign-invested enterprises that are required to respond to the notice with the required information within 10 days of receipt of the notice; otherwise, a penalty will apply.

In accordance with SAT rules[6], if a taxpayer's profitability is lower than the median of the interquartile range established by similar companies, the authority should adjust the profit of the enterprise to not lower than the median of the range. When the pricing of the related party transaction is not in accordance with the arm's-length principle and results to a lower taxable revenue or income after the audit, the tax authorities should make an adjustment following the procedures described as follows:

- Draft the first tax adjustment plan based on the comparability analysis.
- Negotiate with the enterprise.
- If the enterprise disagrees on the preliminary plan, it has to provide other relevant information, which will be verified from tax authorities, who will then make a deliberation.
- The tax authority will issue a "Preliminary Special Tax Audit Adjustment Notice." If the enterprise disagrees with the notice, it needs to communicate it within 7 days of receiving the notice.
- Tax authorities will negotiate and deliberate again.

Table 7.6 Audit process

Audit process	**– Initial screening** **– Selection of TP target** **– Investigation and negotiation** **– Negotiation on the potential TP adjustment** **– Reaching consensus on the adjustment amount and closure of the audit case** **– Five year's postaudit supervision**

- Where the enterprise does not raise any disagreements within the time limit, the tax bureau will consider the preliminary adjustment notice as agreed.
- The tax authorities will determine the final adjustment and issue a "Special Tax Audit Notice" to the enterprise.

Furthermore, the Chinese Transfer Pricing Regulations even provide an adjustment to avoid double taxation; this is an evident sign that SAT appreciates the importance of this aspect in any transfer pricing adjustment. The guidelines in China Transfer Pricing Regulation are explained in art.107. In particular, to apply for a corresponding adjustment involving related parties in a country that has submitted with China an agreement to avoid double taxation, the form has to be written and submitted within 3 years, along with an "Application for Launching Mutual Agreement Procedures" both to SAT and the tax authority in charge.

Furthermore, the SAT shall engage in discussions and negotiations with the competent authority of the other treaty country and provide to the enterprise the outcome in writing through the tax authority in charge. Corresponding adjustments do not apply to situations involving nondeductible interest expense or interest expense deemed as dividend distribution (Table 7.6).

7.9 Advance Pricing Arrangements (APA)

With China's tax reforms, the Chinese tax law, as mentioned several times above, has become more organized and has moved towards international standards.

It is important to underline that in China there are some areas in the transfer pricing matter, showing deviations compared with other countries adopting the OECD guidelines.

In China, the filling requirements are more demanding than in other countries. It is an obligation to submit the nine RPT forms and prepare the documentation required for each enterprise of the cross-border group. It is important to prepare in advance a set of transfer pricing documentation so that the group can comply with the compulsory deadlines.

Furthermore, when setting the transfer prices for the group's transactions, the group should adopt consistent, acceptable, and reasonable transfer pricing policies. The transfer pricing method adopted for related party transactions should be comparable to those used by companies in the same industry and with similar functions, size, sales volume, etc.

This is vital for sustained growth of the enterprises and their investments in China.

A proactive instrument to reduce transfer pricing risks is an APA, which is an arrangement between tax authorities and the taxpayer in respect of the pricing of transactions for a number of years in the future.

An APA ensures taxpayers that their transfer pricing policies and procedures meet the arm's-length principle. The APA is defined in the China Transfer Pricing Regulations, which provide standardization of APA procedures and aim to ensure that tax authority resources are only devoted to APAs when there is an economic benefit to China to justify the effort and resources required to negotiate an APA. The China Transfer Pricing Regulations indicate that the following criteria should be satisfied in order for a taxpayer to be eligible for an APA:

- Annual related party transactions over RMB 40 million;
- Compliance with the related party disclosure requirements;
- Preparation, maintenance, and providing of contemporaneous documentation in accordance with the requirements;
- Submission of a letter of intent for a pre-filling meeting to discuss the following statements:
  - Years to be covered;
  - Information about the parties and about the transactions involved;
  - Overview of the group business operations risks profile.

The taxpayer has 3 months to prepare formal documentation to add to "Formal Application Letter for Advance Pricing Arrangement" and submit to tax authorities. Within 5 months, the tax authorities will examine the application and request any additional information to form their conclusion. Tax authorities, within 30 days of reaching their conclusion, will arrange further discussion and negotiation with the taxpayer. If agreement is reached, the draft APA is submitted to the SAT for review and final approval.

Chapter 8
Anti-Avoidance Rules and Permanent Establishment Concept

8.1 The General Anti-Avoidance Rules in China

Tax avoidance is a legal way to minimize the amount of tax payable. The term must be distinguished from tax evasion, which is illegal and involves fraud, as well as international nondisclosure of income. An international environment easily creates numerous opportunities for tax avoidance, and it is quite difficult to sum it up in its entirety.

Following are some common examples:

- Shift of residence: a taxpayer moves his residence from one country to another in order to get into a better taxation system;
- Establishment of a tax haven subsidiary in order to reduce the withholding taxes on dividends if advantageous treaties exist or in order to earn foreign-source income;
- Establishment of a trust or corporation in a tax heaven with the aim to divert domestic-source income to a controlled foreign entity.

The State Administration of Taxation promulgated GAAR principles for the first time in 2008 in Article 47 of the new PRC Enterprise Income Tax Law ("EIT Law"). Since the promulgation of the EITL law, SAT and other government authorities have issued a number of tax circulars aiming to enforce tax collection with respect to offshore transactions. China's GAAR is actually contained in three legal documents: EITL, EITL Implementing Regulations, and the Notice of State Administration of Taxation on Issuing the Measures for the Implementation of Special Tax Adjustment ("Measure No.2").

Article 47 of EITL basically empowers the SAT to make adjustments where transactions

1. Result in a reduction in taxable income;
2. Have no reasonable business purpose.

The expression "not have a reasonable business purpose" in Article 47 of the EIT Law means that the main purpose of the taxpayer is to reduce, be exempt from, or

DOI 10.1007/978-3-319-00275-0_8,

defer the payment of taxes. Under these rules, the concept "substance over form" is adopted as a guideline for the tax authorities to identify whether an enterprise has tax avoidance arrangements by examining the following factors:

- The form and the substance of an arrangement;
- The time and effective period of an arrangement;
- The implementation method of an arrangement;
- The connection of each step or part of an arrangement;
- The changes in each party's financial situation involved in an arrangement;
- The tax result of an arrangement.

Article 92 of Measures No. 2 then provides that anti-avoidance investigations should target the following arrangements:

- Abusive use of tax preferences;
- Abusive application of tax treaties;
- Abusive use of the forms of enterprise organization;
- Tax avoidance by means of tax havens;
- Other arrangements without reasonable business purposes.

Articles 94, 95, 96, and 97 then provide further detail on how investigations should be conducted:

In conducting a general anti-tax avoidance investigation, the tax authorities may request the planners of the tax avoidance arrangement to provide relevant materials and supporting evidence. If tax authorities issue the "Tax Inspection Notice," the enterprise shall present supporting evidence for justifying its reasonable business purposes within 60 days of receipt.

If the enterprise fails to provide documentation within the period or the evidence provided fails to justify the reasonableness of its business purpose, the tax authorities can make an adjustment based on the information obtained and deliver a "Notice on Special Tax Investigation Adjustment." After investigations, the tax authority has to annul the tax benefit obtained by the enterprise. For enterprises without economic substance, especially incorporated in tax havens, the tax authorities are empowered to deny the existence of the enterprises from a tax collection perspective. Any general anti-avoidance investigation and corresponding tax adjustment shall be reported level by level upward to the State Administration of Taxation for approval.

Circular [2009] No. 698 has the aim of bringing the PRC's GAAR principles from concept to reality. If the actual tax burden is less than 12.5 % in the jurisdiction of the intermediate foreign holding company or if that jurisdiction exempts foreign-sourced income from tax, a foreign seller has to disclose the "indirect" offshore transfer of a Chinese resident company to tax authorities within 30 days after execution of the transfer agreement. Circular 698 has extended compulsory disclosure burdens on the transaction parties, including the following disclosures:

- Equity/share transfer agreement;
- Relationship between the foreign seller and the intermediate holding company, considering funding, operations, sales and purchases, and other related areas;

- Information on operations, employees, bookkeeping, assets, etc. of the intermediate holding company;
- Relationship between the intermediate holding company and the Chinese resident company with respect to funding, operations, sales and purchases, etc.;
- Commercial purpose for the establishment of the offshore intermediate holding company;
- Any additional disclosures required by the tax authorities.

To strengthen the enforcement of GAAR rules, the SAT has set up an administration office for nonresidents under its International Tax Department.

8.2 Anti-Avoidance Mechanisms

Most countries have anti-avoidance measures to deal with a certain type of tax avoidance. Some important examples are described below:

- Judicial anti-avoidance doctrines and statutory anti-avoidance rules;
- Thin capitalization rules;
- Transfer pricing rules;
- Controlled foreign corporation (CFC) legislation.

8.2.1 Thin Capitalization Rules

When a resident corporation pays interest to a nonresident corporation, the interest is deductible by the resident corporation in computing income. Unlike interest, dividends paid by a resident corporation are not deductible. The advantage of paying interest to nonresidents over paying dividends favors the debt financing of resident corporation by nonresident investors. In general, financing a resident corporation with debt is more effective than financing it with equity because the interests are deductible instead of the dividends, as mentioned above. In response to the bias in favor of debt over equity, many countries have introduced thin capitalization rules.

The Ministry of Finance and the State Administration of Taxation issued in 2008 "Notice Cai Shui" (2008) No. 121. The Notice provides guidance for the implementation of the thin capitalization rule introduced by the new Corporate Income Tax Law. China has adopted thin capitalization rules to prevent nonresident shareholders of resident corporations from using excessive debt capital to extract corporate profits in the form of deductible interest instead of nondeductible dividends. An enterprise may deduct interest actually paid to related parties within the permitted debt-to-equity ratio. The deduction should be on an actual payment basis. It is not possible to deduct accrued but not paid related party expenses.

Generally, excessive interest is determinate by reference to debt: equity ratio of the domestic corporations.

In China, the "related-party debt-to-equity ratio" is of 5:1 for financial enterprises and 2:1 for other enterprises. The interest on related party, which exceeds the range, will not be deductible. The related party debt includes not only direct loans from a related party but also a back-to-back loan where a related party provides, through an unrelated party, an unrelated party loan guaranteed by a related party or secured by the assets of a related party and other investment in the nature of a debt indirectly obtained from a related party. In computing the debt-to-equity ratio, only the debt and equity from a related party are considered and unrelated party debt is excluded.

However, the enterprise can produce supporting documentation demonstrating that the financing is respecting the arm's-length principle or that the effective tax rate of the borrowing entity is not higher than the rate of the domestic related party.

8.2.2 Transfer Pricing Rules

Transfer pricing is the common term for the pricing charged on intra-firm, cross-border transactions of associated enterprises established in different tax jurisdictions. China, as most countries, has transfer pricing rules to prevent related taxpayers from carrying out transactions at artificially high or low prices aiming to move income and expenses to various jurisdictions. China's tax system became more rigorous in transfer pricing issues in 2008, with enforcement in 2009 and in 2010 when a new regulation became effective. Transfer pricing rules are discussed in the previous chapter.

8.2.3 Controlled Foreign Corporation Legislation

The EIT Law in Chap. 6 defines the anti-tax avoidance measures for related party transactions using controlled foreign corporation. In general, a CFC is a corporation set up in a foreign law, with or without tax jurisdictions, under the direct or indirect control of a local resident enterprise or a local resident individual. In China, a CFC is defined as a non-Chinese company controlled by Chinese tax residents (both individuals and companies, which must hold a 10 % or greater voting shares and jointly own 50 % or more of the shares) through direct or indirect share ownership. To be a CFC, the company must be incorporated in a country where the effective tax rate is 50 % or less than China's statutory enterprise income tax rate.

The purpose of an anti-tax avoidance law is to tackle situations where the local resident enterprise or individual exercises control on the CFC to defer or avoid tax payment in the local jurisdiction. A Chinese resident enterprise should report annually to the authorities about its overseas investment and its annual tax return.

The competent tax authorities will issue a confirmation notice. If the CFC is located in a "white list" country or its income is derived mainly from active business activities or has an annual profit lower than CNY 5 million, the company can avoid the application of the CFC rules. The concept of CFC was first introduced into the China taxation system with art. 45 of the EIT law, which empowers the Chinese tax authority to treat the profits created by the CFC in a jurisdiction with a tax rate obviously lower than the taxable income of the Chinese resident enterprise or Chinese resident individual. The Implementation Rules of the EIT Law has further clarified that CFC includes foreign corporations where

- The Chinese resident enterprise or individual each directly or indirectly owns 10 % or more of the voting shares of the foreign corporation and jointly own more than 50 % of the shares of the foreign corporation;
- The shareholding percentage of the foreign corporation by the Chinese resident enterprise or individual does not meet the criteria prescribed above but exercised effective control over the foreign corporation by virtue of shares, capital, business operations, purchases and sales, etc.

8.3 Permanent Establishment: Definitions & Exemptions

The term permanent establishment is common in bilateral China treaties against double taxation. Chinese Regulations consider OECD guidelines to define permanent establishments and to allow the source country, where an enterprise is set, to tax the income of an enterprise that is a branch of the company in another contracting state, considering that a permanent establishment is a "fixed place" of business in a contracting state that carried out the business of an enterprise in another contracting state. The profits derived by the PE are taxable in the country where the subsidiary is established.

The foreign company will be considered to have a PE in China if it has an establishment or a place of business in China. Furthermore, the foreign company will be considered to have a PE in China if it has employees working in China for a certain period of time or if the foreign company has an agent in China, which concludes contracts or accepts orders. The basic rule of a PE derives from Art. 5 of the OEC Model, which defines permanent establishment as a "fixed place of business through which the business of an enterprise is wholly or partly carried out":

- *Place of business*: this requirement necessitates some physical presence, e.g. the premises of the business or equipment used in the business;
- *Fixed place*: the place of business must be fixed in the sense that it is a distinct place, which exhibits some degree of permanence;
- *Carrying on of business:* the concepts of PE and carrying on business are bound up together. It is necessary that the enterprise not only has a fixed place of business but also wholly or partly carries on its business through that fixed place;

Article 5 of the Detailed Implementation Regulations of the PRC CIT defines the activities that constitute an establishment or place of business in China:

- Management establishment, business establishment or an office;
- Factory, farm, or place of extraction of natural resources;
- Place where services are provided;
- Place where a project of construction, installation, assembly, repair, exploration, etc. is carried out;
- Other establishments or places of business where production and business operations are carried out.

Some tax treaties also include the following:

- A mine, an oil or gas well, a quarry, or any other place of extraction of natural resources;
- A warehouse in relation to a person providing storage facilities for others;
- A farm or plantation/forest.

An enterprise established in a contracting state that provides services through its employees or other personnel in another contracting state for a prescribed period is considered to have a permanent establishment (the period is different from treaty to treaty). The SAT, through Notice Guoshuifa 3, clarifies that the term "business" refers to manufacturing or operating activities and even to business activities of non-profit organizations.

Furthermore, to consider a fixed place of business auxiliary or preparatory for the head office and not a PE, it is important to understand if it provides services to the head office, if the nature of the business is identical to that of the head office, or if the business of the fixed place constitutes an important part of the business of the head office.

China tax treaties do not include in permanent establishment the following statements:

- The use of facilities solely for the purpose of storage, display, or delivery of goods or merchandise belonging to the enterprise;
- The maintenance of stock of goods or merchandise belonging to the enterprise solely for the purpose of storage, display, or delivery;
- The maintenance of stock of goods or merchandise belonging to the enterprise solely for the purpose of processing by another enterprise;
- The maintenance of a fixed place of business solely for the purpose of purchasing goods or merchandise, advertising, or collecting information for the enterprise;
- The maintenance of a fixed place of business solely for the purpose of carrying on, for the enterprise, any other activities of a preparatory or auxiliary character;
- The maintenance of a fixed place of business solely for any combination of the activities above, provided that the overall activity of the fixed place of business resulting from this combination is of a preparatory or auxiliary character.

The general exemptions above have to be integrated with the following:

- The maintenance of a fixed place of business solely for the purpose of advertising, for the supply of information, for scientific research, or for similar activities of a preparatory or auxiliary character;
- The maintenance of a stock of goods or merchandise solely for the purpose of display in a nonpermanent and temporary trade fair or exhibition and for sale after closing of the said fair or exhibition;
- Assembly services carried on by an enterprise of a contracting state in connection with the sale of machinery or equipment from that contracting state to the other contracting state;
- The temporary maintenance of a stock of goods displayed in a stock fair or an exhibition, which is to be sold after by a contracting state in the other contracting state in connection with the sale of machinery or equipment to the other contracting state.

If an enterprise of a contracting state carries on a part of its business in another contracting state without an affixed place but with an agent, it could be deemed to have a permanent establishment in the other contracting state if the agent is not independent. An agent to be independent should work autonomously and not wholly for the enterprise. In general, a dependent agent has the authority to conclude contracts in a contracting state in the name of the company of the other contracting state.

Chapter 9
International Tax Treaties

9.1 American Area

9.1.1 China–American Area Bilateral Agreements' History

9.1.1.1 China–Brazil Bilateral Agreements' History

Diplomatic ties between China and Brazil officially started in 1974 with the establishment of diplomatic embassies in each country's capital. In 2010, the second BRIC summit was held in Brazil and was attended by China's President Hu. During the meeting, proposals were made for increased cooperation between Brazil and China on political and trade-related issues. During this Second China–Brazil Strategic Dialogue, a number of Subcommittees of the China–Brazil High-level Coordination and Cooperation Committee (CBHCCC) exchanged views on major international topics of common interest (Fig. 9.1).

The two countries had close cooperation within international organizations and multilateral mechanisms, including the UN, the G20, and the BRIC. They also aligned themselves on many major international issues such as the reform of the international financial system, climate change, and cooperation between big emerging countries. With increased trade, Brazil moved up the ranks to becoming China's ninth largest trading partner, while China remained as Brazil's largest trading partner.

In 2010, despite the positive relationship between the two countries, Brazil was one of the few economies to criticize China's policy publicly to allow for a faster appreciation of the Chinese currency, which would better help it compete against Chinese exports. Brazil is rich in natural resources (bauxite, gold, iron ore, manganese, nickel, phosphates, platinum, tin, uranium, petroleum, hydropower, timber). On the other hand, China's economy is dependent on importation of natural resources to sustain its growth. Its trade influences go even further, best exemplified by Brazil's infrastructure upgrading with the proposal the "Accelerated Growth Plan" (which started in 2007 with China acting as chief investor and supplier of technology). Because of China's rising demand for natural resources, Brazil has

L. Riccardi, *Chinese Tax Law and International Treaties*,
DOI 10.1007/978-3-319-00275-0_9,

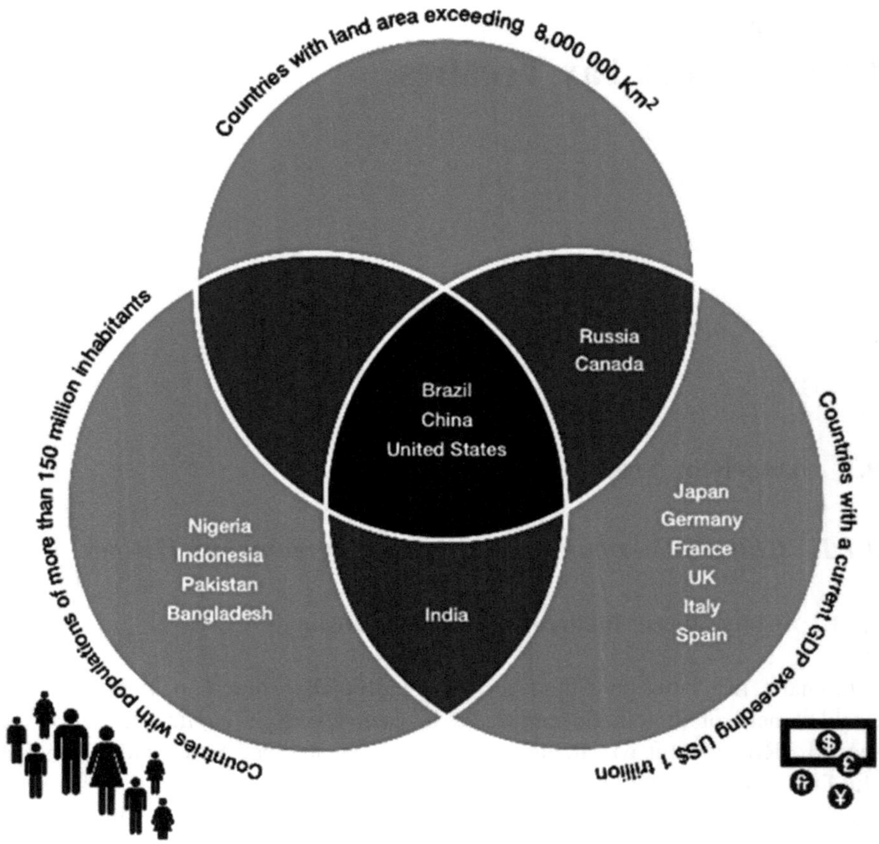

Fig. 9.1 G-20 countries. *Source*: World Bank and United Nations Statistics Division

benefited greatly over the past several years from the high prices of commodities in the global market. Both countries represent a great market for exportations (Fig. 9.2).

However, the increased trade relations resulted in further trading disputes. Brazil imposed its first anti-dumping measure against China in December 1989 regardless of China being granted "market economy status" (November 2004). Brazil continued to impose anti-dumping tariffs against Chinese exports. There is currently an order signed by Brazilian President Luis Ignacio Lula da Silva that allows the government to take measures to temporary restrict imports of Chinese products until 2013.

In the current financial crisis, Brazil and China took common position against the belief of a capacity for self-regulation of the financial markets, agreeing on the necessity to further coordinate their countries' emerging economies. The financial crisis pointed out various aspects on which the two countries can cooperate. The issues on reforming their international financial systems and on better coordinating

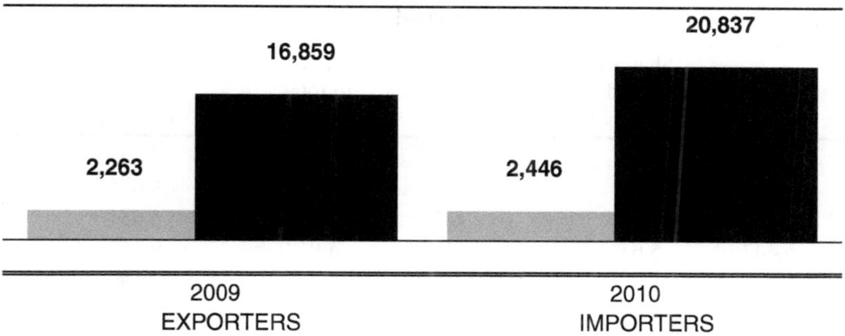

Fig. 9.2 Total number of Brazilian companies working with China. *Source*: Secretariat for Foreign Trade (SECEX) Ministry of Development, Industry and Foreign Trade (MDIC)

with the other BRIC countries could establish a new international financial architecture, enabling China and Brazil to play major roles within the international scene (Table 9.1 and Fig. 9.3).

9.1.1.2 China–Canada Bilateral Agreement's History

It has been more than 40 years of diplomatic ties between the People's Republic of China and Canada. Canada was one of the first western countries to recognize the People's Republic of China. Relations between the two countries have been generally stable, and China is currently Canada's second largest trading partner. During his visit in 2010, President Hu Jintao delivered a speech entitled "Promote the All-round Development of the China-Canada Strategic Partnership" at the welcoming banquet held by Prime Minister Harper. In his speech, he expanded the importance of developing China–Canada relations, emphasizing the need for the two countries to make joint efforts to push forward a strategic partnership. During his speech, he made five proposals: strengthening exchanges between the countries, expanding practical cooperation, widening cultural exchanges, enhancing cooperation in major international and regional affairs, and respecting each other's core interests and major concerns.

The leaders of the two countries reiterated their intentions to develop China–Canada strategic partnership and announced the goal of $60 billion in bilateral trade by 2015. In fact, two-way trade and investment is constantly growing. At the beginning of 2012, China and Canada signed a declaration of intent to negotiate a new bilateral investment treaty (BIT) with the purpose of encouraging foreign investment by providing greater protection against discriminatory and arbitrary practices within the host state, including granting adequate compensation in case of expropriation and enhancing the predictability of changes in regulations regarding foreign investment. Data that describe Canada–China trade and investment flows in this study are quoted in U.S. dollars, the most widely used currency for the settlement of international payments, to draw a comparative statistical

Table 9.1 Trade balance: Brazil–China (US $ million FOB)

Year	Exports to China (*A*)	Shares relative to total exports (%)	Imports from China (*B*)	Shares relative to total imports (%)	Bilateral trade flow (*A* + *B*)	Surplus (*A* − *B*)
2001	1,902	3.3	1,328	2.4	3,231	574
2002	2,521	4.2	1,554	3.3	4,075	967
2003	4,533	6.2	2,148	4.4	6,681	2,386
2004	5,442	5.6	3,710	5.9	9,152	1,731
2005	6,835	5.8	5,355	7.3	12,190	1,480
2006	8,402	6.1	7,990	8.7	16,393	412
2007	10,749	6.7	12,621	10.5	23,370	−1,872
2008	16,523	8.3	20,044	11.6	36,567	−3,522
2009	21,004	13.7	15,911	12.5	36,915	5,093
2010	30,786	15.2	25,593	14.1	56,379	5,193

Source: Secretariat for Foreign Trade (SECEX) Ministry of Development, Industry and Foreign Trade (MDIC)

analysis. National currencies have been converted using annual average exchange rates provided by domestic central banks over the relevant time period as described below in Table 9.2:

It is common to observe differences in the level of trade each country reports in the context of bilateral trade statistics. There are several differences in the level of trade of Canada and China, reported in the context of bilateral trade statistics. Two important differences are the shipment of goods to the trading partner via third economies and differing customs valuation methods. For the purposes of this study, imports from each country will be used to characterize Canada–China bilateral trade wherever possible. In line with this methodology, the import statistics of each country will be summed up when identifying the value of two-way trade. As for stocks of foreign direct investment (FDI), inward investment data will be sourced from the destination country. Unless otherwise noted, merchandise trade statistics have been sourced from the Global Trade Atlas and reference data submitted by Statistics Canada and the General Administration of Customs of China.

The Canadian government stated that the agreement would be focused on nondiscrimination, the grant of a minimum standard of treatment, transparency, transfer of funds between the countries, and rules regulating expropriation. Since 2003, China has been Canada's second largest trading partner, even surpassing Britain and Japan, and now accounts for approximately 6 % of Canada's total world trade. Leading commodities in the trade between the two countries include chemicals, metals, industrial and agricultural machinery, wood, and fishery products (Tables 9.3 and 9.4).

Canada–Chinese trade, even if it has recently faced an important increase, still represents a small percentage of the entire international trade of each country. There is a huge potential to increase the trade between the two countries. In terms of merchandise trade, China is the third largest importer of Canadian products, with imports of US$ 21.6 billion in 2011. Resource-related goods such as wood

BRAZIL

Area	8,511,965 sq. km
Population	193.7m

The Economy

GDP	R3, 185bn
GDP	$1,595bn
Avg. growth 2004-09	3.50%
GDP per head	$8,230
GDP per head PPP (USA=100)	22.5
Economic freedom index	56.3

Components of GDP

	% of total
Private consumption	62
Public consumption	22
Investment	17
Exports	11
Imports	-11

Inflation and Finance

Consumer price inflation 2010	5.0%
Avg. ann. Inflation 2005-10	4.7%
Money market rate, 2010	9.8%
Narrow money (M1)	14.2%
Broad money	17.4%

Trade

Principle exports

	$ bn fob
Primary products	67.3
Semimanufactured products	62.0
Manufactured products	20.5
Total	153.0

Main export destinations

	% of total
China	12.3
United States	10.3
Argentina	8.3
Netherlands	5.3

Fig. 9.3 (continued)

Principal imports	
	$ bn cif
Products & raw materials	59.8
Capital goods	29.7
Consumer goods	21.5
Fuels & lubricants	16.7
Total	127.6

Main origins of imports	
	% of total
United States	17.5
China	13.7
Argentina	9.5
Germany	8.3

Fig. 9.3 Brazil economic indicators. *Source*: The Economist, 2012

Table 9.2 Exchange rates used in the study (against US dollar)

	2001	2002	2003	2004	2005	2006	2007	2008	2009	2010	2011
Canadian Dollar	1.548	1.570	1.401	1.301	1.211	1.134	1.074	1.066	1.141	1.029	0.989
Chinese RMB	8.277	8.277	8.277	8.276	8.193	7.972	7.605	6.947	6.830	6.769	6.463

Source: *Bank of Canada and People's Bank of China*

Table 9.3 Canadian–Chinese merchandise trade (US$ billions)

	2001	2002	2003	2004	2005	2006	2007	2008	2009	2010	2011
Canada exports (China imports)	2.7	2.6	3.4	5.2	6.0	6.9	8.9	9.9	9.7	12.9	17.0
Canada imports (China exports)	8.2	10.2	13.3	18.6	24.4	30.5	35.9	39.9	35.0	43.2	48.6
Total	11.0	12.8	16.7	23.8	30.4	37.3	44.8	49.8	44.7	56.1	65.6

Source: *Global Trade Atlas (Canadian statistics)*

Table 9.4 Canadian–Chinese merchandise trade (US$ billions)

	2001	2002	2003	2004	2005	2006	2007	2008	2009	2010	2011
China exports (Canada imports)	3.3	4.3	5.6	8.2	11.7	15.5	19.4	21.8	17.7	22.2	25.2
China imports (Canada exports)	4.0	3.6	4.4	7.3	7.5	7.7	11.0	12.8	11.9	14.8	21.6
Total trade	7.4	7.9	10.0	15.5	19.2	23.2	30.3	34.6	29.6	37.0	46.8

Source: *Global Trade Atlas (Chinese statistics)*

products, pulp and paper, metals, and minerals account for the majority of China's imports from Canada. China's agricultural imports from Canada are also substantial, particularly oilseeds, fish, and seafood. While there have been upward trends in some sectors, notably in high value-added manufacturing exports such as machinery and equipment, aircraft, and medical instruments, China's demand for resource-related goods remains the primary driver of trade even as Canada looks to broaden its product offerings to an increasingly diversified Chinese economy (Fig. 9.4).

9.1.1.3 China–Mexico Bilateral Agreements' History

China and Mexico issued a Joint Communique on the Establishment of Diplomatic Relations between the two countries on February 14, 1972. Despite subsequent tensions leading up to and around this period, Sino–Mexican relations have developed smoothly since. In recent years, in particular, high levels of cooperation have developed; in 1993, a political consultation mechanism was established between the two foreign ministries of China and Mexico. On his first official visit to Mexico City in December 2003 as China's premier, Wen Jiabao declared Mexico as one of China's "strategic partners" in the western hemisphere. The interest for Mexico is probably due to its location in the center of the American region and its sharing of a 2,000-mile border with the United States. Mexico has taken part since 1994 in the North American Free Trade Agreement (NAFTA), together with Canada and the United States, forming the largest trade bloc in the world (in terms of aggregated GDP).

China and Mexico also share a lot of common views in international affairs and have cooperated in multilateral institutions, with Mexico supporting China on the Human Rights Commission of the UN, for example, by abstaining from voting.

Mexico's links to China are usually related to U.S. and Mexican relations, which have been stressed for many reasons, including widespread violence around the border, result of Mexican drug cartels and the perennial challenges of illegal immigration. Nonetheless, the results of the financial collapse in the United States on the Mexican economy are evident. In the past few years, the decline in trade has accelerated, capital investments have declined, unemployment has risen, and Mexico's GDP has fallen. Regardless, China is the second largest trading partner of Mexico and Mexico is the third largest trading partner of China in Latin America (Tables 9.5 and 9.6).

Mexico was the last country in the world to support China's entry into the World Trade Organization (WTO), mainly due to its deep concern over trade and employment issues, as Mexico has repeatedly charged China with "dumping" accusations within the WTO. Furthermore, China and Mexico compete mostly on the same market (Mexico's top ten exports, except for oil, all compete with Chinese exports); hence, Mexico is the main Latin American country feeling the pressure of the Chinese economy. China is interested in oil, which Mexico exports mainly to the U.S., but in that market it competes with other South American countries that also have bilateral agreements with China.

CANADA

Area	9,970,610 sq. km
Population	33.6m

The Economy

GDP	C $1,527bn
GDP	$1,336bn
Avg. growth 2004-09	1.20%
GDP per head	$39,600
GDP per head PPP (USA=100)	82.2
Economic freedom index	80.8

Components of GDP

	% of total
Private consumption	59
Public consumption	22
Investment	21
Exports	29
Imports	-30

Inflation and Finance

Consumer price inflation 2010	1.8%
Avg. ann. Inflation 2005-10	1.7%
Money market rate, 2010	0.6%
Narrow money (M1)	10.0%
Broad money	7.9%

Trade

Principle exports

	$ bn fob
Machinery & equipment	70.4
Energy Products	69.9
Industrial goods & materials	69.3
Motor vehicles & parts	38.3
Agricultural & fishing products	32.6
Total	323.3

Main export destinations

	% of total
United States	75.1
United Kingdom	3.4
China	3.1
Japan	2.3
EU 27	8.3

Fig. 9.4 (continued)

Principal imports	
	$ bn cif
Machinery & equipment	94.4
Industrial goods & materials	65.7
Consumer goods	50.3
Motor vehicles & parts	48.4
Energy products	29.7
Total	327.3

Main origins of imports	
	% of total
United States	51.1
China	10.9
Mexico	4.6
Japan	3.4
EU 27	12.4

Fig. 9.4 Canada economic indicators. *Source*: The Economist, 2012

Table 9.5 China: economic indicators with Mexico

	2001–2005	2006	2007	2008	2009	2010
GDP (in billion USD at current value)	1,722	2,713	3,499	4,521	4,991	5,879
GDP (annual growth %)	9.6	12.7	14.2	9.6	9.2	10.3
GDP per capita (current USD)	1,334	2,069	2,651	3,414	3,749	4,393
Gross national income per capita PPP (in current international dollar)	3,258	4,790	5,610	6,250	6,860	7,570
Gross capital formation (% GDP)	40	43	42	44	48	–
Total reserves (in billion USD)	4,776	1,080	1,546	1,966	2,452	–
FDI, net inflows (BOP, in billion USD)	54.938	78.095	138.413	147.791	78.193	–

Table 9.6 Mexico: economic indicators with China

	2001–2005	2006	2007	2008	2009	2010
GDP (in billion USD at current value)	716	952	1,036	1,096	0,883	5,879
GDP (annual growth %)	1.4	5.2	3.3	1.5	−6.1	10.3
GDP per capita (current USD)	7,077	9,137	9,840	10,307	8,217	4,393
Gross national income per capita PPP (in current international dollar)	10,620	13,510	14,410	15,120	14,200	7,570
Gross capital formation (% GDP)	23	26	26	27	22	–
Total reserves (in billion USD)	59	76	87	95	100	–
FDI, net inflows (BOP, in billion USD)	23.243	20.103	29.083	24.913	14.462	–

For these reasons, Mexico has always been considered 'at a loss' in the bilateral relation with China, also due to the fact that compared with the other South American countries (foremost among them Chile, Peru, Argentina, and Brazil), Mexico is not a big exporter of natural resources and agricultural commodities, depending more on trade of manufactured items. There are different approaches between these two countries: Chinese goals are sought under substantial government supervision through an integrated development program that is missing in Mexico. Even binational organizations in Mexico have not yet obtained government support to bring all Mexican sectors together to understand and deal with the Chinese products, contrary to the approach of the Chinese entities, which are systematically developing a network of cheap and accessible suppliers that provide components for products, along with stronger incentives for foreign investors, as well as a hardworking and cheaper labor force. Both sides are bound by differences in their natural and cultural resources with each player being able to choose what to bring to the table.

An example of this situation can best be seen through the events of 2009 when, as a consequence of the swine flu (thought to have originated in Mexico), relations between the two countries spilt. Cooling substantially, this showed that the partnership between the two countries was still far from perfect. Despite this, the mutual desire to increase bilateral trade and the shipping of Mexican raw materials into China suggested that these particular diplomatic tensions would only be a temporary consequence of the crisis. In fact, during 2010 the relations continued smoothly and progress was made in their cultural, educational, policing, and tourism exchanges and cooperation (Fig. 9.5).

China represents the third biggest export market outside North America for Mexico, and the two nations compete to sell manufactured goods to U.S. consumers. Despite the recent change of directions, Chinese investment has traditionally been very modest in Mexico. The balance of trade between the two developing economies is heavily tilted in favor of the Asian giant, which now provides Mexico with roughly 15 % of its imports.

Recently Mexico has been moving away from its dependence on the USA, but still its exports have been moving to the United States with a percentage of 80, while the percentage of export to China is 2 %.

The objective to open the Mexican market was discussed during the trade meeting of the Group of 20 economic powers in the Mexican Pacific resort of Puerto Vallarta, where ministers agreed to support open markets and oppose protectionist measures.

9.1.1.4 China–USA Bilateral Agreement's History

The first real intention of forming bilateral relations in modern times comes in the early seventies, with U.S. President Richard Nixon, and the official recognition of the People's Republic of China with the announcement of the "Joint Communiqué

MEXICO	
Area	1,972,545 sq. km
Population	109.6m
The Economy	
GDP	PS11, 822bn
GDP	$875bn
Avg. growth 2004-09	1.30%
GDP per head	$8,140
GDP per head PPP (USA=100)	31
Economic freedom index	67.8
Components of GDP	
	% of total
Private consumption	67
Public consumption	12
Investment	22
Exports	28
Imports	-29
Inflation and Finance	
Consumer price inflation 2010	4.2%
Avg. ann. Inflation 2005-10	4.4%
Money market rate, 2010	4.9%
Narrow money (M1)	11.3%
Broad money	12.2%
Trade	
Principle exports	
	$ bn fob
Manufactured products	189.7
Crude oil & products	30.9
Agricultural products	7.7
Mining products	1.4
Total	229.8

Fig. 9.5 (continued)

on the Establishment of Diplomatic Relations (1979)." China and the U.S. resumed trade relations in 1972 and 1973. A wide variety of manufacturing sectors were covered by direct investment by the U.S. in mainland China, including several large hotel projects, restaurant chains, and petrochemicals. U.S. companies entered into trade agreements establishing more than 20,000 equity joint ventures, contractual joint ventures, and wholly foreign-owned enterprises in mainland China (Table 9.7).

Main export destinations	
	% of total
United States	80.6
Canada	3.6
Germany	1.4
Spain	1.1

Principal imports	
	$ bn cif
Intermediate goods	170.9
Consumer goods	32.8
Capital goods	30.6
Total	234.4

Main origins of imports	
	% of total
United States	52.8
China	15.3
Japan	5.3
South Korea	5.1

Fig. 9.5 Mexico economic indicators. *Source*: The Economist, 2012

Table 9.7 U.S. exports to China ($ millions and % change)

NAIC commodity	2007	2008	2009	2010	2001	2010–2011 % Change
Total exports to China	**65,238**	**71,457**	**69,576**	**91,878**	**103,879**	**13.1**
Waste and scrap	7,331	7,562	7,142	8,561	11,540	34.8
Aerospace products & parts	7,447	5,471	5,344	5,766	6,392	10.9
Motor vehicles	908	1,194	1,134	3,515	5,369	52.7
Basic chemicals	2,914	3,090	3,433	4,202	4,658	10.8
Others (general purpose machinery)	1,885	2,273	1,890	2,445	3,113	27.3
Others (agricultural products)	1,558	1,786	1,008	2,328	2,825	21.4

Source: USITC DataWeb, 2012

The U.S. trade deficit with mainland China exceeded $350 billion in 2006 and was the United States' largest bilateral trade deficit. Some of the factors influencing the U.S. trade deficit with mainland China include the weakening of the U.S. economy: there has been a shift of low-end assembly industries to mainland China from newly industrialized countries in Asia. Mainland China has increasingly become the last link in a long chain of value-added production. Nonetheless, U.S. demand for labor-intensive goods exceeds their domestic output, and China has restrictive trade practices mainland. The People's Republic of China has put up many barriers to foreign goods (such as high tariffs, lack of transparency, the requirement of special permissions), aiming to protect its state-owned companies despite its accession to the WTO (Table 9.8).

Table 9.8 U.S. imports from China ($ millions and % change)

NAIC commodity	2007	2008	2009	2010	2011	2010–2011 % Change
Total imports from China	**321,508**	**337,790**	**296,402**	**364,944**	**399,335**	**9.4**
Computer equipment	44,462	45,820	44,818	59,800	68,276	14.2
Communication equipment	23,192	26,618	26,362	33,464	39,806	19.0
Semiconductors & other components	15,353	13,645	12,363	18,263	19,835	8.6
Audio & video equipment	19,075	19,715	18,253	19,493	15,853	−18.7
Household & institutional furniture	11,872	11,086	9,128	11,123	11,398	2.5
Other fabricated metal products	6,781	7,242	5,690	7,228	8,638	19.5

Source: U.S. International Trade Commission DataWeb, 2012

Nowadays, these two countries' economies are directly correlated as China is the largest foreign holder of U.S. public debt and has been one of the critics of U.S. deficit and fiscal policy. China has repeatedly asked for the safeguarding of Chinese investments in U.S. treasuries (and called for locked rates of purchasing power of the dollar). Despite the financial crisis, trade between these two countries is growing fast. The two countries have been each other's second largest trading partners; the U.S. was China's second largest export market and the sixth largest source of imports, while China was the third largest export market and the biggest source of imports (for 9 consecutive years). By the end of 2010, the United States, as one of China's largest sources of foreign investment, had invested in 59,500 projects and Chinese businesses had made $4.42 billion (nonfinancial direct investment in a wide variety of projects within the United States).

Since the beginning of 2009, the U.S. and Chinese have agreed to hold regular high-level talks about economic issues and mutual concerns by establishing the China–U.S. Strategic Economic Dialogue (SED). The SED mechanism replaced the former Senior Dialogue and Strategic Economic Dialogue, which started with the George W. Bush administration. The first meeting of the SED was held in Washington, on July 2009, with representatives of both countries meeting annually to coordinate their economic developments. The SED addressed challenges and opportunities to ensure that both economies covered a wide scope of bilateral and long-term strategic/economic interests.

Despite this mechanism, economic nationalism seems to have risen between the countries. In September 2009, the US imposed 35 % tariffs on Chinese tire imports (a large trade dispute emerged). The Chinese accused the U.S. of acting as trade protectionists, while the Americans stated that the tariff was in accordance with their international agreements. Again in 2010, the U.S. launched six anti-dumping and countervailing investigations against China, costing over $850 million. The United States (including Canada and Mexico) and China are members of the Asia-Pacific Economic Cooperation (APEC) forum, an organization that seeks to promote free trade and economic cooperation in the Asia-Pacific region. APEC seeks to raise the living standards and promote sustainable economic growth. Its efforts

UNITED STATES

Area	9,372,610 sq. km
Population	314.7m

The Economy

GDP	$14,119bn
Avg. growth 2004-09	1.00%
GDP per head	$45,990
Economic freedom index	77.8

Components of GDP

	% of total
Private consumption	71
Public consumption	17
Investment	14
Exports	11
Imports	-14

Inflation and Finance

Consumer price inflation 2010	1.6%
Avg. ann. Inflation 2005-10	2.2%
Money market rate, 2010	0.2%
Narrow money (M1)	4.2%
Broad money	7.2%

Trade

Principle exports

	$ bn fob
Capital goods	390.4
Industrial supplies	296.3
Consumer goods	150
Vehicles & products	81.6
Total	1056.0

Fig. 9.6 (continued)

are carried throughout three main areas: Trade and Investment Liberalization, Business Facilitation, and Economic and Technical Cooperation.

China and the United States engaged in many fruitful and mutually beneficial efforts on energy and environment issues. Cooperation in energy conservation, pollution, renewable energy, clean energy, energy efficient buildings, and environmental governance became a new highlight in their bilateral relations. The development of U.S. and Chinese relations shows that between these countries, shared interests come first, while their bilateral relations are challenged with dialogue and

Main export destinations	
	% of total
Canada	19.4
Mexico	12.2
China	6.6
Japan	4.8
United Kingdom	4.3
Germany	4.2
EU 27	20.9

Principal imports	
	$ bn cif
Industrial supplies	461.2
Consumer goods	428.4
Capital goods	369.3
Vehicles & products	160
Total	1,559.60

Main origins of imports	
	% of total
China	19.8
Canada	14.6
Mexico	11.4
Japan	6.3
Germany	4.7
United Kingdom	3.1
EU 27	17.9

Fig. 9.6 United States economic indicators

deliberation. The importance of their trade influences in the Asia-Pacific region is unconceivable, and despite the trade protectionist events of 2010 it does not overshadow the crucial reliance of these two countries' share (Fig. 9.6).

U.S. trade deficit with China rose from $273.1 billion in 2010 to an all-time high of $295.5 billion in 2011. The increase in the imbalance accounts for three-quarters of the growth in the U.S. trade deficit for 2011. The following month, the United States, the EU, and Japan filed a "request for consultations" with China at the WTO over its restrictions on exporting rare earth metals. The United States challenged China's quota on rare earth exports forcing multinational companies that use the metals in manufacturing to relocate to China (Fig. 9.7).

9.1.2 Brazil–China Treaty

The Government of the People's Republic of China and the Government of the Federative Republic of Brazil, desiring to conclude an Agreement for the avoidance of double taxation and the prevention of fiscal evasion with respect to taxes on income, have agreed as follows:

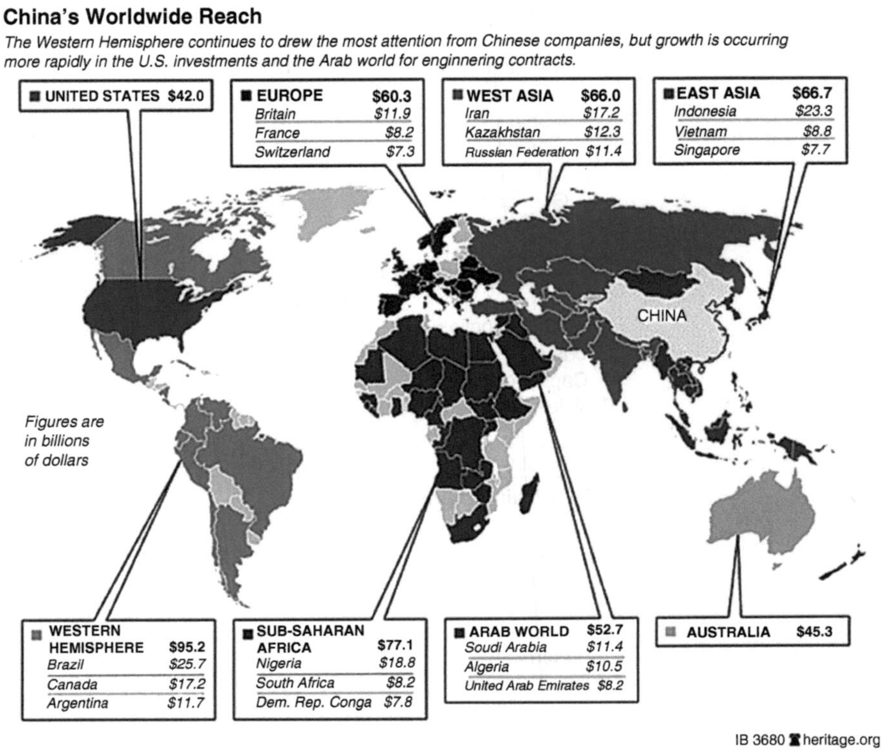

Fig. 9.7 China's worldwide reach. *Source*: The Heritage Foundation, China Global Investment Tracker dataset, updated July 2012, https://thf_media.s3.amazonaws.com/2012/xls/China-Global-Investment-Tracker2012.xls

Article 1 - Personal Scope

This Agreement shall apply to persons who are residents of one or both of the Contracting States.

Article 2 - Taxes Covered

1. The existing taxes to which the Agreement shall apply are:
   a) in the case of the People's Republic of China:
      I) the individual income tax;
      II) the income tax concerning joint ventures with Chinese and foreign investment;
      III) the income tax concerning foreign enterprises; and
      IV) the local income tax (hereinafter referred to as "Chinese tax").
   b) in the case of the Federative Republic of Brazil: the federal income tax, excluding the supplementary income tax and the tax on activities of minor importance (hereinafter referred to as "Brazilian tax");
2. The Agreement shall also apply to any identical or substantially similar taxes which are imposed after the date of signature of the Agreement in addition to, or in place of, the above-mentioned existing taxes. The competent authorities of the Contracting states

shall notify each other of any substantial changes that have been made in their respective taxation laws.

Article 3 - General Definitions

1. For the purposes of this Agreement, unless the context otherwise requires:

   a) the term "China" means the People's Republic of China; when used in geographical sense, means all the territory of the People's Republic of China, including its territorial sea, in which the Chinese laws relating to taxation apply, and any area beyond its territorial sea, within which the People's Republic of China has sovereign rights of exploration for and exploitation of resources of the seabed and its sub-soil and superjacent water resources in accordance with international law;
   b) the term "Brazil" means the Federative Republic of Brazil;
   c) the terms "a Contracting State" and "the other Contracting State" mean China or Brazil as the context requires;
   d) the term "tax" means Chinese tax or Brazilian tax, as the context requires;
   e) the term "person" includes an individual, a company and any other body of persons;
   f) the term "company" means any corporate or any entity which is treated as a body corporate for tax purposes;
   g) the terms "enterprise of a Contracting State" and "enterprise of the other Contracting State" mean respectively an enterprise carried on by a resident of a Contracting State and an enterprise carried on by a resident of the other Contracting State;
   h) the term "nationals" means all individuals possessing the nationality of a Contracting State and all juridical persons created or organized under the laws of that Contracting State; as well as any organization without juridical personality treated for tax purposes as juridical person created or organized under the laws of that Contracting State;
   i) the term "international traffic" means any transport by a ship or aircraft operated by an enterprise which has its head office (i.e. effective management) in a Contracting State, except when the ship or aircraft is operated solely between places in the other contracting State;
   j) the term "competent authority" means:

      I) in the case of China, the State Tax Bureau or its authorized representative;
      II) in the case of Brazil, the Minister of Economy, Finance and Planning, the Department of Federal Revenue or their authorized representatives.

2. As regards the application of this Agreement by a Contracting State, any term not defined therein shall, unless the context otherwise requires, have the meaning which it has under the laws of that Contracting State concerning the taxes to which this Agreement applies.

Article 4 - Resident

1. For the purposes of this Agreement, the term "resident of a Contracting State" means any person who, under the laws of that Contracting State, is liable to tax therein by reason of his domicile, residence, place of head office (i.e. effective management) of any other criterion of a similar nature.
2. Where by reason of the provisions of paragraph 1, an individual is a resident of both Contracting States, then his status shall be determined as follows:

   a) he shall be deemed to be a resident of the Contracting State in which he has a permanent home available to him; if he has a permanent home available to him in both Contracting States, he shall be deemed to be a resident of the Contracting State with which his personal and economic relations are closer (center of vital interests);

b) if the State in which he has center of vital interests cannot be determined, or if he has not a permanent home available to him in either Contracting State, he shall be deemed to be a resident of the State in which he has a habitual abode;
c) if he has a habitual abode in both Contracting States or in neither of them, he shall be deemed to be a resident of the Contracting State of which he is a national;
d) if he is a national of both Contracting States or of neither of them, the competent authorities of the Contracting States shall settle the question by mutual agreement.

3. Where by reason of the provisions of paragraph 1, a person other than an individual is a resident of both Contracting States, then it shall be deemed to be a resident of the Contracting State in which its place of head office (i.e. effective management) is situated.

Article 5 - Permanent Establishment

1. For the purposes of this Agreement, the term "permanent establishment" means affixed place of business through which the business of an enterprise is wholly or partly carried on.
2. The term "permanent establishment" includes especially:

   a) a place of management;
   b) a branch;
   c) an office;
   d) a factory;
   e) a workshop; and
   f) a mine, an oil or gas well, a quarry or any other place of extraction of natural resources.

3. The term "permanent establishment" likewise encompasses:

   a) a building site, a construction, assembly or installation project or supervisory activities in connection therewith, but only where such site, project or activities continue for a period of more than six months;
   b) the furnishing of services, including consultancy services, by an enterprise of a Contracting State through employees or other engaged personnel in the other Contracting State, provided that such activities continue for the same project or a connected project for a period or periods aggregating more than six months within any twelve-month period.

4. Not withstanding the provisions of paragraphs 1 to 3, the term "permanent establishment" shall be deemed not to include:

   a) the use of facilities solely for the purpose of storage, display or delivery of goods of merchandise belonging to the enterprise;
   b) the maintenance of a stock of goods or merchandise belonging to the enterprise solely for the purpose of storage, display or delivery;
   c) the maintenance of a stock of goods or merchandise belonging to the enterprise solely for the purpose of processing by another enterprise;
   d) the maintenance of a fixed place of business solely for the purpose of purchasing goods or merchandise or of collecting information, for the enterprise;
   e) the maintenance of a fixed place of business solely for the purpose of carrying on, for the enterprise, any other activity of a preparatory or of auxiliary character.

5. Notwithstanding the provisions of paragraphs 1 and 2, where a person—other than an agent of an independent status to whom the provisions of paragraph 6 apply—is acting

in a Contracting State on behalf of an enterprise of the other Contracting State, has and habitually exercises an authority to conclude contracts in the name of the enterprise, that enterprise shall be deemed to have a permanent establishment in the first-mentioned Contracting State in respect of any activities which that person undertakes for the enterprise, unless the activities of such personage limited to those mentioned in paragraph 4 which, if exercised through a fixed place of business, would not make this fixed place of business a permanent establishment under the provisions of that paragraph.

6. An enterprise of a Contraction State shall not be deemed to have a permanent establishment in the other Contracting State merely because it carries on business in that other Contracting State through a broker, general commission agent or any other agent of an independent status, provided that such persons are acting in the ordinary course of their business. However, when the activities of such an agent are devoted wholly or almost wholly on behalf of that enterprise, he will not be considered an agent of an independent status within the meaning of this paragraph.
7. The fact that a company which is a resident of a Contracting State controls or is controlled by a company which is a resident of the other Contracting State, or which carries on business in that other State (whether through a permanent establishment or otherwise), shall not of itself constitute either company a permanent establishment of the other.

Article 6 - Income From Immovable Property

1. Income derived by a resident of a Contracting State from immovable property (including income from agriculture or forestry) situated in the other Contracting State may be taxed in that other Contracting State.
2. The term "immovable property" shall have the same meaning under the law of the Contracting State in which the property in question is situated. The term shall in any case include property accessory to immovable property, livestock and equipment used in agriculture and forestry, rights to which the provisions of general law respecting landed property apply, usufruct of immovable property and rights to variable or fixed payments as consideration for the working of, or the right to work, mineral deposits, sources and other natural resources. Ships and aircraft shall not be regarded as immovable property.
3. The provisions of paragraph 1 shall apply to income derived from the direct use, letting, or use in any other form of immovable property.
4. The provisions of paragraphs 1 and 3 shall also apply to the income from immovable property of an enterprise and to income from immovable property used for the performance of independent personal services.

Article 7 - Business Profits

1. The profits of an enterprise of a Contracting State shall be taxable only in that Contracting State unless the enterprise carries on business in the other contracting State through a permanent establishment situated therein. If the enterprise carries on business as foresaid, the profits of the enterprise may be taxed in the other Contracting State but only so much of them as is attributable to that permanent establishment.
2. Subject to the provisions of paragraph 3, where an enterprise of a Contracting State carries on business in the other Contracting State through a permanent establishment situated therein, there shall in each Contracting State be attributed to that permanent establishment the profits which it might be expected to make if it were a distinct and separate enterprise engaged in the same or similar activities under the same or similar conditions and dealing wholly independently with the enterprise of which it is a permanent establishment.
3. In determining the profits of a permanent establishment, there shall be allowed as deductions expenses which are incurred for the purposes of the permanent establishment, including executive and general administrative expenses so incurred.

4. In so far as it has been customary in a Contracting State to determine the profits to be attributed to a permanent establishment on the basis of an apportionment of the total profits of the enterprise to its various parts, nothing in paragraph 2 shall preclude that Contracting State from determining the profits to be taxed by such an apportionment as may be customary. The method of apportionment adopted shall, however, be such that the result shall be in accordance with the principles contained in this Article.
5. No profits shall be attributed to a permanent establishment by reason of the mere purchase by that permanent establishment of goods or merchandise for the enterprise.
6. For the purpose of paragraphs 1 to 5, the profits to be attributed to the permanent establishment shall be determined by the same method year by year unless there is good and sufficient reason to the contrary.
7. Where profits include items of income which are dealt with separately in other Articles of this Agreement, then the provisions of those Articles shall not be affected by the provisions of this Article.

Article 8 - Shipping And Air Transport

1. Profits from the operation of ships or aircraft in international traffic shall be taxable only in the Contracting State in which the place of head office (i.e. effective management) of the enterprise is situated.
2. If the place of head office of a shipping enterprise is aboard a ship, then it shall be deemed to be situated in the Contracting State in which the home harbor of the ship is situated, or if there is no such home harbor, in the Contracting State of which the operator of the ship is a resident.
3. The provisions of paragraph 1 shall also apply to profits from the participation in a pool, a joint business or an international operating agency.

Article 9 - Associated Enterprises

Where:

a) an enterprise of a Contracting State participates directly or indirectly in the management, control or capital of an enterprise of the other Contracting State, or
b) the same persons participate directly or indirectly in the management, control or capital of an enterprise of a Contracting State and an enterprise of the other Contracting State, and in either case conditions are made or imposed between the two enterprises in their commercial or financial relations which differ from those which would be made between independent enterprises, then any profits which would, but for those conditions, have accrued to one of the enterprises, but, by reason of those conditions, have not so accrued, may be included in the profits of that enterprise and taxed accordingly.

Article 10 – Dividends

1. Dividends paid by a company which is a resident of a Contracting State to a resident of the other Contracting State may be taxed in that other Contracting State.
2. However, such dividends may also be taxed in the Contracting State of which the company paying the dividends is a resident and according to the laws of that9Contracting State, but if the recipient is the beneficial owner of the dividends the tax so charged shall not exceed 15 per cent of the gross amount of the dividends, the provisions of this paragraph shall not affect the taxation of the company in respect of the profits out of which the dividends are paid.
3. The term "dividends" as used in this Article means income from shares, "jouissance" shares or "jouissance" rights. mining shares, founders shares or other rights, not being debt-claims, participating in profits, as well as income from other corporate rights which is subjected to the same taxation treatment as income from shares by the laws of the State of which the company making the distribution is a resident.

4. The provisions of paragraphs 1 and 2 shall not apply if the beneficial owner of the dividends, being a resident of a Contracting State, carries on business in the other Contracting State of which the company paying the dividends is a resident, through a permanent establishment situated therein, or performs in that Contracting State independent personal services from a fixed base situated therein, and the holding in respect of which the dividends are paid is effectively connected with such permanent establishment or fixed base. In such case the provisions of Article 7 or Article 14, as the case may be, shall apply.
5. Where a resident of a Contracting State has a permanent establishment in the other Contracting State, this permanent establishment may be subject to a tax with held at source in accordance with the law of that other Contracting State.

However, such tax cannot exceed 15 percent of gross amount of the profits of that permanent establishment determined after the payment of the corporate tax related to such profits.

6. Where a company which is a resident of a Contracting State derives profits or income from the other Contracting State, that other Contracting State may not impose any tax on the dividends paid by the company, except in so far as such dividends are paid to a resident of that other Contracting State or in so far as the holding in respect of which the dividends are paid is effectively connected with a permanent establishment or a fixed base situated in that other Contracting State, nor subject the company's undistributed profits to a tax on the company's undistributed profits, even if the dividends paid or the undistributed profits consist wholly or partly of profits or income arising in such other Contracting State.

Article 11 – Interest

1. Interest arising in a Contracting State and paid to a resident of the other Contracting State may be taxed in that other Contracting State.
2. However, such interest may also be taxed in the Contracting State in which in arises and according to the laws of that Contracting State, but if the recipient is the beneficial owner of the interest the tax so charged shall not exceed 15 percent of the gross amount of the interest.
3. Not withstanding the provisions of paragraphs 1 and 2, interest arising in a Contracting State and derived by the Government of the other Contracting State, a political subdivision, a local authority and the Central Bank thereof or any financial institution wholly owned by that Government, including interest from government securities, bonds or debentures issued by them, shall be exempt from tax in the first mentioned Contracting State.
4. The term "interest" as used in this Article means income from debt-claims of every kind, whether or not secured by mortgage and whether or not carrying a right to participate in the debtor's profits, and in particular, income from government securities and income from bonds or debentures, including premiums and prizes attaching to such securities, bonds or debentures. Penalty charges for late payment shall not be regarded as interest for the purpose of this Article.
5. The provisions of paragraphs 1, 2 and 3 shall not apply if the beneficial owner of the interest, being a resident of a Contracting State, carries on business in the other Contracting State in which the interest arises, through a permanent establishment situated therein, or performs in that other Contracting State independent personal services from a fixed base situated therein, and the debt-claim in respect of which the interest is paid is effectively connected with such permanent establishment or fixed base. In such case the provisions of Article 7 or Article 14, as the case may be, shall apply.
6. Interest shall be deemed to arise in a Contracting State when the payer is the Government of that Contracting State, a political subdivision, a local authority thereof or a

resident of that State. Where, however, the person paying the interest, whether he is a resident of a Contracting State or not, has in a Contracting State a permanent establishment or a fixed base in connection with which the indebtedness on which the interest is paid was incurred, and such interest is borne by such permanent establishment or fixed base, then such interest shall be deemed to arise in the Contracting State in which the permanent establishment or fixed base is situated.

7. Where, by reason of a special relationship between the payer and the beneficial owner or between both of them and some other person, the amount of the interest, having regard to the debt-claim for which it is paid, exceeds the amount which would have been agreed upon by the payer and the beneficial owner in the absence of such relationship, the provisions of this Article shall apply only to the last-mentioned amount. In such case, the excess part of the payments shall remain taxable according to the laws of each Contracting State, due regard being had to the other provisions of this Agreement.
8. The tax rate limitation provided for in paragraph 2 shall not apply to interest arising in a Contracting State and paid to a permanent establishment of an enterprise of the other Contracting State which is situated in a third State.

Article 12 - Royalties

1. Royalties arising in a Contracting State and paid to a resident of the other Contracting State may be taxed in that other Contracting State.
2. However, such royalties may also be taxed in the Contracting State in which they arise and according to the laws of that Contracting State, but if the recipient is the beneficial owner of the royalties the tax so charged shall not exceed:

   a) 25 per cent of the gross amount of the royalties arising from the use or the right to use trademarks;
   b) 15 per cent of the gross amount of the royalties in all other cases.

3. The term "royalties" as used in this Article means payments of any kind received as a consideration for the use of, or the right to use, any copyright of literary, artistic or scientific work including cinematograph films and films or tapes for radio or television broadcasting, any patent, know-how, trade mark, design or model, plan, secret formula or process, or for the use of, or the right to use, industrial, commercial or scientific equipment, or for information concerning industrial, commercial or scientific experience.
4. The provisions of paragraphs 1 and 2 shall not apply if the beneficial owner of the royalties, being a resident of a Contracting State, carries on business in the other Contracting State in which the royalties arise, through a permanent establishment situated therein, or performs in that other Contracting State independent personal services from a fixed base situated therein, and the right or property in respect of which the royalties are paid is effectively connected with such permanent establishment of fixed base. In such case the provisions of Article 7 or Article 14, as the case may be, shall apply.
5. Royalties shall be deemed to arise in a Contracting State when the payer is the Government of that Contracting State, a political subdivision, a local authority thereof or a resident of that Contracting State. Where, however, the person paying the royalties, whether he is a resident of a Contracting State or not, has in a Contracting State a permanent establishment or a fixed base in connection with which the liability to pay the royalties was incurred, and such royalties are borne by such permanent establishment of fixed base, then such royalties shall be deemed to arise in the Contracting State in which the permanent establishment or fixed base is situated.
6. Where, by reason of a special relationship between the payer and the beneficial owner or between both of them and some other person, the amount of the royalties, having regard to the use, right or information for which they are paid, exceeds the amount which would

have been agreed upon by the payer and the beneficial owner in the absence of such relationship, the provisions of this Article shall apply only to the last-mentioned amount. In such case, the excess part of the payment shall remain taxable according to the laws of each Contracting State, due regard being had to the other provisions of this Agreement.

Article 13 - Capital Gains

1. Gains derived by a resident of a Contracting State from the alienation of immovable property referred to in Article 6 and situated in the other Contracting State may be taxed in that other Contracting State.
2. Gains from the alienation of movable property forming part of the business property of a permanent establishment which an enterprise of a Contracting State has in the other Contracting State or of movable property pertaining to a fixed base available to a resident of a Contracting State in the other Contracting State for the purpose of performing independent personal services, including such gains from the alienation of such a permanent establishment (alone or together with the whole enterprise) or of such a fixed base, may be taxed in that other Contracting State.
3. Gains from the alienation of ships or aircraft operated in international traffic or movable property pertaining to the operation of such ships or aircraft shall be taxable only in the Contracting State in which the place of head office (i.e. effective management) of the enterprise is situated.
4. Gains from the alienation of any property other than that referred to in paragraphs1, 2 and 3, may be taxed in both Contracting State.

Article 14 - Independent Personal Services

1. Income derived by a resident of a Contracting State, in respect of professional services or other activities of an independent character shall be taxable only in that Contracting State except in one of the following circumstances, when such income may also be taxed in the other Contracting State:

   a) if he has a fixed base regularly available to him in the other Contracting State for the purpose of performing his activities; in that case, only so much of the income as is attributable to that fixed base may be taxed in that other Contracting State;
   b) if the remuneration for his activities in the other Contracting State is paid by a resident of that other Contracting State or is borne by a permanent establishment or fixed base situated in that other Contracting State; in that case, only so much of the remuneration as derived therefrom may be taxed in that other Contracting State.

2. The term "professional services" includes especially independent scientific, literary, artistic, educational or teaching activities as well as the independent activities of physicians, lawyers, engineers, architects, dentists and accountants.

Article 15 - Dependent Personal Services

1. Subject to the provisions of Articles 16, 18, 19, 20 and 21, salaries, wages and other similar remuneration derived by a resident of a Contracting State in respect of an employment shall be taxable only in that Contracting State unless the employment is exercised in the other Contracting State. If the employment is so exercised, such remuneration as is derived therefrom may be taxed in that other Contracting State.
2. Notwithstanding the provision of paragraph 1, remuneration derived by resident of a Contracting State in respect of an employment exercised in the other Contracting State shall be taxable only in the first mentioned State if:

   a) the recipient is present in the other Contracting State for a period or periods not exceeding in the aggregate 183 days in the calendar year concerned; and

b) the remuneration is paid by, or on behalf of, an employer who is not a resident of the other Contracting State; and
c) the remuneration is not borne by a permanent establishment or a fixed base which the employer has in the other Contracting State.

3. Notwithstanding the provisions of paragraphs 1 and 2 of this Article, remuneration derived in respect of an employment exercised aboard a ship or aircraft operated by an enterprise of a Contracting State in international traffic, shall be taxable only in the Contracting State in which the place of head office (i.e. effective management) of the enterprise is situated.

Article 16 - Directors' Fees

Directors' fees and other similar payments derived by a resident of a Contracting State in his capacity as a member of the board of directors or similar council of accompany which is a resident of the other Contracting State may be taxed in that other Contracting State.

Article 17 - Artistes And Athletes

1. Not withstanding the provisions of Articles 14 and 15, income derived by a resident of a Contracting State as an entertainer, such as a theatre, motion picture, radio or television artiste, or a musician, or as an athlete, from his personal activities as such exercised in the other Contracting State, may be taxed in that other Contracting State.
2. Where income in respect of personal activities exercised by an entertainer or an athlete in his capacity as such accrues not to the entertainer or athlete himself but to another person, that income may, notwithstanding the provisions of Articles 7, 14 and15, be taxed in the Contracting State in which the activities of the entertainer or athlete are exercised.
3. Notwithstanding the provisions of paragraphs 1 and 2, income derived by entertainers or athletes who are residents of a Contracting State from the activities exercised in the other Contracting State under a plan of cultural exchange between the Governments of both Contracting States shall be exempt from tax in that other Contracting State.

Article 18 – Pensions

1. Subject to the provisions of paragraph 2 of Article 19, pensions and other similar remuneration paid to a resident of a Contracting State in consideration of past employment shall be taxable only in that Contracting State.
2. Notwithstanding the provisions of paragraph 1, pensions paid and other similar payments made by the Government of a Contracting State, a political subdivision or a local authority thereof under a public welfare scheme of the social security system of that Contracting State shall be taxable only in that Contracting State.
3. However, such pensions and other similar remuneration may also be taxed in the other Contracting State if the payment is made by a resident of that other Contracting State or a permanent establishment situated therein.

Article 19 - Government Service

1. a) Remuneration, other than pension, paid by the Government of a Contracting State, a political subdivision or a local authority thereof to an individual in respect of services rendered to the Government of that Contracting State, apolitical subdivision or a local authority thereof, shall be taxable only in that Contracting State.
   b) However, such remuneration shall be taxable only in the other Contracting State if the services are rendered in that other Contracting State and the individual is a resident of that other Contracting State who:

      i) is a national of that other Contracting State; or
      ii) did not become a resident of that other Contracting State solely for the purpose of rendering the services.

2. a) Any pension paid by, or out of funds to which contributions are made by, the Government of a Contracting State, a political subdivision or a local authority thereof to an individual in respect of services rendered to the Government of that Contracting State, a political subdivision or a local authority thereof shall be taxable only in that Contracting State.
   b) However, such pension shall be taxable only in the other Contracting State if the individual is a resident of, and a national of, that other Contracting State.
3. The provisions of Articles 15, 16, 17 and 18 shall apply to remuneration and pensions in respect of services rendered in connection with a business carried on by the Government of a Contracting State, a political subdivision or a local authority thereof.

Article 20 - Teachers And Researchers

An individual who is, or was immediately before visiting a Contracting State, a resident of the other Contracting State and who, at the invitation of the first-mentioned Contracting State or of a university, college, school, museum or other cultural institution in that first-mentioned Contracting State or under an official program of cultural exchange, is present in that Contracting State for a period not exceeding two years solely for the purpose of teaching, giving lectures or carrying out research at such institution shall be exempt from tax in that Contracting State on his remuneration for such activity, provided he is subject to tax thereon in the other Contracting State.

Article 21 - Students And Trainees

1. Payments which a student or business apprentice who is or was immediately before visiting a Contracting State a resident of the other Contracting State and who is present in the first-mentioned Contracting State solely for the purpose of his education or training receives for the purpose of his maintenance, education or training shall not be taxed in that Contracting State, provided that such payments arise from sources outside that Contracting State.
2. In respect of grants, scholarships and remuneration from employment not covered by paragraph 1, a student or business apprentice described in paragraph 1 shall, in addition, be entitled during such education or training to the same exemptions, reliefs or reductions in respect of taxes available to residents of the Contracting State which he is visiting.

Article 22 - Other Income

Items of income of a resident of a Contracting State, arising in the other Contracting State and not dealt with in the foregoing Articles of this Agreement, maybe taxed in that other Contracting State.

Article 23 - Methods For Elimination Of Double Taxation

1. In China, double taxation shall be eliminated as follows:

   a) where a resident of China derives income from Brazil, the amount of tax on that income payable in Brazil in accordance with the provisions of this Agreement, shall be credited against the Chinese tax imposed on that resident. The amount of credit, however, shall not exceed the amount of the Chinese tax on that income computed in accordance with the taxation laws and regulations of China;
   b) in addition to the provisions of subparagraph (a), where the income derived from Brazil is a dividend paid by a company which is a resident of Brazil to a company which is a resident of China and which owns not less than 10 per cent of the shares of the company paying the dividend, the credit shall take into account the tax paid in Brazil by the company paying the dividend in respect of its income.

2. In Brazil, double taxation shall be eliminated as follows:

   Where a resident of Brazil derives income from China, the amount of tax on that income payable in China in accordance with the provisions of this Agreement shall be credited against the Brazilian tax imposed on that resident. The amount of credit, however, shall not exceed the amount of the Brazilian tax on that income computed in accordance with the taxation laws and regulations of Brazil.

Article 24 - Non-Discrimination

1. Nationals of a Contracting State shall not be subjected in the other Contracting State to any taxation or any requirement connected therewith, which is other or more burdensome than the taxation and connected requirements to which nationals of that other Contracting State in the same circumstances are or may be subjected.
2. The taxation on a permanent establishment which an enterprise of a Contracting State has in the other Contracting State shall not be less favorably levied in that other Contracting State than the taxation levied on enterprises of that other Contracting State carrying on the same activities. The provisions of this paragraph shall not be construed as obliging a Contracting State to grant to residents of the other Contracting State any personal allowances, reliefs and reductions for taxation purposes on account of civil status of family responsibilities which it grants to its own residents.
3. Except where the provisions of Article 9, paragraph 7 of Article 11, or paragraph6 of Article 12, apply, interest, royalties and other disbursements paid by an enterprise of a Contracting State to a resident of the other Contracting State shall, for the purpose of determining the taxable profits of such enterprise, be deductible under the same conditions as if they had been paid to a resident of the first-mentioned State.
4. Enterprises of a Contracting State, the capital of which is wholly or partly owned or controlled, directly or indirectly, by one or more residents of the other Contracting State, shall not be subjected in the first-mentioned State to any taxation or any requirement connected therewith which is other or more burdensome than the taxation and connected requirements to which other similar enterprises of the first-mentioned State are or may be subjected.
5. In this Article, the term "taxation" means taxes to which this Agreement applies.

Article 25 - Mutual Agreement Procedure

1. Where a resident considers that the actions of one or both of the Contracting State result or will result for him in taxation not in accordance with the provisions of this Agreement, he may, irrespective of the remedies provided by the domestic law of those States, present his case to the competent authority of the Contracting State of which he is a resident. The case must be presented within 3 years from the first notification of the action resulting in taxation not in accordance with the provisions of the Agreement.
2. The competent authority shall endeavor, if the objection appears to it to be justified and if it is not itself able to arrive at a satisfactory solution, to resolve the case by mutual agreement with the competent authority of the other Contracting State, with a view to the avoidance of taxation which is not in accordance with the provisions of the Agreement.
3. The competent authorities of the Contracting States shall endeavor to resolve by mutual agreement any difficulties or doubts arising as to the interpretation or application of the Agreement. They may also consult together for the elimination of double taxation in cases not provided for in this Agreement.

4. The competent authorities of the Contracting States may communicate with each other directly for the purpose of reaching an agreement in the sense of paragraphs 2 and 3.

Article 26 - Exchange Of Information

1. The competent authorities of the Contracting States shall exchange such information as is necessary for carrying out the provisions of this Agreement or of the domestic laws of the Contracting States concerning taxes covered by the Agreement, insofar as the taxation there under is not contrary to this Agreement, in particular for the prevention of evasion of such taxes. The exchange of information is not restricted by Article 1. Any information received by a Contracting State shall be treated as secret and shall be disclosed only to persons or authorities (including courts and administrative bodies) involved in the assessment or collection of, the enforcement or prosecution in respect of, or the determination of appeals in relation to, the taxes covered by the Agreement. Such persons or authorities shall use the information only for such purposes. They may disclose the information in public court proceedings or in judicial decisions.
2. In no case shall the provisions of paragraph 1 be construed so as to impose on a Contracting State the obligation:

   a) to carry out administrative measures at variance with the laws and the administrative practice of that or of the other Contracting State;
   b) to supply information which is not obtainable under the laws or in the normal course of the administration of that or of the other Contracting State;
   c) to supply information that would disclose any trade, business, industrial, commercial or professional secret or trade process, or information, the disclosure of which would be contrary to public policy (*order public*).

Article 27 - Diplomatic Agents And Consular Officers

Nothing in this Agreement shall affect the fiscal privileges of diplomatic agents or consular officers under the general rules of international law or under the provisions of special agreements.

Article 28 - Entry Into Force

1. Each Contracting State shall notify the other, through diplomatic channels, of the fulfillment of all internal legal procedures necessary for the entry into force of this Agreement. This Agreement shall enter into force on the thirtieth day after the date of the second notification.
2. This Agreement shall take effect as follows:

   a) in respect of taxes withheld at source, to payments received on or after the first day of January of the calendar year immediately following that in which the Agreement enters into force;
   b) in respect of other taxes covered by the Agreement, for taxable years beginning on or after the first day of January of the calendar year immediately following that in which the Agreement enters into force.

Article 29 – Termination

This Agreement shall continue in effect indefinitely but either of the Contracting State may, on or before the thirtieth day of June in any calendar year beginning after the expiration of a period of five years from the date of its entry into force, give written notice of termination to the other Contracting State through the diplomatic channels. In such event this Agreement shall cease to have effect:

a) in respect of taxes withheld at source, to payments received on or after the first day of January of the calendar year immediately following that in which the notice of termination is given;

b) in respect of other taxes covered by the Agreement, for taxable years beginning on or after the first day of January of the calendar year immediately following that in which the notice of termination is given.

DONE at Beijing this 5th day of August 1991, in duplicate, in the Chinese, Portuguese and English Languages, all three texts being equally authentic. In case of any divergence of interpretation, the English text shall prevail.

9.1.3 Canada–China Treaty

The Government of the People's Republic of China and the Government of Canada, desiring to conclude an Agreement for the avoidance of double taxation and the prevention of fiscal evasion with respect to taxes on income, have agreed as follows:

Article 1 - Personal Scope

This Agreement shall apply to persons who are residents of one or both of the Contracting States.

Article 2 - Taxes Covered

1. The existing taxes to which this Agreement shall apply are, in particular:

   a) in the case of Canada:

      I) the income taxes imposed by the Government of Canada (hereinafter referred to as "Canadian tax");

   b) in the case of the People's Republic of China:

      I) the individual income tax;
      II) the income tax concerning joint ventures with Chinese and foreign investment;
      III) the income tax concerning foreign enterprises; and
      IV) the local income tax (hereinafter referred to as "Chinese tax").

2. This Agreement shall also apply to any identical or substantially similar taxes which are imposed after the date of signature of this Agreement in addition to, or in place of, those referred to in paragraph 1. The relevant authorities of the Contracting States shall notify each other of any substantial changes which have been made in their respective taxation laws within a reasonable period of time after such changes.

Article 3 - General Definitions

1. For the purposes of this Agreement, unless the context otherwise requires:

   a) the term "Canada" used in a geographical sense means the territory of Canada, including any area beyond the territorial seas of Canada which, in accordance with international law and under the laws of Canada, is an area within which Canada may exercise rights with respect to the seabed and sub-soil and their natural resources;
   b) the term "the People's Republic of China", when used in a geographical sense, means all the territory of the People's Republic of China, including its territorial sea, in which the laws relating to Chinese tax apply, and all the area beyond its territorial

sea, including the seabed and sub-soil thereof, over which the People's Republic of China has jurisdiction in accordance with international law and in which the laws relating to Chinese tax apply;

c) the terms "a Contracting State" and "the other Contracting State" mean the People's Republic of China or Canada, as the context requires;
d) the term "tax" means Chinese tax or Canadian tax, as the context requires;
e) the term "person" includes an individual, a company and any other body of persons;
f) the term "company" means any corporate or any entity which is treated as a body corporate for tax purposes;
g) the terms "enterprise of a Contracting State" and "enterprise of the other Contracting State" mean respectively an enterprise carried on by a resident of a Contracting State and an enterprise carried on by a resident of the other Contracting State;
h) the term "nationals" means all individuals having the nationality of a Contracting State and all legal persons, partnerships and other bodies of persons deriving their status as such from the law in force in a Contracting State;
i) the term "international traffic" means any transport by a ship or aircraft operated by an enterprise of a Contracting State, except when the ship or aircraft is operated solely between places in the other Contracting State;
j) the term "competent authority" means, in the case of the People's Republic of China, the Ministry of Finance or its authorized representative, and in the case of Canada, the Minister of National Revenue or his authorized representative.

2. As regards the application of this Agreement by a Contracting State any term not defined in this Agreement shall, unless the context otherwise requires, have the meaning which it has under the law of that Contracting State concerning the taxes to which this Agreement applies.

Article 4 – Resident

1. For the purposes of this Agreement, the term "resident of a Contracting State" means any person who, under the laws of that Contracting State, is liable to tax therein by reason of his domicile, residence, place of head office, place of management or any other criterion of a similar nature.
2. Where by reason of the provisions of paragraph 1 an individual is a resident of both Contracting States, then his status shall be determined as follows:

   a) he shall be deemed to be a resident of the Contracting State in which he has a permanent home available to him; if he has a permanent home available to him in both Contracting States, he shall be deemed to be a resident of the Contracting State with which his personal and economic relations are closer (center of vital interests);
   b) if the Contracting State in which he has his center of vital interests cannot be determined, or if he has not a permanent home available to him in either Contracting State, he shall be deemed to be a resident of the Contracting State in which he has a habitual abode;
   c) if he has an habitual abode in both Contracting States or in neither of them, he shall be deemed to be a resident of the Contracting State of which he is a national;
   d) if he is a national of both Contracting States or of neither of them, the competent authorities of the Contracting States shall settle the question by mutual agreement.

3. Where by reason of the provisions of paragraph 1 a person other than an individual is a resident of both Contracting States, the competent authorities of the Contracting States shall by mutual agreement endeavor to settle the question and to determine the mode of application of this Agreement to such person.

Article 5 - Permanent Establishment

1. For the purposes of this Agreement, the term "permanent establishment" means a fixed place of business through which the business of an enterprise is wholly or partly carried on.
2. The term "permanent establishment" includes especially:

   a) a place of management;
   b) a branch;
   c) an office;
   d) a factory;
   e) a workshop; and
   f) a mine, an oil or gas well, a quarry or any other place of extraction of natural resources.

3. The term "permanent establishment" likewise encompasses:

   a) a building site, a construction, assembly or installation project or supervisory activities in connection therewith, but only where such site, project or activities continue for a period of more than six months;
   b) the furnishing of services, including consultancy services, by an enterprise of a Contracting State through employees or other personnel in the other Contracting State, provided that such activities continue (for the same project or a connected project) for a period or periods aggregating more than six months within any twelve-month period.

4. Notwithstanding the provisions of paragraphs 1 to 3, the term "permanent establishment" shall be deemed not to include:

   a) the use of facilities solely for the purpose of storage, display or delivery of goods or merchandise belonging to the enterprise;
   b) the maintenance of a stock of goods or merchandise belonging to the enterprise solely for the purpose of storage, display or delivery;
   c) the maintenance of a stock of goods or merchandise belonging to the enterprise solely for the purpose of processing by another enterprise;
   d) the maintenance of a fixed place of business solely for the purpose of purchasing goods or merchandise or for collecting information, for the enterprise;
   e) the maintenance of a fixed place of business solely for the purpose of carrying on, for the enterprise, any other activity of a preparatory or auxiliary character;
   f) the maintenance of a fixed place of business solely for any combination of activities mentioned in subparagraphs a) to e) provided that the overall activity of the fixed place of business resulting from this combination is of a preparatory or auxiliary character.

5. Notwithstanding the provisions of paragraphs 1 and 2, where a person—other than an agent of an independent status to whom the provisions of paragraph 6applies—is acting in a Contracting State on behalf of an enterprise of the other Contracting State and has, and habitually exercises, in the first-mentioned Contracting State an authority to conclude contracts in the name of the enterprise, that enterprise shall be deemed to have a permanent establishment in the first-mentioned Contracting State in respect of any activities which that person undertakes for the enterprise, unless his activities are limited to those mentioned in paragraph 4 which, if exercised through a fixed place of business, would not make that fixed place of business a permanent establishment under the provisions of that paragraph.
6. An enterprise of a Contracting State shall not be deemed to have a permanent establishment in the other Contracting State merely because it carries on business in that other

Contracting State through a broker, general commission agent or any other agent of an independent status, provided that such persons are acting in the ordinary course of their business. However, when the activities of such an agent are devoted wholly or almost wholly on behalf of that enterprise, he will not be considered an agent of an independent status within the meaning of this paragraph.

7. The fact that a company which is a resident of a Contracting State controls or is controlled by a company which is a resident of the other Contracting State, or which carries on business in that other Contracting State (whether through a permanent establishment or otherwise), shall not of itself constitute either company a permanent establishment of the other.

Article 6 - Income From Immovable Property

1. Income derived by a resident of a Contracting State from immovable property situated in the other Contracting State may be taxed in that other Contracting State.
2. The term "immovable property" shall have the meaning which it has under the law of the Contracting State in which the property in question is situated. The term shall in any case include property accessory to immovable property, livestock and equipment used in agriculture and forestry, rights to which the provisions of general law respecting landed property apply, usufruct of immovable property and rights to variable or fixed payments as consideration for the working of, or the right to work, mineral deposits, sources and other natural resources; ships and aircraft shall not be regarded as immovable property.
3. The provisions of paragraph 1 shall apply to income derived from the direct use, letting, or use in any other form of immovable property.
4. The provisions of paragraphs 1 and 3 shall also apply to the income from immovable property of an enterprise and to income from immovable property used for the performance of independent personal services.

Article 7 - Business Profits

1. The profits of an enterprise of a Contracting State shall be taxable only in that Contracting State unless the enterprise carries on business in the other Contracting State through a permanent establishment situated therein. If the enterprise carries on or has carried on business as aforesaid, the profits of the enterprise may be taxed in the other Contracting State but only so much of them as is attributable to that permanent establishment.
2. Subject to the provisions of paragraph 3, where an enterprise of a Contracting State carries on business in the other Contracting State through a permanent establishment situated therein, there shall in each Contracting State be attributed to that permanent establishment the profits which it might be expected to make if it were a distinct and separate enterprise engaged in the same or similar activities under the same or similar conditions and dealing wholly independently with the enterprise of which it is a permanent establishment.
3. In determining the profits of a permanent establishment, there shall be allowed as deductions expenses which are incurred for the purposes of the business of the permanent establishment, including executive and general administrative expenses so incurred, whether in the Contracting State in which the permanent establishment is situated or elsewhere. However, no such deduction shall be allowed in respect of amounts, if any, paid (otherwise than towards reimbursement of actual expenses) by the permanent establishment to the head office of the enterprise or any of its other offices, by way of royalties, fees or other similar payments in return for the use of patents or other rights, or by way of commission, for specific services performed or for management, or, except in the case of a banking enterprise, by way of interest on moneys lent to the permanent establishment. Likewise, no account shall be taken, in the determination of the profits of a permanent establishment, for amounts charged (otherwise than towards reimbursement of actual expenses), by the permanent

establishment to the head office of the enterprise or any of its other offices, by way of royalties, fees or other similar payments in return for the use of patents or other rights, or by way of commission for specific services performed or for management, or, except in the case of a banking enterprise, by way of interest on moneys lent to the head office of the enterprise or any of its other offices.

4. Insofar as it has been customary in a Contracting State to determine the profits to be attributed to a permanent establishment on the basis of an apportionment of the total profits of the enterprise to its various parts, nothing in paragraph 2 shall preclude that Contracting State from determining the profits to be taxed by such an apportionment as may be customary; the method of apportionment adopted shall, however, be such that the result shall be in accordance with the principles contained in this Article.
5. No profits shall be attributed to a permanent establishment by reason of the mere purchase by that permanent establishment of goods or merchandise for the enterprise.
6. For the purposes of paragraphs 1 to 5, the profits to be attributed to the permanent establishment shall be determined by the same method year by year unless there is good and sufficient reason to the contrary.
7. Where profits include items of income which are dealt with separately in other Articles of this Agreement, then, the provisions of those Articles shall not be affected by the provisions of this Article.

Article 8 - Shipping And Air Transport

1. Profits from the operation of ships or aircraft in international traffic shall be taxable only in the Contracting State in which the place of head office or the place of effective management is situated.
2. Notwithstanding the provisions of paragraph 1 and Article 7, profits derived from the operation of ships or aircraft used principally to transport passengers or goods exclusively between places in a Contracting State may be taxed in that Contracting State.
3. The provisions of this Article shall also apply to profits from participation in a pool, a joint business or an international operating agency.

Article 9 - Associated Enterprises

Where:

a) an enterprise of a Contracting State participates directly or indirectly in the management, control or capital of an enterprise of the other Contracting State, or
b) the same persons participate directly or indirectly in the management, control or capital of an enterprise of a Contracting State and an enterprise of the other Contracting State, and in either case conditions are made or imposed between the two enterprises in their commercial or financial relations which differ from those which would be made between independent enterprises, then any profits which would, but for those conditions, have accrued to one of the enterprises, but, by reason of those conditions, have not so accrued, may be included in the profits of that enterprise and taxed accordingly.

Article 10 – Dividends

1. Dividends paid by a company which is a resident of a Contracting State to a resident of the other Contracting State may be taxed in that other Contracting State.
2. However, such dividends may also be taxed in the Contracting State of which the company paying the dividends is a resident, and according to the laws of that Contracting State, but if the recipient is the beneficial owner of the dividends the tax so charged shall not exceed:

a) 10 percent of the gross amount of the dividends if the beneficial owner is a company which owns at least 10 per cent of the voting stock of the company paying the dividends;
b) 15 percent of the gross amount of the dividends in all other cases. The provisions of this paragraph shall not affect the taxation of the company in respect of the profits out of which the dividends are paid.

3. The term "dividends" as used in this Article means income from shares or other rights, not being debt-claims, participating in profits, as well as income from other rights which is subjected to the same taxation treatment as income from shares by the taxation laws of the Contracting State of which the company making the distribution is a resident.
4. The provisions of paragraphs 1 and 2 shall not apply if the beneficial owner of the dividends, being a resident of a Contracting State, carries on business in the other Contracting State of which the company paying the dividends is a resident, through a permanent establishment situated therein, or performs in that other Contracting State independent personal services from a fixed base situated therein, and the holding in respect of which the dividends are paid is effectively connected with such permanent establishment or fixed base. In such case the provisions of Article 7 or Article 14, as the case may be, shall apply.
5. Where a company which is a resident of a Contracting State derives profits or income from the other Contracting State, that other Contracting State may not impose any tax on the dividends paid by the company, except insofar as such dividends are paid to a resident of that other Contracting State or insofar as the holding in respect of which the dividends are paid is effectively connected with a permanent establishment or a fixed base situated in that other Contracting State, nor subject the company's undistributed profits to a tax on the company's undistributed profits, even if the dividends paid or the undistributed profits consist wholly or partly of profits or income arising in that other Contracting State.
6. Notwithstanding any provision in this Agreement, a company which is a resident of the People's Republic of China and which has permanent establishments in Canada, shall, in accordance with the provisions of Canadian law, remain subject to the additional tax on companies other than Canadian corporations, but the rate of such additional tax shall not exceed 10 per cent. For the purpose of this paragraph, the term "earnings" means the profits attributable to such permanent establishments in Canadian a year and previous years after deducting therefrom:

   a) business losses attributable to such permanent establishments (including losses from the alienation of property forming part of the business property of such permanent establishments) in such year and previous years,
   b) all taxes chargeable in Canada on such profits, other than the additional tax referred to herein, and
   c) the profits reinvested in Canada, provided that the amount of such deduction shall be determined in accordance with the existing provisions of the law of Canada regarding the computation of the allowance in respect of investment in property in Canada, and any subsequent modification of those provisions which shall not affect the general principle hereof.

7. The additional tax referred to in paragraph 6 shall be levied only to the extent that the cumulative amount of earnings of the company, or of a person related there to from the same or similar business as that carried on by the company, exceeds five hundred thousand Canadian dollars ($ 500, 000).

Article 11 – Interest

1. Interest arising in a Contracting State and paid to a resident of the other Contracting State may be taxed in that other Contracting State.

2. However, such interest may also be taxed in the Contracting State in which it arises, and according to the laws of that Contracting State, but if the recipient is the beneficial owner of the interest the tax so charged shall not exceed 10 per cent of the gross amount of the interest.
3. Notwithstanding the provisions of paragraph 2, interest arising in a Contracting State is exempt from tax in that Contracting State, if it is paid:

   a) in the case of Canada:

      i) to the Government of Canada;
      ii) to the Bank of Canada;
      iii) on a loan directly or indirectly financed or guaranteed by the Canadian Export Development Corporation;
      iv) to a financial establishment owned by the Government of Canada and mutually agreed upon by the competent authorities of the Contracting States;

   b) in the case of the People's Republic of China:

      i) to the Government of the People's Republic of China;
      ii) to the People's Bank of China;
      iii) on a loan directly or indirectly financed or guaranteed by the Bank of China or the Chinese International Trust and Investment Company (CITIC);
      iv) to a financial establishment owned by the Government of the People's Republic of China and mutually agreed upon by the competent authorities of the Contracting States.

4. The term "interest" as used in this Article includes income from debt-claims of every kind, whether or not secured by mortgage, and whether or not carrying a right to participate in the debtor's profits, and in particular, income from Government securities and income from bonds or debentures, as well as premiums and bonuses attaching to such securities, bonds or debentures.
5. The provisions of paragraphs 1, 2 and 3 shall not apply if the beneficial owner of the interest, being a resident of a Contracting State, carries on business in the other Contracting State in which the interest arises, through a permanent establishment situated therein, or performs in that other Contracting State independent personal services from a fixed base situated therein, and the debt-claim in respect of which the interest is paid is effectively connected with such permanent establishment or fixed base. In such case the provisions of Article 7 or Article 14, as the case may be, shall apply.
6. Interest shall be deemed to arise in a Contracting State when the payer is the Government of that Contracting State, a political subdivision, a local authority or a resident of that Contracting State. Where, however, the person paying the interest, whether he is a resident of a Contracting State or not, has in a Contracting State a permanent establishment or a fixed base in connection with which the indebtedness on which the interest is paid was incurred, and such interest is borne by such permanent establishment or fixed base, then such interest shall be deemed to arise in the Contracting State in which the permanent establishment or fixed base is situated.
7. Where, by reason of a special relationship between the payer and the beneficial owner or between both of them and some other person, the amount of the interest, having regard to the debt-claim for which it is paid, exceeds the amount which would have been agreed upon by the payer and the beneficial owner in the absence of such relationship, the provisions of this Article shall apply only to the last-mentioned amount. In such case, the excess part of the payments shall remain11taxable according to the laws of each Contracting State, due regard being had to the other provisions of this Agreement.

Article 12 – Royalties

1. Royalties arising in a Contracting State and paid to a resident of the other Contracting State may be taxed in that other Contracting State.
2. However, such royalties may also be taxed in the Contracting State in which they arise, and according to the laws of that Contracting State, but if the recipient is the beneficial owner of the royalties the tax so charged shall not exceed 10 percent of the gross amount of the royalties.
3. The term "royalties" as used in this Article means payments of any kind received as a consideration for the use of, or the right to use, any copyright of literary, artistic or scientific work including cinematograph films and films or tapes for radio or television broadcasting, any patent, know-how, trade mark, design or model, plan, secret formula or process, or for the use of, or the right to use, industrial, commercial or scientific equipment, or for information concerning industrial, commercial or scientific experience.
4. The provisions of paragraphs 1 and 2 shall not apply if the beneficial owner of the royalties, being a resident of a Contracting State, carries on business in the other Contracting State in which the royalties arise, through a permanent establishment situated therein, or performs in that other Contracting State independent personal services from a fixed base situated therein, and the right or property in respect of which the royalties are paid is effectively connected with such permanent establishment or fixed base. In such case the provisions of Article 7 or Article 14, as the case may be, shall apply.
5. Royalties shall be deemed to arise in a Contracting State when the payer is the Government of that Contracting State, a political subdivision, a local authority or a resident of that Contracting State. Where, however, the person paying the royalties, whether he is a resident of a Contracting State or not, has in a Contracting State a permanent establishment or a fixed base in connection with which the liability to pay the royalties was incurred, and such royalties are borne by such permanent establishment or fixed base, then such royalties shall be deemed to arise in the Contracting State in which the permanent establishment or fixed base is situated.
6. Where, by reason of a special relationship between the payer and the beneficial owner or between both of them and some other person, the amount of the royalties, having regard to the use, right or information for which they are paid, exceeds the amount which would have been agreed upon by the payer and the beneficial owner in the absence of such relationship, the provisions of this Article shall apply only to the last-mentioned amount. In such case, the excess part of the payments shall remain taxable according to the laws of each Contracting State, due regard being had to the other provisions of this Agreement.

Article 13 - Capital Gains

1. Gains derived by a resident of a Contracting state from the alienation of immovable property referred to in Article 6 and situated in the other Contracting state may be taxed in that other Contracting state.
2. Gains from the alienation of movable property forming part of the business property of a permanent establishment which an enterprise of a Contracting State has in the other Contracting State or of movable property pertaining to a fixed base available to a resident of a Contracting State in the other Contracting State for the purpose of performing independent personal services, including such gains from the alienation of such a permanent establishment (alone or with the whole enterprise) or of such a fixed base, may be taxed in that other Contracting State.

3. Gains from the alienation of ships or aircraft operated in international traffic and movable property pertaining to the operation of such ships or aircraft which are received by a resident of a Contracting State shall be taxable only in that Contracting State.
4. Gains from the alienation of shares in the capital of a Company, the assets of which consist mainly, directly or indirectly, of immovable property situated in a Contracting State, may be taxed in that Contracting State.
5. Gains derived by a resident of a Contracting State from the alienation of any property other than that referred to in paragraphs 1 to 4 above, may be taxed in the Contracting State in which they arise.

Article 14 - Independent Personal Services

1. Income derived by a resident of a Contracting State in respect of professional services or other activities of an independent character shall be taxable only in that Contracting State except in the following circumstances, when such income may also be taxed in the other Contracting State:

    a) if he has a fixed base regularly available to him in the other Contracting State for the purpose of performing his activities; in that case, only so much of the income as is attributable to that fixed base may be taxed in that other Contracting State; or
    b) if his stay in the other Contracting State for a period or periods exceeding in the aggregate 183 days in the calendar year concerned; in that case, only so much of the income as is derived from his activities performed in that other Contracting State may be taxed in that other Contracting State.

2. The term "professional services" includes especially independent scientific, literary, artistic, educational or teaching activities as well as the independent activities of physicians, lawyers, engineers, architects, dentists and accountants.

Article 15 - Dependent Personal Services

1. Subject to the provisions of Articles 16, 18 and 19, salaries, wages and other similar remuneration derived by a resident of a Contracting State in respect of an employment shall be taxable only in that Contracting State unless the employment is exercised in the other Contracting State. If the employment is so exercised, such remuneration as is derived therefrom may be taxed in that other Contracting State.
2. Notwithstanding the provisions of paragraph 1, remuneration derived by a resident of a Contracting State in respect of an employment exercised in the other Contracting State shall be taxable only in the first-mentioned Contracting State if:

    a) the recipient is present in that other Contracting State for a period or periods not exceeding in the aggregate 183 days in the calendar year concerned; and
    b) the remuneration is paid by, or on behalf of, an employer who is not a resident of that other Contracting State; and
    c) the remuneration is not borne by a permanent establishment or a fixed base which the employer has in that other Contracting State.

3. Notwithstanding the provisions of paragraphs 1 and 2, remuneration in respect of an employment exercised aboard a ship or aircraft operated in international traffic by an enterprise of a Contracting State, shall be taxable only in that Contracting State.

Article 16 - Directors' Fees And Remuneration Of Top-Level Managerial Officials

1. Directors' fees and other similar payments derived by a resident of a Contracting State in his capacity as a member of the board of directors of a company which is a resident of the other Contracting State may be taxed in that other Contracting State.

2. Salaries, wages and other similar remuneration derived by a resident of a Contracting State in his capacity as an official in a top-level managerial position of accompany which is a resident of the other Contracting State may be taxed in that other Contracting State.

Article 17 - Artistes And Athletes

1. Notwithstanding the provisions of Articles 14 and 15, income derived by a resident of a Contracting State as an entertainer, such as a theatre, motion picture, radio or television artiste, or a musician, or as an athlete, from his personal activities as such exercised in the other Contracting State, may be taxed in that other Contracting State.
2. Where income in respect of personal activities exercised by an entertainer or an athlete in his capacity as such accrues not to the entertainer or athlete himself but to another person, that income may, notwithstanding the provisions of Articles 7, 14and 15, be taxed in the Contracting State in which the activities of the entertainer or athlete are exercised.
3. Notwithstanding the provisions of paragraphs 1 and 2, income derived from the activities of an entertainer or an athlete who is a resident of a Contracting State, exercised in the other Contracting State within the framework of an official cultural exchange program between the Contracting States, shall not be taxed in that other Contracting State.

Article 18 - Government Service

a) Remuneration, other than a pension, paid by a Contracting State or a political subdivision or a local authority thereof to an individual in respect of services rendered to that Contracting State or subdivision or authority shall be taxable only in that Contracting State.
b) However, such remuneration shall be taxable only in the other Contracting State if the services are rendered in that Contracting State and the individual is a resident of that Contracting State who:

   i) is a national of that Contracting State; or
   ii) did not become a resident of that Contracting State solely for the purpose of rendering the services.

   The provisions of Articles 15, 16 and 17 shall apply to remuneration in respect of services rendered in connection with a business carried on by a Contracting State or a political subdivision or a local authority thereof.

Article 19 – Students

Payments which a student, apprentice or business trainee who is, or was immediately before visiting a Contracting State, a resident of the other Contracting State and who is present in the first-mentioned Contracting State solely for the purpose of his education or training receives for the purpose of his maintenance, education or training shall not be taxed in that Contracting State.

Article 20 - Other Income

1. Items of income of a resident of a Contracting State, wherever arising, not dealt with in the foregoing Articles of this Agreement shall be taxable only in that Contracting State.
2. The provisions of paragraph 1 shall not apply to income, other than income from immovable property as defined in paragraph 2 of Article 6, if the recipient of such income, being a resident of a Contracting State, carries on business in the other Contracting State through a permanent establishment situated therein, or performs in that other Contracting State independent personal services from a fixed base situated therein, and the right or property in respect of which the income is paid is effectively

connected with such permanent establishment of fixed base. In such case the provisions of Article 7 or Article 14, as the case may be, shall apply.

3. Notwithstanding the provisions of paragraphs 1 and 2, items of income of a resident of a Contracting State not dealt with in the foregoing Articles of this Agreement, and arising in the other Contracting State may be taxed in that other Contracting State.

Article 21 - Methods For Elimination Of Double Taxation

1. In the case of Canada, double taxation shall be avoided as follows:

   a) Subject to the existing provisions of the law of Canada regarding the deduction from tax payable in Canada of tax paid in a territory outside Canada and to any subsequent modification of those provisions which shall not affect the general principle hereof and unless a greater deduction or relief is provided under the laws of Canada, tax payable in the People's Republic of China on profits, income or gains arising in the People's Republic of China shall be deducted from any Canadian tax payable in respect of such profits, income or gains.
   b) Subject to the existing provisions of the law of Canada regarding the determination of the exempt surplus of a foreign affiliate and to any subsequent modification of those provisions—which shall not affect the general principle hereof—for the purpose of computing Canadian tax, a company resident in Canada shall be allowed to deduct in computing its taxable income any dividend received by it out of the exempt surplus of a foreign affiliate resident in the People's Republic of China, and for this purpose, the Canadian participant in a Chinese-Canadian joint venture established according to the law of the People's Republic of China concerning joint ventures with Chinese and foreign investment shall be treated as having a foreign affiliate in respect of its interest in the joint venture.

2. For the purposes of paragraph 1 a), tax payable in the People's Republic of China by a company which is a resident of Canada shall be deemed to include any amount which would have been payable as Chinese tax for any year but for an exemption from, or reduction of, tax granted for that year or any part thereof under any of the following provisions of Chinese law:

   a) Articles 5 and 6 of the Income Tax Law of the People's Republic of China concerning Joint Venture with Chinese and Foreign Investment and Article 3 of the Detailed Rules and Regulations for the Implementation of the Income Tax Law of the People's Republic of China concerning Joint Ventures with Chinese and Foreign Investment;
   b) Articles 4 and 5 of the Income Tax Law of the People's Republic of China concerning Foreign Enterprises;
   c) Articles I, II, III, IV and X of Part I, Articles I, II, III and IV of Part II and Articles I, II and III of part III of the interim provisions of the State Council of the People's Republic of China concerning reduction or exemption from enterprise income tax in special economic zones and coastal cities; so far as they were in force on, and have not been modified since, the date of signature of this Agreement, or have been modified only in minor respects so as not to affect their general character; or (d) any other provision which may subsequently be made granting an exemption or reduction of tax which is agreed by the competent authorities of the Contracting States to be of a substantially similar character, if it has not been modified thereafter or has been modified only in minor respects so as not to affect its general character.
   e) For the application of this paragraph, the amount of Chinese tax shall be deemed to be:

i) in the case of dividends: 10 per cent if the recipient of the dividends is the beneficial owner of at least 10 per cent of the voting stock of the company paying the dividends; 15 per cent in all other cases;
ii) in the case of interest 10 per cent; and
iii) in the case of royalties 15 per cent.

3. In the case of the People's Republic of China, double taxation shall be avoided as follows:

a) Where a resident of the People's Republic of China derives income from Canada, the amount of tax payable in Canada in respect of that income in accordance with the provisions of this Agreement shall bellowed as a credit against the Chinese tax imposed on that resident.
The amount of credit, however, shall not exceed the amount of the Chinese tax computed as appropriate to that income in accordance with the taxation laws and regulations of the People's Republic of China.
b) Where the income derived from Canada is a dividend paid by a company which is a resident of Canada to a company which is a resident of the People's Republic of China and which owns not less than 10 per cent of the shares of the company paying the dividend, the credit shall take into account the tax payable in Canada by the company paying the dividend in respect of its income.

4. For the purposes of this Article, profits, income or gains of a resident of a Contracting State which are taxed in the other Contracting State in accordance with this Agreement shall be deemed to arise from sources in that other Contracting State.

Article 22 - Non-Discrimination

1. Nationals of a Contracting State shall not be subjected in the other Contracting State to any taxation or any requirement connected therewith which is other or more burdensome than the taxation and connected requirements to which nationals of that other Contracting State in the same circumstances are or may be subjected. The provisions of this paragraph shall, notwithstanding the provisions of Article 1, also apply to individuals who are not residents of one or both of the Contracting States.
2. The taxation on a permanent establishment which an enterprise of a Contracting State has in the other Contracting State shall not be less favorably levied in that other Contracting State than the taxation levied on enterprises of that other Contracting State carrying on the same activities. The provisions of this paragraph shall not be construed as obliging a Contracting State to grant to residents of the other Contracting State any personal allowances, reliefs and reductions for taxation purposes on account of civil status or family responsibilities which it grants to its own residents.
3. Enterprises of a Contracting State, the capital of which is wholly or partly owned or controlled, directly or indirectly, by one or more residents of the other Contracting State, shall not be subjected in the first-mentioned Contracting State to any taxation or any requirement connected therewith which is other or more burdensome than the taxation and connected requirements to which other similar enterprises of the first-mentioned Contracting State, the capital of which is wholly or partly owned or controlled, directly or indirectly, by one or more residents of a third State, are or may be subjected.

Article 23 - Mutual Agreement Procedure

1. Where a person considers that the actions of one or both of the Contracting States result or will result for him in taxation not in accordance with the provisions of this Agreement, he may, irrespective of the remedies provided by the domestic law of those Contracting States, address to the competent authority of the Contracting State of which he is a resident, or to that of the Contracting State of which he is a national if

his case comes under paragraph 1 of Article 22, an application in writing stating the grounds for claiming the revision of such taxation.

2. The competent authority shall endeavor, if the objection appears to it to be justified and if it is not itself able to arrive at a satisfactory solution, to resolve the case by mutual agreement with the competent authority of the other Contracting State, with a view to the avoidance of taxation which is not in accordance with the provision of this Agreement.
3. The competent authorities of the Contracting States shall endeavor to resolve by mutual agreement any difficulties or doubts arising as to the interpretation or application of this Agreement. They may also consult together for the elimination of double taxation in cases not provided for in this Agreement.
4. The competent authorities of the Contracting States may communicate with each other directly for the purpose of reaching an agreement in the sense of paragraphs 2 and 3. When it seems advisable for the purpose of reaching agreement, the competent authorities may meet together for an oral exchange of opinions.

Article 24 - Exchange Of Information

1. The competent authorities of the Contracting States shall exchange such information as is necessary for carrying out the provisions of this Agreement or of the domestic laws of the Contracting States concerning taxes covered by this Agreement, insofar as the taxation thereunder is not contrary to this Agreement, in particular for the prevention of fraud or evasion of such taxes. The exchange of information is not restricted by Article 1. Any information so exchanged shall be treated as secret and shall be disclosed only to persons or authorities, including courts, involved in the assessment or collection of the taxes covered by this Agreement or the determination of appeals in relation thereto. Such information may be disclosed in public court proceedings or in judicial decisions.
2. In no case shall the provisions of paragraph 1 be construed so as to impose on a Contracting State the obligation:

   a) to carry out administrative measures at variance with the laws and the administrative practice of that or of the other Contracting State;
   b) to supply information which is not obtainable under the laws or in the normal course of the administration of that or of the other Contracting state; or
   c) to supply information which would disclose any trade, business, industrial, commercial or professional secret or trade process, or information, the disclosure of which would be contrary to public policy.

Article 25 - Diplomatic Agents And Consular Officers

Nothing in this Agreement shall affect the fiscal privileges of diplomatic agents or consular officers under the general rules of international law or under the provisions of special agreements.

Article 26 - Entry Into Force

This Agreement shall enter into force on the thirtieth day after the date on which diplomatic notes indicating the completion of internal legal procedures necessary in each country for the entry into force of this Agreement have been exchanged. This Agreement shall have effect:

a) in respect of tax withheld at the source on amounts paid or credited to non-residents on or after the first day of January next following that in which this Agreement enters into force; and (b) in respect of other taxes for taxation years beginning on or after the first day of January next following that in which this Agreement enters into force.

Article 27 – Termination

This Agreement shall continue in effect indefinitely but either of the Contracting States may, on or before the thirtieth day of June in any calendar year beginning after the expiration of a period of five years from the date of its entry into force, give to the other Contracting State, through diplomatic channels, written notice of termination. In such event, this Agreement shall cease to have effect:

a) in respect of tax withheld at the source on amounts paid or credited to non-residents on or after the first day of January in the calendar year next following that in which the notice of termination is given; and) in respect of other taxes for taxation years beginning on or after the first day of January in the calendar year next following that in which the notice of termination is given.

IN WITNESS WHEREOF the undersigned, duly authorized to that effect, have signed this Agreement.

DONE in duplicate at Beijing, this twelfth day of May 1986, in the Chinese, English and French languages, each version being equally authentic.

9.1.4 USA–China Treaty

The Government of the People's Republic of China and the Government of the United States of America, desiring to conclude an Agreement for the avoidance of double taxation and the prevention of tax evasion with respect to taxes on income, have agreed as follows:

Article 1 - Personal Scope

This Agreement shall apply to persons who are residents of one or both of the Contracting States.

Article 2 - Taxes Covered

1. The taxes to which this Agreement applies are

   a) in the People's Republic of China:

      I) the individual income tax;
      II) the income tax concerning joint ventures with Chinese and foreign investment;
      III) the income tax concerning foreign enterprises;
      IV) the local income tax (hereinafter referred to as "Chinese tax")

   b) in the United States of America: the Federal income taxes imposed by the Internal Revenue Code (hereinafter referred to as "United States tax")

2. The Agreement shall apply also to any identical or substantially similar taxes which are imposed after the date of signature of the Agreement in addition to, or in place of, those referred to in paragraph 1. Within an appropriate time period, the competent authorities of the Contracting States shall notify each other of any substantial changes which have been made in their respective taxation laws.

Article 3 - General Definitions

1. In this Agreement unless the context otherwise requires,

   a) the term "the People's Republic of China", when used in a geographical sense, means all the territory of the People's Republic of China, including its territorial sea, in which the laws relating to Chinese tax are in force, and all the area beyond its territorial sea, including the seabed and subsoil thereof, over which the People's Republic of China has jurisdiction in accordance with international law and in which the laws relating to Chinese tax are in force;
   b) the term "United States of America", when used in a geographical sense, means all the territory of the United States of America, including its territorial sea, in which the laws relating to United States tax are in force, and all the area beyond its territorial sea, including the seabed and subsoil thereof, over which the United States of America has jurisdiction in accordance with international law and in which the laws relating to United States tax are in force;
   c) the terms "a Contracting State" and "the other Contracting State" mean the People's Republic of China or the United States of America, as the context requires;
   d) the term "tax" means Chinese tax or United States tax, as the context requires;
   e) the term "person" includes an individual, a company, a partnership and any other body of persons;
   f) the term "company" means any corporate or any entity which is treated as a body corporate for tax purposes;
   g) the terms "enterprise of a Contracting State" and "enterprise of the other Contracting State" mean respectively an enterprise carried on by a resident of a Contracting State and an enterprise carried on by a resident of the other Contracting State;
   h) the term "nationals" means all individuals having the nationality of a Contracting State and all legal persons, partnerships and other bodies of persons deriving their status as such from the law in force in a Contracting State;
   i) the term "competent authority" means:

      (i) in the People's Republic of China, the Ministry of Finance or its authorized representative; and
      (ii) in the United States of America, the Secretary of the Treasury or his authorized representative.

2. As regards the application of the Agreement by a Contracting State any term not defined therein shall, unless the context otherwise requires, have the meaning which it has under the laws of that Contracting State concerning the taxes to which the Agreement applies.

Article 4 – Resident

1. For the purposes of this Agreement, the term "resident of a Contracting State" means any person who, under the laws of that Contracting State, is liable to tax therein by reason of his domicile, residence, place of head office, place of incorporation or any other criterion of a similar nature.
2. Where by reason of the provisions of paragraph 1 an individual is a resident of both Contracting States, then the competent authorities of the Contracting States shall determine through consultations the Contracting State of which that individual shall be deemed to be a resident for the purposes of this Agreement.
3. Where by reason of the provisions of paragraph 1 a company is a resident of both Contracting States, then the competent authorities of the Contracting States shall determine through consultations the Contracting State of which the company shall be deemed to be a resident for the purposes of this Agreement, and, if they are unable to so

determine, the company shall not be considered to be a resident of either Contracting State for purposes of enjoying benefits under this Agreement.

4. Where by reason of the provisions of paragraph 1 a company is a resident of the United States of America, and, under a tax agreement between the People's Republic of China and a third country is also a resident of that third country, the company shall not be considered to be a resident of the United States of America for purposes of enjoying benefits under this Agreement.

Article 5 - Permanent Establishment

1. For the purposes of this Agreement, the term "permanent establishment" means affixed place of business through which the business of an enterprise is wholly or partly carried on.
2. The term "permanent establishment" includes especially:

   a) a place of management;
   b) a branch;
   c) an office;
   d) a factory;
   e) a workshop; and
   f) a mine, an oil or gas well, a quarry, or any other place of extraction of natural resources.

3. The term "permanent establishment" also includes:

   a) a building site, a construction, assembly or installation project, or supervisory activities in connection therewith, but only where such site, project or activities continue for a period of more than six months;
   b) an installation, drilling rig or ship used for the exploration or exploitation of natural resources, but only if so used for a period of more than three months; and
   c) the furnishing of services, including consultancy services, by an enterprise through employees or other personnel engaged by the enterprise for such purpose, but only where such activities continue (for the same or a connected project) within the country for a period or periods aggregating more than six months within any twelve month period.

4. Notwithstanding the provisions of paragraphs 1 through 3, the term "permanent establishment" shall be deemed not to include:

   a) the use of facilities solely for the purpose of storage, display or delivery of goods or merchandise belonging to the enterprise;
   b) the maintenance of a stock of goods or merchandise belonging to the enterprise solely for the purpose of storage, display or delivery;
   c) the maintenance of a stock of goods or merchandise belonging to the enterprise solely for the purpose of processing by another enterprise;
   d) the maintenance of a fixed place of business solely for the purpose of purchasing goods or merchandise, or of collecting information, for the enterprise;
   e) the maintenance of a fixed place of business solely for the purpose of carrying on, for the enterprise, any other activity of a preparatory or auxiliary character;
   f) the maintenance of a fixed place of business solely for any combination of the activities mentioned in sub-paragraphs (a) through (e), provided that the overall activity of the fixed place of business resulting from this combination is of a preparatory or auxiliary character.

5. Notwithstanding the provisions of paragraphs 1 and 2, where a person, other than an agent of an independent status to whom paragraph 6 applies, is acting on behalf of an enterprise and has and habitually exercises in a Contracting State an authority to

conclude contracts in the name of the enterprise, that enterprise shall be deemed to have a permanent establishment in that Contracting State in respect of any activities which that person undertakes for the enterprise, unless the activities of such personage limited to those mentioned in paragraph 4 which, if exercised through a fixed place of business, would not make this fixed place of business a permanent establishment under the provisions of that paragraph.

6. An enterprise of a Contracting State shall not be deemed to have a permanent establishment in the other Contracting State merely because it carries on business in that other Contracting State through a broker, general commission agent or any other agent of an independent status, provided that such persons are acting in the ordinary course of their business. However, when the activities of such an agent are devoted wholly or almost wholly on behalf of that enterprise, he will not be considered an agent of an independent status within the meaning of this paragraph if it is shown that the transactions between the agent and the enterprise were not made underarm's-length conditions.
7. The fact that a company which is a resident of a Contracting State controls or is controlled by a company which is a resident of the other Contracting State, or which carries on business in that other Contracting State (whether through a permanent establishment or otherwise), shall not of itself constitute either company a permanent establishment of the other.

Article 6 - Income From Immovable Property

1. Income derived by a resident of a Contracting State from real property situated in the other Contracting State may be taxed in that other Contracting State.
2. The term "real property" shall have the meaning which it has under the laws of the Contracting State in which the property in question is situated. The term shall in any case include property accessory to real property, livestock and equipment used in agriculture and forestry, rights to which the provisions of general law respecting landed property apply, usufruct of real property and rights to variable or fixed payments as consideration for the working of, or the right to work, mineral deposits, sources and other natural resources; ships and aircraft shall not be regarded as real property.
3. The provisions of paragraph 1 shall apply to income derived from the direct use, letting or use in any other form of real property.
4. The provisions of paragraphs 1 and 3 shall also apply to the income from real property of an enterprise and to income from real property used for the performance of independent personal services.

Article 7 - Business Profits

1. The profits of an enterprise of a Contracting State shall be taxable only in that Contracting State unless the enterprise carries on business in the other Contracting State through a permanent establishment situated therein. If the enterprise carries on business as aforesaid, the profits of the enterprise may be taxed in the other Contracting State but only so much of them as is attributable to that permanent establishment.
2. Subject to the provisions of paragraph 3, where an enterprise of a Contracting State carries on business in the other Contracting State through a permanent establishment situated therein, there shall in each Contracting State be attributed to that permanent establishment the profits which it might be expected to make if it were a distinct and separate enterprise engaged in the same or similar activities under the same or similar conditions and dealing wholly independently with the enterprise of which it is a permanent establishment.
3. In the determination of the profits of a permanent establishment, there shall be allowed as deductions expenses which are incurred for the purposes of the permanent establishment, including executive and general administrative expenses so incurred, whether in the State in which the permanent establishment is situated or elsewhere. However, no

such deduction shall be allowed in respect of amounts, if any, paid (otherwise than towards reimbursement of actual expenses) by the permanent establishment to the head office of the enterprise or any of its other offices, by way of royalties or other similar payments or by way of interest on money lent to the permanent establishment. Likewise, no account shall be taken, in the determination of the profits of a permanent establishment, for amounts charged (otherwise than towards reimbursement of actual expenses) by the permanent establishment to the head office of the enterprise or any of its other offices, by way of royalties or other similar payments or by way of interest on money lent to the head office of the enterprise or any of its other offices.

4. Insofar as the tax law of a Contracting State provides with respect to a specific industry that the profits to be attributed to a permanent establishment are to be determined on the basis of a deemed profit, nothing in paragraph 2 shall preclude that Contracting State from applying those provisions of its law, provided that the result is in accordance with the principles contained in this Article.
5. No profits shall be attributed to a permanent establishment by reason of the mere purchase by that permanent establishment of goods or merchandise for the enterprise.
6. For the purposes of paragraphs 1 through 5, the profits to be attributed to the permanent establishment shall be determined by the same method year by year unless there is good and sufficient reason to the contrary.
7. Where profits include items of income which are dealt with separately in other Articles of this Agreement, the provisions of those Articles shall not be affected by the provisions of this Article.

Article 8 - Associated Enterprises

1. Where:

   a) an enterprise of a Contracting State participates directly or indirectly in the management, control or capital of an enterprise of the other Contracting State; or
   b) the same persons participate directly or indirectly in the management, control or capital of an enterprise of a Contracting State and an enterprise of the other Contracting State, and in either case the relationship between the two enterprises in their commercial or financial relations differs from that which would exist between independent enterprises, then any profits which, but for those conditions would have accrued to one of the enterprises, but by reason of those conditions have not so accrued, may be included in the profits of that enterprise and taxed accordingly.

2. Where a Contracting State includes in the profits of an enterprise of that Contracting State-and taxes accordingly-profits on which an enterprise of the other Contracting State has been charged to tax in that other Contracting State, and the profits so included are profits which would have accrued to the enterprise of the first-mentioned State if the conditions made between the two enterprises had been those which would have been made between independent enterprises, then that other Contracting State shall make an appropriate adjustment to the amount of the tax charged therein on those profits. In determining such adjustment, due regard shall be paid to the other provisions of this Agreement and the competent authorities of the Contracting States shall if necessary consult each other.

Article 9 –Dividends

1. Dividends paid by a company that is a resident of a Contracting State to a resident of the other Contracting State may be taxed in that other Contracting State.

2. However, such dividends may also be taxed in the Contracting State of which the company paying the dividends is a resident, and according to the laws of that Contracting State, but if the recipient is the beneficial owner of the dividends the tax so charged shall not exceed 10 percent of the gross amount of the dividends. This paragraph shall not affect the taxation of the company in respect of the profits out of which the dividends are paid.
3. The term "dividends" as used in this Article means income from shares or other rights, not being debt-claims, participating in profits, as well as income from other corporate rights which is subjected to the same taxation treatment as income from shares by the taxation laws of the Contracting State of which the company making the distribution is a resident.
4. The provisions of paragraphs 1 and 2 shall not apply if the beneficial owner of the dividends, being a resident of a Contracting State, carries on business in the other Contracting State, of which the company paying the dividends is a resident, through a permanent establishment situated therein, or performs in that other Contracting State independent personal services from a fixed base situated therein, and the holding or other corporate rights in respect of which the dividends are paid is effectively connected with such permanent establishment or fixed base. In such case the provisions of Article 7 or 13, as the case may be, shall apply.
5. Where a company which is a resident of a Contracting State derives profits or income from the other Contracting State, that other Contracting State may not impose any tax on the dividends paid by the company, except insofar as such dividends are paid to a resident of that other Contracting State or insofar as the holding or other corporate rights in respect of which the dividends are paid is effectively connected with a permanent establishment or a fixed base situated in that other Contracting State, nor subject the company's undistributed profits to a tax on the company's undistributed profits, even if the dividends paid or the undistributed profits consist wholly or partly of profits or income arising in that other Contracting State.

Article 10 – Interest

1. Interest arising in a Contracting State and paid to a resident of the other Contracting State may be taxed in that other Contracting State.
2. However, such interest may also be taxed in the Contracting State in which it arises and according to the laws of that Contracting State, but if the recipient is the beneficial owner of the interest, the tax so charged shall not exceed 10 percent of the gross amount of the interest.
3. Notwithstanding the provisions of paragraph 2, interest arising in a Contracting State and derived by the government of the other Contracting State, a political subdivision or local authority thereof, the Central Bank of that other Contracting State or any financial institution wholly owned by that government, or by any resident of the other Contracting State with respect to debt-claims indirectly financed by the government of that other Contracting State, a political subdivision or local authority thereof, the Central Bank of that other Contracting State or any financial institution wholly owned by that government, shall be exempt from tax in the first-mentioned Contracting State.
4. The term "interest" as used in this Article means income from debt-claims of every kind, whether or not secured by mortgage, and whether or not carrying a righto participate in the debtor's profits, and in particular, income from government securities, and income from bonds or debentures, including premiums or prizes attaching to such securities, bonds, or debentures.
5. The provisions of paragraphs 1, 2 and 3 shall not apply if the beneficial owner of the interest, being a resident of a Contracting State, carries on business in the other Contracting State in which the interest arises, through a permanent establishment situated therein, or performs in that other Contracting State independent personal

services from a fixed base situated therein, and the debt-claim in respect of which the interest is paid is effectively connected with such permanent establishment or fixed base. In such case the provisions of Article 7 or 13, as the case may be, shall apply.

6. Interest shall be deemed to arise in a Contracting State when the payer is the government of that Contracting State itself, a political subdivision, a local authority or a resident of that Contracting State. Where, however, the person paying the interest, whether he is a resident of a Contracting State or not, has in a Contracting State a permanent establishment or a fixed base in connection with which the indebtedness on which the interest is paid was incurred, and such interest is borne by such permanent establishment or fixed base, then such interest shall be deemed to arise in the Contracting State in which the permanent establishment or fixed base is situated.
7. Where, by reason of a special relationship between the payer and the beneficial owner or between both of them and some other person, the amount of the interest, having regard to the debt-claim for which it is paid, exceeds the amount which would have been agreed upon by the payer and the beneficial owner in the absence of such relationship, the provisions of this Article shall apply only to the last-mentioned amount. In such case the excess part of the payments shall remain taxable according to the laws of each Contracting State, due regard being had to the other provisions of this Agreement.

Article 11 – Royalties

1. Royalties arising in a Contracting State and paid to a resident of the other Contracting State may be taxed in that other Contracting State.
2. However, such royalties may also be taxed in the Contracting State in which they arise and according to the laws of that Contracting State, but if the recipient is the beneficial owner of the royalties, the tax so charged shall not exceed 10 percent of the gross amount of the royalties.
3. The term "royalties" as used in this Article means payments of any kind received as a consideration for the use of, or the right to use, any copyright of literary, artistic or scientific work, including cinematographic films or films or tapes used for radio or television broadcasting, any patent, technical know-how, trademark, design or model, plan, secret formula or process, or for the use of, or the right to use, industrial commercial or scientific equipment, or for information concerning industrial, commercial or scientific experience.
4. The provisions of paragraphs 1 and 2 shall not apply if the beneficial owner of the royalties, being a resident of a Contracting State, carries on business in the other Contracting State in which the royalties arise, through a permanent establishment situated therein, or performs in that other Contracting State independent personal services from a fixed base situated therein, and the right or property in respect of which the royalties are paid is effectively connected with such permanent establishment or fixed base. In such case the provisions of Article 7 or 13, as the case may be, shall apply.
5. a) Royalties will be deemed to arise in a Contracting State when the payer is the government of that Contracting State itself, a political subdivision, a local authority or a resident of that Contracting State. Where, however, the person paying the royalties, whether he is a resident of a Contracting State or not, has in a Contracting State a permanent establishment or a fixed base in connection with which the liability to pay the royalties was incurred, and such royalties are borne by such permanent establishment or fixed base, then such royalties shall be deemed to arise in the Contracting State in which the permanent establishment or fixed base is situated.
   b) Where under sub-paragraph a) royalties do not arise in one of the Contracting States, and the royalties relate to the use of, or the right to use, the right or property in one of the Contracting States, the royalties shall be deemed to arise in that Contracting State.

6. Where, by reason of a special relationship between the payer and the beneficial owner or between both of them and some other person, the amount of the royalties, having regard to the use, right, or information for which they are paid, exceeds the amount which would have been agreed upon by the payer and the beneficial owner in the absence of such relationship, the provisions of this Article shall apply only to the last-mentioned amount. In such case the excess part of the payments shall remain taxable according to the laws of each Contracting State, due regard being had to the other provisions of this Agreement.

Article 12 - Capital Gains

1. Gains derived by a resident of a Contracting State from the alienation of real property referred to in Article 6 and situated in the other Contracting State may be taxed in that other Contracting State.
2. Gains from the alienation of movable (personal) property forming part of the business assets of a permanent establishment which an enterprise of a Contracting State has in the other Contracting State, or of movable (personal) property pertaining to a fixed base available to a resident of a Contracting State in the other Contracting State for the purpose of performing independent personal services, including such gains from the alienation of such a permanent establishment (alone or together with the whole enterprise) or such a fixed base, may be taxed in that other Contracting State.
3. Gains derived by a resident of a Contracting State from the alienation of ships or aircraft operated in international traffic and of movable (personal) property pertaining to the operation of such ships or aircraft shall be taxable only in that Contracting State.
4. Gains from the alienation of shares of the capital stock of a company the property of which consists directly or indirectly principally of real property situated in a Contracting State may be taxed in that Contracting State.
5. Gains from the alienation of shares other than those mentioned in paragraph 4 representing a participation of 25 percent in a company that is a resident of a Contracting State may be taxed in that Contracting State.
6. Gains derived by a resident of a Contracting State from the alienation of any property other than that referred to in paragraphs 1 through 5 and arising in the other Contracting State may be taxed in that other Contracting State.

Article 13 - Independent Personal Services

1. Income derived by an individual who is a resident of a Contracting State in respect of professional services or other activities of an independent character shall be taxable only in that Contracting State, unless he has a fixed base regularly available to him in the other Contracting State for the purpose of performing his activities or he is present in that other Contracting State for a period or periods exceeding in the aggregate 183 days in the calendar year concerned. If he has such a fixed base or remains in that other Contracting State for the aforesaid period or periods, the income may be taxed in that other Contracting State, but only so much of it as is attributable to that fixed base or is derived in that other Contracting State during the aforesaid period or periods.
2. The term "professional services" includes, especially, independent scientific, literary, artistic, educational or teaching activities as well as the independent activities of physicians, lawyers, engineers, architects, dentists and accountants.

Article 14 - Dependent Personal Services

1. Subject to the provisions of Articles 15, 17, 18, 19 and 20, salaries, wages and other similar remuneration derived by a resident of a Contracting State in respect of an employment shall be taxable only in that Contracting State unless the employment is exercised in the other Contracting State. If the employment is so exercised, such remuneration as is derived therefrom may be taxed in that other Contracting State.

2. Notwithstanding the provisions of paragraph 1, remuneration derived by a resident of a Contracting State in respect of an employment exercised in the other Contracting State shall be taxable only in the first-mentioned State if:

   a) the recipient is present in the other Contracting State for a period or periods not exceeding in the aggregate 183 days in the calendar year concerned; and
   b) the remuneration is paid by, or on behalf of, an employer who is not a resident of the other Contracting State; and
   c) the remuneration is not borne by a permanent establishment or a fixed base which the employer has in the other Contracting State.

Article 15 -Directors' Fees

Directors' fees and other similar payments derived by a resident of a Contracting State in his capacity as a member of the board of directors of a company which is a resident of the other Contracting State may be taxed in that other Contracting State.

Article 16 -Artistes And Athletes

1. Notwithstanding the provisions of Articles 13 and 14, income derived by a resident of a Contracting State as an entertainer, such as a theatre, motion picture, radio, or television artiste, or a musician, or as an athlete, from his personal activities as such exercised in the other Contracting State, may be taxed in that other Contracting State. However, income derived by a resident of a Contracting State as an entertainer or athlete from activities exercised in accordance with a special program for cultural exchange agreed upon by the governments of both Contracting States shall be exempt from tax by the other Contracting State.
2. Where income in respect of personal activities exercised by an entertainer or an athlete in his capacity as such accrues not to the entertainer or athlete himself but to another person, that income may, notwithstanding the provisions of Articles 7, 13 and14, be taxed in the Contracting State in which the activities of the entertainer or athlete are exercised. However, if those activities are exercised in accordance with a special program for cultural exchange agreed upon by the governments of both Contracting States, the income so derived shall be exempt from tax by the other Contracting State.

Article 17 – Pensions

1. Subject to the provisions of paragraph 2 of Article 18, pensions and other similar remuneration paid to a resident of a Contracting State in consideration of past employment shall be taxable only in that Contracting State.
2. Notwithstanding the provisions of paragraph 1, pensions and other payments made by the government, a political subdivision or a local authority of a Contracting State under its social security system or public welfare plan shall be taxable only in that Contracting State.

Article 18 - Government Service

1. a) Remuneration, other than a pension, paid by the government or a political subdivision or a local authority of a Contracting State to an individual in respect of services rendered to that government or subdivision or authority should be taxable only in that Contracting State.
   b) However, such remuneration shall be taxable only in the other Contracting State if the services are rendered in that other Contracting State and the individual is a resident of that other Contracting State who:

      i) is a national of that other Contracting State; or
      ii) did not become a resident of that other Contracting State solely for the purpose of rendering the services.

2. a) Any pension paid by, or out of funds created by, the government or a political subdivision or a local authority of a Contracting State to an individual in respect of services rendered to that government or subdivision or authority shall be taxable only in that Contracting State.
   b) However, such pension shall be taxable only in the other Contracting State if the individual is a resident of, and a national of, that other Contracting State.

3. The provisions of Articles 14, 15, 16 and 17 shall apply to remuneration and pensions in respect of services rendered in connection with a business carried on by the government or a political subdivision or a local authority of a Contracting State.

Article 19 -Teachers And Researchers

An individual who is, or immediately before visiting a Contracting State was, a resident of the other Contracting State and is temporarily present in the first-mentioned Contracting State for the primary purpose of teaching, giving lectures or conducting research at a university, college, school or other accredited educational institution or scientific research institution in the first-mentioned Contracting State shall be exempt from tax in the first-mentioned Contracting State for a period not exceeding three years in the aggregate in respect of remuneration for such teaching, lectures or research.

Article 20 - Students And Trainees

A student, business apprentice or trainee who is or was immediately before visiting a Contracting State, a resident of the other Contracting State and who is present in the first-mentioned Contracting State solely for the purpose of his education, training or obtaining special technical experience shall be exempt from tax in that Contracting State with respect to:

a) payments received from abroad for the purpose of his maintenance, education, study, research or training;
b) grants or awards from a government, scientific, educational or other tax-exempt organization; and
c) income from personal services performed in that Contracting State in an amount not in excess of 5, 000 United States dollars or its equivalent in Chinese Yuan for any taxable year.

The benefits provided under this Article shall extend only for such period of time as is reasonably necessary to complete the education or training.

Article 21 - Other Income

1. Items of income of a resident of a Contracting State, wherever arising, not dealt with in the foregoing Articles of this Agreement shall be taxable only in that Contracting State.
2. The provisions of paragraph 1 shall not apply to income other than that from real property as defined in paragraph 2 of Article 6 if the recipient of such income, being a resident of a Contracting State, carries on business in the other Contracting State through a permanent establishment situated therein, or performs in that other Contracting State independent personal services from a fixed base situated therein, and the right or property in respect of which the income is paid is effectively connected with such permanent establishment or fixed base. In such case the provisions of Article 7 or 13, as the case may be, shall apply.
3. Notwithstanding the provisions of paragraphs 1 and 2, items of income of a resident of a Contracting State not dealt with in the foregoing Articles of this Agreement and arising in the other Contracting State may also be taxed in that other Contracting State.

Article 22 - Methods For Elimination Of Double Taxation

1. In the People's Republic of China, double taxation shall be eliminated as follows:

   a) Where a resident of China derives income from the United States, the amount of the United States income tax payable in respect of that income in accordance with the provisions of this Agreement shall be allowed as a credit against the Chinese tax imposed on that resident. The amount of credit, however, shall not exceed the amount of the Chinese tax computed with respect to that income in accordance with the taxation laws and regulations of China.
   b) Where the income derived from the United States is a dividend paid by a company which is a resident of the United States to a company which is a resident of China and which owns not less than 10 percent of the shares of the company paying the dividend, the credit shall take into account the United States income tax payable by the company paying the dividend in respect of the profits out of which the dividends are paid.

2. In the United States of America, in accordance with the provisions of the law of the United States, the United States shall allow to a resident or citizen of the United States as a credit against the United States tax on income:

   a) the income tax paid to China by or on behalf of such resident or citizen; and
   b) in the case of a United States company owning at least 10 percent of the voting rights in a company which is a resident of China and from which the United States company receives dividends, the income tax paid to China by or on behalf of the distributing company with respect to the profits out of which the dividends are paid.

For the purposes of this paragraph of this Agreement, the taxes referred to in paragraphs 1 a) and 2 of Article 2 shall be considered income taxes.

3. Income derived by a resident of a Contracting State which may be taxed in the other Contracting State in accordance with this Agreement shall be deemed to arise in that other Contracting State.

Article 23 - Non-Discrimination

1. Nationals of a Contracting State shall not be subjected in the other Contracting State to any taxation or any requirement connected therewith which is other or more burdensome than the taxation and connected requirements to which nationals of that other Contracting State in the same circumstances are or may be subjected. This provision shall, notwithstanding the provisions of Article 1, apply to persons who are not residents of one or both of the Contracting States.
2. The taxation on a permanent establishment which an enterprise of a Contracting State has in the other Contracting State shall not be less favorably levied in that other Contracting State than the taxation levied on enterprises of that other Contracting State carrying on the same activities. This provision shall not be construed as obliging

   A Contracting State to grant to residents of the other Contracting State any personal allowances, reliefs and reductions for taxation purposes on account of civil status or family responsibilities which it grants to its own residents.

3. Except where the provisions of Article 8, paragraph 7 of Article 10 or paragraph6 of Article 11 apply, interest, royalties and other disbursements paid by a resident of a Contracting State to a resident of the other Contracting State shall, for the purposes of determining the taxable profits of the first-mentioned resident, be deductible under the same conditions as if they had been paid to a resident of the first-mentioned Contracting State.

4. Enterprises of a Contracting State, the capital of which is wholly or partly owned or controlled, directly or indirectly, by one or more residents of the other Contracting State, shall not be subjected in the first-mentioned Contracting State to any taxation or any requirement connected therewith which is other or more burdensome than the taxation and connected requirements to which other similar enterprises of the first-mentioned Contracting State are or may be subjected.

Article 24 - Mutual Agreement Procedure

1. Where a person considers that the actions of one or both of the Contracting States result or will result for him in taxation not in accordance with the provisions of this Agreement, he may, irrespective of the remedies provided by the domestic law of those Contracting States, present his case to the competent authority of the Contracting State of which he is a resident or, if his case comes under paragraph 1 of Article 23, to that of the Contracting State of which he is a national. The case must be presented within three years from the first notification of the action resulting in taxation not in accordance with the provisions of this Agreement.
2. The competent authority shall endeavor, if the objection appears to it to be justified and if it is not itself able to arrive at a satisfactory solution, to resolve the case through consultation with the competent authority of the other Contracting State, with a view to the avoidance of taxation which is not in accordance with this Agreement. Any agreement reached shall be implemented notwithstanding any time limits in the domestic law of the Contracting States.
3. The competent authorities of the Contracting States shall endeavor to resolve by mutual agreement any difficulties or doubts arising as to the interpretation or application of this Agreement. They may also consult together for the elimination of double taxation in cases not provided for in this Agreement.
4. The competent authorities of the Contracting States may communicate with each other directly for the purpose of reaching an agreement in the sense of paragraphs 2and 3. To facilitate reaching a mutual agreement, the competent authorities of both Contracting States may meet for an oral exchange of opinions.

Article 25 - Exchange Of Information

1. The competent authorities of the Contracting States shall exchange such information as is necessary for carrying out the provisions of this Agreement or of the domestic laws of the Contracting States concerning taxes covered by this Agreement insofar as the taxation thereunder is not contrary to this Agreement, in particular for the prevention of fraud or evasion of such taxes. The exchange of information is not restricted by Article 1. Any information received by a Contracting State shall be treated as secret and shall be disclosed only to persons or authorities (including courts and administrative bodies) involved in the assessment, collection, or administration of, the enforcement or prosecution in respect of, or the determination of appeals in relation to, the taxes covered by this Agreement. Such persons or authorities shall use the information only for such purposes. They may disclose the information in public court proceedings or in judicial decisions.
2. In no case shall the provisions of paragraph 1 be construed so as to impose on a Contracting State the obligation:

   a) to carry out administrative measures at variance with the laws and administrative practice of that or of the other Contracting State;
   b) to supply information which is not obtainable under the laws or in the normal course of the administration of that or of the other Contracting State;
   c) to supply information which would disclose any trade, business, industrial, commercial or professional secret or trade process, or information the disclosure of which would be contrary to public policy.

Article 26 -Diplomatic Agents And Consular Officers

Nothing in this Agreement shall affect the fiscal privileges of diplomatic agents or consular officers under the general rules of international law or under the provisions of special agreements.

Article 27 -Entry Into Force

Each of the Contracting States shall notify the other Contracting State in writing, through diplomatic channels, upon the completion of their respective legal procedures to bring this Agreement into force. The Agreement shall enter into force on the thirtieth day after the date of the latter of such notifications and shall take effect as respects income derived during taxable years beginning on or after the first day of January next following the date on which this Agreement enters into force.

Article 28 – Termination

This Agreement shall remain in force indefinitely, but either Contracting State may terminate the Agreement by giving notice to the other Contracting State in writing through diplomatic channels on or before June 30 in any calendar year after five years from the date on which this Agreement enters into force. In such event, the Agreement shall cease to have effect with respect to income derived during taxable years beginning on or after the first day of January of the year following that in which the notice of termination is given.

DONE at Beijing on the 30th day of April 1984, in duplicate, in the Chinese and English languages, the two texts having equal authenticity.

9.2 Asian Area

9.2.1 China–Asian Area Bilateral Agreements' History

9.2.1.1 China–Hong Kong Bilateral Agreements' History

2012 marked the 15th year since the reversion of Hong Kong from British to Chinese sovereignty. In the 15 years, much has changed. Economically, Hong Kong is still a major international financial center and a leading gateway into China. Hong Kong's economic interaction with the Chinese mainland has also grown deeper and broader. The city's closer tie to the mainland was also bolstered on June 29, 2003 when the Special Administrative Region (SAR) of Hong Kong and mainland China signed a bilateral trade agreement, known as the Closer Economic Partnership Agreement (CEPA). The agreement was the result of an initiative on the part of business circles of the two regions, especially by the Hong Kong General Chamber of Commerce in response to anxieties about Hong Kong's relationship with China, with its role as the 'gateway' between China and the rest of the world.

Prior to CEPA, trade between China and Hong Kong was effectively treated as trade across an international border. Bilateral shipments of goods and materials were to first clear either Hong Kong or Chinese Customs, the same applying to people movements through the two countries' immigration systems. By negotiating a free trade agreement, Hong Kong bolstered its competitive advantage on the Chinese mainland, where over 1,400 products of Hong Kong were initially allowed to be imported into China tariff-free. A wide variety of service sectors were also provided greater access to the mainland market, allowing some Hong Kong companies to establish wholly owned subsidiaries in the Chinese mainland that can compete domestically. In the financial sector, for example, Hong Kong banks were allowed to offer bank accounts, credit cards, and remittances denominated in RMB.

Since the initial agreement, a series of annexures and amendments have been made, including in January 1, 2004 where China agreed to unilateral tariff reductions in 273 categories of Hong Kong products originally subject to import duties in the mainland. This number greatly increased in subsequent years, where in 2006 all exports of products originating in Hong Kong were exempted from import duties.

According to research done by the Hong Kong Trade Development Council (HKTDC), CEPA has led to an increase in Hong Kong exports to China. The impact of CEPA on Hong Kong was strong but not without some repercussions. The influx of mainland tourist to Hong Kong was initially accepted, bringing welcome relief to Hong Kong's ailing hotel, retail, restaurant, and manufacturing industries. Soon after, pressure mounted on local Hong Kong service sectors to learn a third business language, *Putonghua* (Mandarin Chinese), as well as to conduct business in RMB.

Hong Kong's role as China's gateway between itself and the West can be described as the 'One Country, Two Systems' policy. This policy essentially exempts Hong Kong from adopting China's socialist system and policies for 50 years, therefore offering a high degree of autonomy for Hong Kong, allowing it to exercise full political rights such as the right to participate in elections and freedom of expression. Financially and economically, it could play a larger role by reaching out to research, media, and educational sectors. The rise of Shanghai as a powerful financial center has challenged Hong Kong's competitiveness in the Asian region as a financial hub; however, it may still hold a comparative advantage over Shanghai due to its solid legal and judicial systems.

Current economic and trade dynamics have raised concerns, however, that Hong Kong's relationship with China will shift in the long run from one of synergy to full integration, undermining the aforementioned autonomy (Tables 9.9 and 9.10).

Although operating under different systems, Hong Kong's economy is inevitably linked to China's, visible in the two countries' comparative monetary systems. The two monetary systems are described as 'mutually independent', implying that neither is superior nor subsidiary to the other, and further China has specified that Hong Kong assets and liabilities would be treated as foreign on the mainland and vice versa. The Hong Kong currency is pegged to the US dollar at 7.8 to 1, also being fully convertible, while the RMB is not.

Table 9.9 Hong Kong's trade with main partners (millions of Euro) 2011—imports

The major imports partners			
1	**China**	**164,507.8**	**48.1 %**
2	Japan	30,908.0	9.0 %
3	EU 27	29,485.8	8.6 %
4	Singapore	24,485.8	7.2 %
5	US	20,672.0	6.0 %
6	South Korea	14,541.6	4.3 %
7	Malaysia	8,628.5	2.5 %
8	India	8,401.7	2.5 %
9	Switzerland	7,672.2	2.2 %
10	Thailand	7,424.2	2.2 %

Source: European Commission

Table 9.10 Hong Kong's trade with main partners (millions of Euro) 2011—exports

The major exports partners			
1	**China**	**169,395.8**	**53.7 %**
2	EU 27	34,877.9	11.1 %
3	US	32,169.0	10.2 %
4	Japan	13,108.9	4.2 %
5	India	9,076.2	2.9 %
6	South Korea	5,938.8	1.9 %
7	Singapore	5,451.4	1.7 %
8	Vietnam	4,474.0	1.4 %
9	Thailand	4,122.2	1.3 %
10	Australia	4,030.1	1.3 %

Source: European Commission

9.2.1.2 China–India Bilateral Agreements' History and Evolution

Both being the world's oldest civilizations, China and India have maintained a strong relationship since ancient times. Since late 1980s, bilateral trade grew rapidly and economic cooperation expanded into more areas. India was China's major overseas project contracting market, and by the end of 2010, China had signed $41.576 billion worth of project and labor contracts in India. In 2012, Indian Minister of Commerce and Industry Anand Sharma traveled to China for the eighth meeting of China–India Joint Group on Trade, Science and Technology. Both sides held the China–India Trade and Investment Cooperation Forum and signed the *Memorandum of Understanding on Extending Trade and Economic Cooperation of the Joint Group on Economy of the Ministry of Commerce of the People's Republic of China and the Ministry of Commerce and Industry of the Republic of India*.

India and China are emerging as economic powerhouses not only in Asia but also in the world. With their high growth rates and huge markets, these two Asian giants have attracted the attention of international business mangers to take a fresh look at the rapidly emerging opportunities in the two countries. It is held that with the rapid growth of India and China, Asia is expected to regain its place as a center of gravity of the world economy. While comparisons of the Indian and Chinese

Table 9.11 Indian–Chinese trade

Year	Exports	Imports	Total Trade
2003–2004	2,955	4,053	7,008
2004–2005	5,615	7,097	12,712
2005–2006	6,759	10,868	17,627
2006–2007	8,321	17,475	25,796
2007–2008	10,871	27,146	38,017
2008–2009	9,353	32,497	41,850
2009–2010	11,617	30,824	42,441
2010–2011	3,626	12,492	16,118

Source: Indian Ministry of Trade, 2012

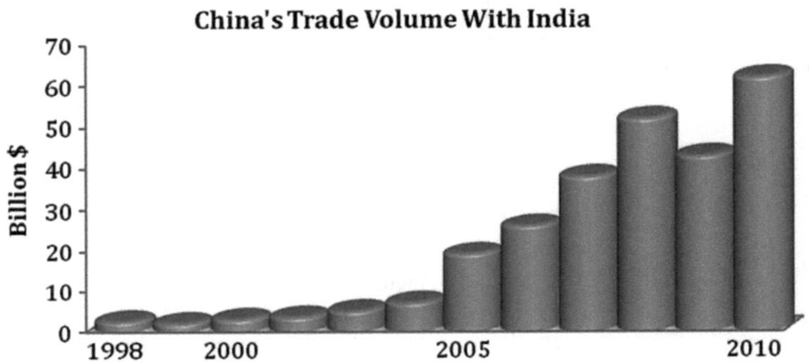

Fig. 9.8 China's trade volume with India. *Source*: National Bureau of Statistics, China Monthly Statistic, Beijing Vol. I

economic performance and their shares in the world market in various sectors continue unabated, the recent trend in bilateral trade and an emerging strategy of close economic cooperation between the two countries represent a significant development in the region. Moreover, the importance of both countries in international business is becoming apparent each passing day (Table 9.11).

The relationship between China and India is currently evolving based on the energy requirements of their industrial expansion. Furthermore, cooperation in the global oil market was sealed in Beijing on January 12, 2006 when the Indian Minister of Petroleum and Natural Gas Mani Shankar Aiyar signed an agreement to promote joint projects elsewhere between ONGC Videsh Ltd (OVL) and the China National Petroleum Corporation (CNPC) (Fig. 9.8).

In addition, on July 6, 2006, China and India reopened Nathula, an ancient trade route that was part of the Silk Road. During the BRICS summit, an international relations conference attended by the heads of state or heads of government of the five member states Brazil, Russia, India, China, and South Africa further facilitated the cooperation between the two countries. The two countries had extensive agreement and maintained sound cooperation on major international and regional issues. Under the framework of such mechanisms as China–India–Russia cooperation, the BRICs, and the G-20, China and India maintained close communication and cooperation and kept coordinated positions on the international financial crisis, climate change, energy and food security, and other major issues (on behalf of the legitimate interests of developing countries).

9.2.1.3 China–Japan Bilateral Agreements' History and Evolution

Japan is an important neighbor of the People's Republic of China. The China–Japan relationship is one of the most important bilateral relationships for both sides. The two countries are building a strategic relationship of mutual benefit. The China–Japan relationship went through ups and downs in 2010; since then it has maintained a sound momentum of growth.

Japan is a member of the G8, APEC, and "ASEAN Plus Three" and is a participant in the East Asia Summit (EAS). The history of Japan and China relation is long and complicated. Putting the political disputes aside, China and Japan are developing closer economic ties in recent decades. As a major economic power, Japan has the world's third largest economy by nominal GDP and fourth largest economy by purchasing power parity. It is also the world's fourth largest exporter and fourth largest importer. Japan's exports amounted to $4,210 (U.S.) per capita in 2005. China is Japan's largest export market, taking up 18.88 %, and also the largest import market, taking up 22.2 % (Hong Kong excluded) (Fig. 9.9).

In the first part of 2001, Japan's investment in China enjoyed a relatively fast speed. The agreed investment was $2.9 billion, and the actual figure was $1.9 billion, up 86 % and 26 %, respectively, compared to the same period of the year before. Up till the end of 2000, there were 20,340 Japanese investment projects in China with a total of $38.634 billion and an actual figure of $28.161 billion. In 2011, the Agreement on the Establishment of the Trilateral Cooperation Secretariat among the Governments of the People's Republic of China, Japan and the Republic of Korea was established, indicating further development of cooperation in East Asia (Fig. 9.10).

In 2012, total trade remained at modest growth, while trade deficit with China was the largest ever. On the back of China's slowing economy, the Chinese government has been further easing its monetary policies such as by decreasing the reserve requirement ratio and interest rates. On the other hand, they seem to be cautious about implementing large-scale economic stimulus measures and easing regulations of real estate investment based on the past experience of having an overheated economy emerge after the implementation of an economic stimulus package of 4 trillion yuan. Any increase in demand due to future economic measures is therefore considered to be limited, and it is also believed that industrial production will only post a modest rise. As a result, these factors will probably force

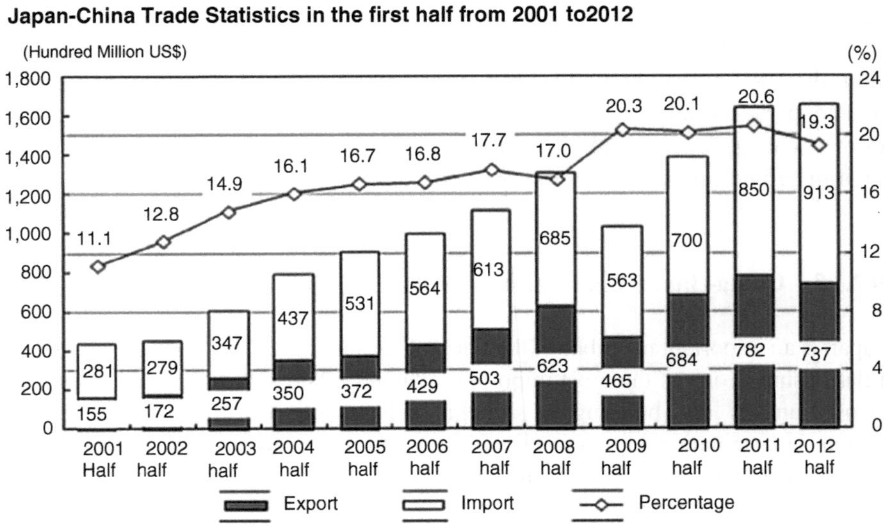

Fig. 9.9 Japan–China trade statistics. *Source*: Japan External Trade Organization, 2012

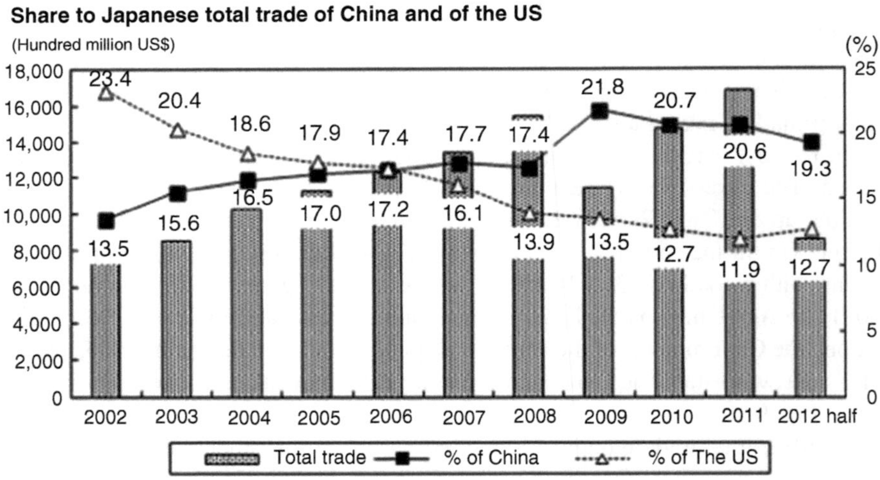

Fig. 9.10 Share to Japanese total trade of China and the US. *Source*: Japan External Trade Organization, 2012

a downturn in Japanese exports to China. Japanese imports from China are expected to increase continuously but modestly led by communication devices. Considering the above, the trade value between China and Japan is expected to increase modestly in comparison to that of 2011 but is unlikely to see a large-scale growth. The trade deficit is expected to grow, reflecting the downturn in exports and the modest rise in imports. There is a strong possibility that the degree of Japan's deficit will surpass the US$28.8 billion marked in 2005 and become the largest ever.

9.2.1.4 China–Korea Bilateral Agreements' History

On August 24, 1992, a diplomatic relationship between Beijing and Seoul was formally established; since then, the trade between the two countries has highly increased. South Korea had long been an ally of the Republic of China. In fact, after the KORUS FTA (United States–Korea Free Trade Agreement) was finalized on June 30, 2007, the Chinese government tried to seal an FTA agreement with South Korea. Both officially announced a joint study on the China–ROK FTA involving several parts as government agencies, industries, and the academia and also agreed to launch the intergovernmental negotiation within the first half of 2011.

China remained the largest trading partner and export and import market of the ROK. The ROK was the third largest trading partner and the fourth largest source of FDI in China. On January 10, 2001, the Ministry of Foreign Affairs and Trade (MOFAT) established two teams of Chinese experts and language specialists under its department handling Chinese affairs in an effort to strengthen diplomacy. The Institute of Foreign Affairs and National Security (IFANS), a think-tank affiliated to MOFAT, launched another center dedicated to China's affairs, which will be a hub to collate research on China undertaken in Korea.

The two countries strengthened cultural and people-to-people exchanges. Leaders of the two countries designated the year 2010 as the "Visit China Year," which was also the year for the Shanghai World Expo. Taking this opportunity, the two sides increased visits and exchanges between delegations and personnel. The ROK instituted 17 Confucius Institutes and four Confucius Classrooms, allowing about 75,000 Chinese students to study in the ROK and around 68,000 students from the ROK to study in China (Tables 9.12 and 9.13).

9.2.1.5 China–Malaysia Bilateral Agreements' History and Evolution

It can be concluded that relations between China and Malaysia was established officially on May 31, 1974, when the then Premier Zhou Enlai and Malasian Prime Minister Tun Razak signed Joint Communique, announcing the normalization and establishment of diplomatic relations between the two countries. From 1985 onwards, the Malaysian Government made gradual readjustment of its policies towards China, with contract continuously increasing between the two countries. Bilateral ties then are said to be entering into a new stage of maturity and all-round development. On 31 May 2004, Chinese Premier Wen Jiabao and Malaysian Prime Minister Abdullah Badawi signed another Joint Communique, outlining the future development of bilateral relations.

Historically since 1974, more than ten agreements on economic trade cooperation have been signed between the two countries, such as the Agreement on

Table 9.12 Export by region

Exports by region ($ million)									
	1990	1995	2000	2005	2006	2007	2008	2009	2010
Asia	24,639	61,565	81,093	146,914	168,447	188,790	214,051	190,761	255,178
Japan	12,638	17,049	20,456	24,027	26,534	26,370	28,252	21,771	28,176
China	585	9,144	18,455	61,915	69,459	81,985	91,389	86,703	116,838
Middle East	2,619	4,880	7,586	12,241	14,463	19,721	26,647	34,039	28,369
Europe	12,001	20,854	28,141	52,853	60,282	71,198	76,697	56,014	69,625
EU	10,003	16,301	23,424	43,659	48,450	55,982	58,375	46,608	53,507
Germany	2,882	5,965	5,154	10,304	10,056	11,543	10,523	8,821	10,702
North America	21,091	25,922	40,037	44,789	46,804	49,273	50,434	41,089	53,918
USA	19,360	24,131	37,611	41,343	43,184	45,766	46,377	37,650	49,816
South America	2,102	7,370	9,369	14,987	20,591	25,781	33,267	26,763	36,187
Oceania	1,214	1,896	3,522	6,018	6,781	7,983	11,216	16,320	13,396
Africa	892	2,227	2,240	6,203	7,730	8,257	9,388	8,466	9,618
Total	**65,016**	**125,058**	**172,268**	**284,419**	**325,465**	**371,489**	**422,007**	**363,533**	**466,384**

Source: Korea International Trade Association

Table 9.13 Import by region

Imports by region ($ million)									
	1990	1995	2000	2005	2006	2007	2008	2009	2010
Asia	28,515	54,921	70,262	126,033	146,049	170,549	199,784	154,114	202,341
Japan	18,574	32,606	31,828	48,403	51,925	56,250	60,956	49,428	64,296
China	2,268	7,401	12,799	38,648	48,557	63,028	76,930	4,246	71,574
Middle East	6,188	11,837	25,793	47,395	62,531	67,541	101,645	61,613	80,815
Europe	10,501	22,452	20,070	33,610	37,410	47,987	53,697	43,862	55,760
EU	9,066	18,191	15,788	27,296	30,061	36,824	39,981	32,232	38,721
Germany	3,284	6,584	4,625	9,774	11,365	13,534	14,769	12,298	14,305
North America	18,408	33,068	31,349	33,190	36,745	40,474	42,768	32,575	44,754
USA	16,942	30,404	29,242	30,586	33,645	37,219	38,365	29,039	–
South America	1,726	3,964	3,263	7,017	9,732	11,324	13,756	11,648	14,645
Oceania	3,201	6,501	6,898	10,971	12,436	14,592	19,519	16,044	22,140
Africa	363	1,962	2,814	2,946	4,732	4,317	4,052	3,185	4,684
Total	**69,844**	**135,119**	**160,481**	**261,238**	**309,383**	**356,846**	**435,275**	**323,084**	**425,212**

Source: Korea International Trade Association

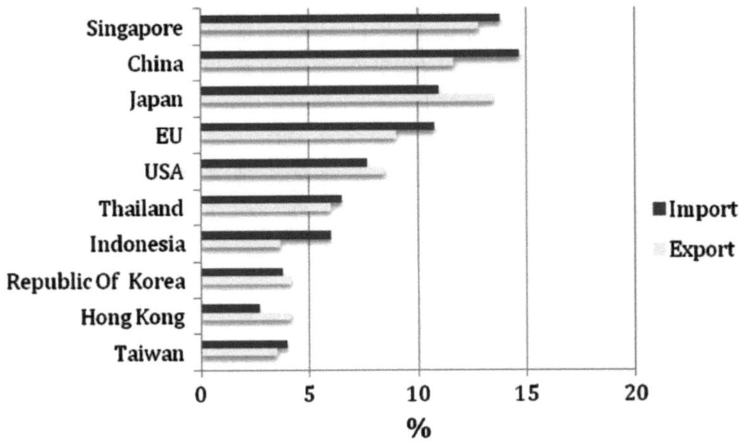

Fig. 9.11 Exports and imports by major countries (Jan–Mar 2012 % share). *Source*: Malaysia External Trade Statistic, 2012

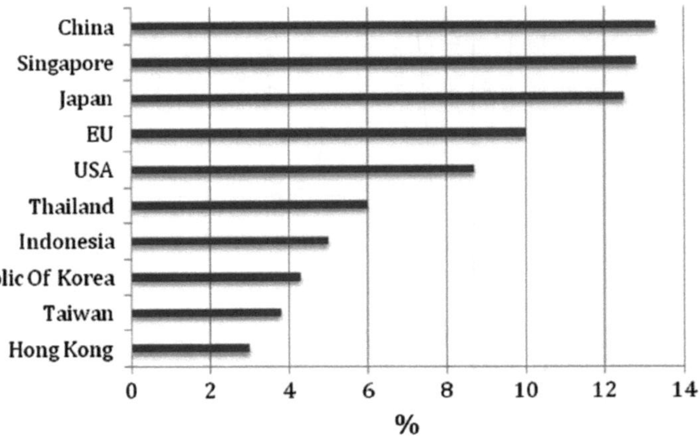

Fig. 9.12 Total trade by country (Jan 2012 % share). *Source*: Malaysia External Trade Statistic, 2012

Avoidance of Double Taxation, Trade Agreement, Agreement on Investment Protection, Shipping Agreement and Air Transport Agreement. With the sound development of economic cooperation between the two countries, relations have moved forward at considerable pace. In 2000, Bank of China and Bank of Malaysia set up their own branches in Kuala Lumpur and Shanghai, respectively, and in 2002 the Chinese People's Bank and the National Bank of Malaysia signed the agreement on bilateral exchange of currencies (Figs. 9.11 and 9.12).

Cooperation in other areas proceeded easily. In 2012, Secretary General of UMNO Datuk Seri Tengku Adnan visited China to meet the CPC's Central Committee Minister of the International Department, Wang Jiarui. The two sides signed the *Memorandum on Exchanges and Cooperation Between the Communist*

Fig. 9.13 Example of flow of goods between three economies. *Source*: International Merchandise Trade Statistics National Compilation and Reporting Practices

Table 9.14 China–Singapore bilateral trade

China–Singapore bilateral trade ($ thousands)		
	2010	2011
Imports	45,844,341	47,747,745
Exports	49,467,859	53,650,725
Total trade	95,312,201	101,398,469

Source: IE Singapore's StateLink

Party of China and the United Malays National Organization (UMNO) of Malaysia. In the same month, Chinese National Tourism Administrator Shao Qiwei visited Malaysia to meet Dato' Sri Ng Yen Yen and discuss about ecotourism, recreational tourism, and cruiser tourism.

9.2.1.6 China–Singapore Bilateral Agreements' History and Evolution

The bilateral trade between China and Singapore started during the 1990s after a diplomatic mission based on trade and the warming of ties from other ASEAN countries towards mainland China. Now Singapore is the first Asiatic country having trade relations with China (Fig. 9.13).

China's exports to Singapore include clothing, agriculture produce, metals, electromechanical equipment, and electronic components. Increased trade, economic and investment cooperation continued to grow. Exchanges in culture, education, training of professionals, and environmental protection produced positive results. Furthermore, a Chinese Cultural Center in Singapore was built, and several Chinese officials visited Singapore (Table 9.14).

Companies such as CapitaLand and Breadtalk have made substantial inroads into China's domestic economy. Others such as Temasek Holdings and Singapore Airlines have each invested in China Eastern Airlines. Singapore attracts a lot of FDI because of its location, corruption-free environment, skilled workforce, low tax rates, and advanced infrastructure. There are more than 7,000 multinational

Table 9.15 Thailand's trade with main partners (millions of Euro) 2011—imports

The major imports partners			
1	Japan	31,883.4	19.1 %
2	**China**	**23,046.9**	**13.8 %**
3	EU 27	13,457.7	8.1 %
4	United Arab Emirates	10,457.7	8.1 %
5	US	10,184.4	6.1 %
6	Malaysia	9,317.3	5.6 %
7	South Korea	6,965.2	4.2 %
8	Switzerland	6,690.1	4.0 %
9	Australia	5,997.2	3.6 %
10	Singapore	5,886.1	3.5 %

Source: European Commission

corporations from the United States, Japan, and Europe in Singapore (there are also 1,500 companies from China and 1,500 from India). Foreign firms are established in virtually every sector of its economy. Singapore has also cocreated the Sino–Singapore Tianjin Eco-city and Suzhou Industrial Park in China.

9.2.1.7 China–Thailand Bilateral Agreements' History and Evolution

The Sino–Thai relations started from the 1970s and especially during the Cambodia's internal conflict when China and Thailand together supported the Khmer Rouge against the communist forces from Vietnam. From the trade point of view, Sino–Thai relations continued to develop and Thailand continues to sustain the One China Policy maintaining unofficial relations with Taiwan. This helps Thailand gain access to capital and the huge Chinese mainland market (Table 9.15).

Cooperation in many fields continued to grow especially in 2010, when cultural activities celebrating the Chinese New Year were held in Bangkok and later the two Ministries of Education renewed the *Agreement on Mutual Recognition of Academic Degrees and Credentials of Higher Education*. In October, the "Strike 2010" Sino–Thai special force anti-terrorist joint training was held. In November, the "Blue Strike" Sino–Thai marine joint training commenced. By the end of 2010, 12 Confucius Colleges and 11 Confucius Classrooms were established in Thailand. The bilateral trade relations have grown from year to year. Sino–Thailand bilateral trade volume in 1999 was $4.22 billion. Trade volume between the two countries reached $25.3 billion in 2006, $31.07 billion in 2007, and $36.2 billion in 2008 (Table 9.16).

China is Thailand's second largest export market and also the largest importer of goods. In 2003, the two countries signed a Free Trade Agreement related to agricultural products. Furthermore, China has planned to create the "China City Complex" in Thailand to boost trade in Asia and in other large foreign markets, which Thailand has trade agreements with. In January 1, 2010 an ASEAN–China Free Trade Area became effective and China was allowed to export its goods throughout ASEAN countries with limited or zero trade barriers.

Table 9.16 Thailand's trade with main partners (millions of Euro) 2011—exports

The major exports partners			
1	**China**	**19,588.6**	**12.0 %**
2	EU 27	17,883.7	11.0 %
3	Japan	17,811.9	10.9 %
4	US	16,281.7	10.0 %
5	Malaysia	9,252.1	5.7 %
6	Hong Kong	8,921.0	5.5 %
7	Singapore	8,524.5	5.2 %
8	Indonesia	7,521.7	4.6 %
9	Australia	5,971.7	3.7 %
10	Vietnam	5,269.4	3.2 %

Source: European Commission

Table 9.17 Vietnam's trade with main partners (millions of Euro) 2011—imports

The major imports partners			
1	**China**	**18,551.5**	**25.6 %**
2	South Korea	9,938.8	13.7 %
3	Japan	7,845.1	10.8 %
4	EU 27	5,843.8	8.1 %
5	Singapore	4,820.5	6.7 %
6	Thailand	4,815.3	6.7 %
7	US	3,416.5	4.7 %
8	Malaysia	2,956.7	4.1 %
9	India	1,769.9	2.4 %
10	Indonesia	1,695.4	2.3 %

Source: European Commission

9.2.1.8 China–Vietnam Bilateral Agreements' History and Evolution

The bilateral relations between the Socialist Republic of Vietnam and the People's Republic of China (PRC) have been turbulent despite their shared socialist background. Bilateral business cooperation grew rapidly. China had been Vietnam's largest trading partner for seven consecutive years. Large cooperation projects made headways to varying degrees. Growth in annual bilateral trade increased from $32 million in 1991 to almost $7.2 billion in 2004. By 2011, the trade volume had totaled to $25 billion. China has become Vietnam's second largest trading partner and the largest source of imports. Both nations are working to establish an economic relation between China's Yunnan Province and Vietnam's northern provinces and cities (Table 9.17).

In July 2010, several demarcation documents between the two countries, which provided a positive progress in boundary negotiations, were issued.

The two sides held several rounds of negotiations on the agreement on basic principles guiding the settlement of maritime issues.

Table 9.18 Vietnam's trade with main partners (millions of Euro) 2011—exports

The major exports partners			
1	US	12,769.0	18.6 %
2	EU 27	12,480.4	18.2 %
3	**China**	**8,391.8**	**12.2 %**
4	Japan	8,132.4	11.8 %
5	South Korea	3,557.0	5.2 %
6	Malaysia	2,136.5	3.1 %
7	Australia	1,900.2	2.8 %
8	Cambodia	1,815.5	2.6 %
9	Indonesia	1,779.4	2.6 %
10	Singapore	1,724.1	2.5 %

Source: European Commission

China and Vietnam started cooperation in culture, education, defense, and security. Nongovernmental exchanges became closer (Table 9.18).

Currently, the first importer of goods in Vietnam is China and the importing value is increasing over the years. Meanwhile, Vietnam's export turnover to China has also been constantly increasing since 2009.

Since Vietnam's major imported goods from China are machineries, spare parts, and materials for products while Vietnam's export commodities to China are mainly agricultural products, seafood, grain, and rubber, there is a high yearly trade deficit with China increasing over the years.

Initially, businesses in export and import sectors with China will directly face difficulties in business activities. In the near future, increasing trade deficit with China may cause instabilities in Forex rate and the macro economy. According to the figures from General Department of Vietnam Customs, in the first six months of 2012, Vietnam's import spending from China was over $13 billion with major items such as machineries, equipment and spare parts (over $2.4 billion), telephones and components (over $1.4 billion), clothes (over $1.4 billion), computers, electronic products and components (more than $1.4 billion).

9.2.2 India–China Treaty

Agreement Between the Government of the Republic of India and the Government of the People's Republic of China for the Avoidance of Double Taxation and the Prevention of Fiscal Evasion with Respect to Taxes on Income: the Government of the Republic of India and the Government of the People's Republic of China, desiring to conclude an Agreement for the avoidance of double taxation and the prevention of fiscal evasion with respect to taxes on income, have agreed as follows:

Article 1 - Personal Scope

This Agreement shall apply to persons who are residents of one or both of the Contracting States.

Article 2 - Taxes Covered

1. This Agreement shall apply to taxes on income imposed on behalf of a Contracting State or of its political subdivisions or local authorities, irrespective of the manner in which they are levied.
2. There shall be regarded as taxes on income all taxes imposed on total income, or on elements of income, including taxes on gains from the alienation of movable or immovable property, as well as taxes on capital appreciation.
3. The existing taxes to which the Agreement shall apply are:

   a) in China:

      i. the individual income-tax;
      ii. the income-tax for enterprises with foreign investment and foreign enterprises;
      iii. the local income tax; (hereinafter referred to as "Chinese Tax").

   b) in India: the income tax including any surcharge thereon; (hereinafter referred to as "Indian tax").

4. This Agreement shall also apply to any identical or substantially similar taxes which are imposed after the date of signature of this Agreement in addition to, or in place of, the existing taxes referred to in paragraph 3. The competent authorities of the Contracting States shall notify each other of any substantial changes which have been made in their respective taxation laws within a reasonable period of time after such changes.

Article 3 - General Definitions

1. For the purposes of this Agreement, unless the context otherwise requires:

   a. the term "China" means the People's Republic of China; when used in geographical sense, means all the territory of the People's Republic of China, including its territorial sea, in which the Chinese laws relating to taxation apply, and any area beyond its territorial sea, within which the People's Republic of China has sovereign rights of exploration for any exploitation of resources of the sea-bed and its sub-soil and superjacent water resources in accordance with international law;
   b. the term "India" means the territory of the Republic of India and includes the territorial sea and airspace above it, as well as any other maritime zone in which India has sovereign rights, other rights and jurisdictions, according to the Indian law and in accordance with international law;
   c. the term "a Contracting State" and "the other Contracting State" means China or India as the context requires;
   d. the term "tax" means Chinese tax or Indian tax, as the context requires;
   e. the term "person" includes an individual, a company and any other entity which is treated as a taxable unit under the taxation laws in force in the respective Contracting States;
   f. the term "company" means any body corporate or any entity which is treated as a body corporate for tax purposes;
   g. the terms "enterprise of a Contracting State" and "enterprise of the other Contracting State" mean, respectively, an enterprise carried on by a resident of a Contracting State and an enterprise carried on by a resident of the other Contracting State;
   h. the term "nationals" means any individual possessing the nationality of a Contracting State and any legal person, partnership or association deriving its status from the laws in force in the Contracting State;

i. the term “international traffic” means any transport by a ship or aircraft operated by an enterprise which is a resident of a Contracting State, except when the ship or aircraft is operated solely between places in the other Contracting State;
j. the term “competent authority” means, in the case of China, the State Administration of Taxation or its authorized representative, and in the case of India, the Central Government in the Ministry of Finance (Department of Revenue) or their authorized representative.

2. As regards the application of this Agreement by a Contracting State, any term not defined therein shall, unless the context otherwise requires, have the meaning which it has under the laws of that Contracting State concerning the taxes to which this Agreement applies.

Article 4 – Resident

1. For the purposes of this agreement, the term “resident of a Contracting State” means any person who, under the laws of that Contracting State, is liable to tax therein by reason of his domicile, residence, place of head office or any other criterion of a similar nature.
2. Where by reason of the provisions of paragraph 1 an individual is a resident of both Contracting States, then his status shall be determined as follows:

   a. He shall be deemed to be a resident of the Contracting State in which he has a permanent home available to him; if he has a permanent home available to him in both Contracting States, he shall be deemed to be a resident of the Contracting State with which his personal and economic relations are closer (center of vital interests);
   b. If the State in which he has his center of vital interests cannot be determined, or if he has not a permanent home available to him in either Contracting State, he shall be deemed to be a resident of the State in which he has an habitual abode;
   c. If he has an habitual abode in both Contracting States or in neither of them, he shall be deemed to be a resident of the Contracting State of which he is a national;
   d. If he is a national of both Contracting States or of neither of them, the competent authorities of the Contracting States shall settle the question by mutual agreement.

3. Where by reason of the provisions of paragraph 1 a person other than an individual is a resident of both Contracting States, then it shall be deemed to be a resident of the Contracting State in which its head office is situated.

Article 5 - Permanent Establishment

1. For the purposes of this Agreement, the term “permanent establishment” means a fixed place of business through which the business of an enterprise is wholly or partly carried on.
2. The term “permanent establishment” includes especially:

   a. a place of management;
   b. a branch;
   c. an office;
   d. a factory;
   e. a workshop;
   f. a mine, an oil or gas well, a quarry or any other place of extraction of natural resources;
   g. a warehouse, in relation to a person providing storage facilities for others;
   h. a farm, plantation or other place where agriculture, forestry, plantation or related activities are carried on;
   i. an installation or structure used for the exploration or exploitation of natural resources, but only if so used for a period of more than 185 days;
   j. a building site or construction, installation or assembly project or supervisory activities in connection therewith, where such site, project or activities (together

with other such sites, projects or activities, if any) continue for a period of more than 188 days;

k. the furnishing of services other than technical services as defined in Article 12 (Royalties and Fees for Technical Services), by an enterprise of a Contracting State through employees or other personnel in the other Contracting State, but only if activities of that nature continue within that other Contracting State for a period or periods aggregating more than 183 days.

3. Notwithstanding the preceding provisions of this Article, the term "permanent establishment" shall be deemed not to include:

   a. the use of facilities solely for the purpose of storage, display or delivery of goods or merchandise belonging to the enterprise;
   b. the maintenance of a stock of goods or merchandise belonging to the enterprise solely for the purpose of storage, display or delivery;
   c. the maintenance of a stock of goods or merchandise belonging to the enterprise solely for the purpose of processing by another enterprise;
   d. the maintenance of a fixed place of business solely for the purpose of purchasing goods or merchandise or of collecting information, for the enterprise;
   e. the maintenance of a fixed place of business solely for the purpose of carrying on, for the enterprise, any other activity of a preparatory or auxiliary character.

4. Notwithstanding the provisions of paragraphs 1 and 2, where a person other than an agent of an independent status to whom the provisions of paragraph 5 apply is acting in a Contracting State on behalf of an enterprise of the other Contracting State, has and habitually exercises an authority to conclude contracts in the name of the enterprise, that enterprise shall be deemed to have a permanent establishment in the first-mentioned Contracting State in respect of any activities which that person undertakes for the enterprise, unless the activities of such person are limited to these mentioned in paragraph 3 which, if exercised through a fixed place of business, would not make this fixed place of business a permanent establishment under the provisions of that paragraph.
5. An enterprise of a Contracting State shall not be deemed to have a permanent establishment in the other Contracting State merely because it carries on business in that other Contracting State through a broker, general commission agent or any other agent of an independent status, provided that such persons are acting in the ordinary course of their business. However, when the activities of such an agent are devoted wholly or almost wholly on behalf of that enterprise, he will not be considered an agent of an independent status within the meaning of this paragraph.
6. The fact that a company which is a resident of a Contracting State controls or is controlled by a company which is a resident of the other Contracting State, or which carries on business in that other State (whether through a permanent establishment or otherwise), shall not of itself constitute either company a permanent establishment of the other.

Article 6 - Income From Immovable Property

1. Income derived by a resident of a Contracting State from immovable property situated in the other Contracting State may be taxed in that other Contracting State.
2. The term "immovable property" shall have the meaning which it has under the law of the Contracting State in which the property in question is situated. The term shall in any case include property accessory to immovable property, livestock and equipment used in agriculture and forestry, rights to which the provisions of general law respecting landed property apply, usufruct of immovable property and rights to variable or fixed payments

as consideration for the working of, or the right to work, mineral deposits, sources and other natural resources. Ships and aircraft shall not be regarded as immovable property.

3. The provisions of paragraph 1 shall apply to income derived from the direct use, letting, or use in any other form of immovably property.
4. The provisions of paragraphs 1 and 3 shall also apply to the income from immovable property of an enterprise and to income from movable property used for the performance of independent personal services.

Article 7 - Business Profits

1. The profits of an enterprise of a Contracting State shall be taxable only in that Contracting State unless the enterprise carries business in the other Contracting State through a permanent establishment situated therein. If the enterprise carries on business as aforesaid, the profits of the enterprise may be taxed in the other Contracting State but only so much of them as is directly or indirectly attributable to that permanent establishment.

The provisions of this paragraph shall, however, not apply if the enterprise proves that the above activities could not have been undertaken by the permanent establishment or have no relation with the permanent establishment.

2. Subject to the provisions of paragraph 3, where an enterprise of a Contracting State carries on business in the other Contracting State through a permanent establishment situated therein, there shall in each Contracting State be attributed to that permanent establishment the profits which it might be expected to make if it were a distinct and separate enterprise engaged in the same or similar activities under the same or similar conditions and dealing wholly independently with the enterprise of which it is a permanent establishment.
3. Insofar as the tax law of a Contracting State provides with respect to a specific business activity that the profits to be attributed to a permanent establishment are to be determined on the basis of a deemed profit, nothing in paragraph 2 shall preclude that Contracting State from applying those provisions of its law, provided that the result is in accordance with the principles contained in this Article.
4. In determining the profits of a permanent establishment, there shall be allowed as deductions expenses which are incurred for the purposes of the business of the permanent establishment, including executive and general administrative expenses so incurred, whether in the Contracting State in which the permanent establishment is situated or elsewhere in accordance with the provisions of tax law of that Contracting State.
5. No profits shall be attributed to a permanent establishment by reason of the mere purchase by that permanent establishment of goods or merchandise for the enterprise.
6. For the purposes of paragraphs 1 to 5, the profits to be attributed to the permanent establishment shall be determined by the same method year by year unless there is good and sufficient reason to the contrary.
7. Where profits include items of income which are dealt with separately in other Articles of this Agreement, then the provisions of those Articles shall not be affected by the provisions of this Article.

Article 8 - Shipping and Air Transport

1. Profits derived by an enterprise which is a resident of a Contracting State from the operation by that enterprise of ships or aircraft in international traffic shall be taxable only in that Contracting State.
2. For the purposes of this Article, profits from the operation of ships or aircraft in international traffic shall mean profits derived by an enterprise described in paragraph

1 from the transportation by sea or air respectively of passengers, mail, livestock or goods carried on by the owners or lessees or charterers of ships or aircraft including:

a. the sale of tickets for such transportation;
b. the rental of ships or aircraft connected with such transportation, and (c) income from use, maintenance, or rental of containers (including trailers, barges, and related equipment for the transport of containers) operated in international traffic.

3. For the purposes of this Article, interest on funds directly connected with the operation of ships or aircraft in international traffic shall be regarded as profits described in this Article, and the provisions of Article 11 (interest) shall not apply in relation to such interest.
4. The provisions of paragraph 1 shall also apply to profits from the participation in a pool, a joint business or an international operating agency.

Article 9 - Associated Enterprises

1. Where:

a. an enterprise of a Contracting State participates directly or indirectly in the management, control or capital of an enterprise of the other Contracting State, or
b. the same persons participate directly or indirectly in the management, control or capital of an enterprise of a Contracting State and an enterprise of the other Contracting State, and in either case conditions are made or imposed between the two enterprises in their commercial or financial relations which differ from those which would be made between independent enterprises, then any profits which would, but for those conditions, have accrued to one of the enterprises, but, by reason of those conditions, have not so accrued, may be included in the profits of that enterprise and taxed accordingly.

2. Where a Contracting State includes in the profits of an enterprise of that Contracting State–and taxes accordingly–profits on which an enterprise of the other Contracting State has been charged to tax in that other Contracting State, and the profits so included are profits which would have accrued to the enterprise of the first-mentioned Contracting State if the conditions made between the two enterprises had been those which would have been made between independent enterprises, then that other State shall make an appropriate adjustment to the amount of tax charged therein on those profits. In determining such adjustment, due regard shall be had to the other provisions of this Agreement and the competent authorities of the Contracting States shall, if necessary, consult each other.

Article 10 – Dividends

1. Dividends paid by a company which is a resident of a Contracting State to a resident of the other Contracting State may be taxed in that other Contracting State.
2. However, such dividends may also be taxed in the Contracting State of which the company paying the dividends is a resident and according to the laws of that Contracting State, but if the recipient is the beneficial owner of the dividends the tax so charged shall not exceed 10 per cent of the gross amount of the dividends. The provisions of this paragraph shall not affect the taxation of the company in respect of the profits out of which the dividends are paid.
3. The term "dividends" as used in this Article means income from shares, or other rights, not being debt-claims, participating in profits, as well as income from other corporate rights which is subjected to the same taxation treatment as income from shares by the laws of the State of which the company making the distribution is a resident.
4. The provisions of paragraphs 1 and 2 shall not apply if the beneficial owner of the dividends, being a resident of a Contracting State, carries on business in the other Contracting State of which the company paying the dividends is a resident, through a

permanent establishment situated therein, or performs in that other Contracting State independent personal services from a fixed base situated therein, and the holding in respect of which the dividends are paid is effectively connected with such permanent establishment or fixed base, in such case the provisions of Article 7 or Article 14, as the case may be, shall apply.

5. Where a company which is a resident of a Contracting State derives profits or income from the other Contracting State, that other Contracting State may not impose any tax on the dividends paid by the company, except insofar as such dividends are paid to a resident of that other Contracting State or insofar as the holding in respect of which the dividends are paid is effectively connected with a permanent establishment or a fixed base situated in that other Contracting State, nor subject the company's undistributed profits to a tax on the company's undistributed profits, even if the dividends paid or the undistributed profits consist wholly or partly of profits or income arising in such other Contracting State.

Article 11 - Interest

1. Interest arising in a Contracting State and paid to a resident of the other Contracting State may be taxed in that other Contracting State.
2. However, such interest may also be taxed in the Contracting State in which it arises and according to the laws of that Contracting State, but if the recipient is the beneficial owner of the interest the tax so charged shall not exceed 10 per cent of the gross amount of the interest.
3. Notwithstanding the provisions of paragraph 2, interest arising in a Contracting State and derived by the Government of the other Contracting State, a political subdivision, a local authority and the Central Bank thereof or any financial institution wholly owned by that Government, or by any other resident of that other Contracting State with respect to debt-claims indirectly financed by the Government of that other Contracting State, a political subdivision, a local authority, and the Central Bank thereof or any financial institution wholly owned by that Government shall be exempt from tax in the first-mentioned Contracting State.
4. The term "interest" as used in this Article means income from debt-claims of every kind, whether or not secured by mortgage and whether or not carrying a right to participate in the debtor's profits, and in particular, income from government securities and income from bonds or debentures, including premiums and prizes attaching to such securities, bonds or debentures. Penalty charges for late payment shall not be regarded as interest for the purpose of this Article.
5. The provisions of paragraphs 1 and 2 shall not apply if the beneficial owner of the interest, being a resident of a Contracting State, carries on business in the other Contracting State in which the interest arises, through a permanent establishment situated therein, or performs in that other Contracting State independent personal services from a fixed base situated therein, and the debt-claim in respect of which the interest is paid is effectively connected with such permanent establishment or fixed base. In such case the provisions of Article 7 or Article 14, as the case may be, shall apply.
6. Interest shall be deemed to arise in a Contracting State when the payer is the Government of that Contracting State, a political subdivision, a local authority thereof or a resident of that Contracting State. Where, however, the person paying the interest, whether he is a resident of a Contracting State or not, has in a Contracting State a permanent establishment or a fixed base in connection with which the indebtedness on which the interest is paid was incurred, and such interest is borne by such permanent establishment or fixed base, then such interest shall be deemed to arise in the Contracting State in which the permanent establishment or fixed base is situated.
7. Where, by reason of a special relationship between the payer and the beneficial owner or between both of them and some other person, the amount of the interest, having regard to the debt-claim for which it is paid, exceeds the amount which would have been agreed

upon by the payer and the beneficial owner in the absence of such relationship, the provisions of this Article shall apply only to the last-mentioned amount. In such case, the excess part of the payments shall remain taxable according to the laws of each Contracting State, due regard being had to the other provisions of this Agreement.

Article 12 - Royalties and Fees for Technical Services

1. Royalties or fees for technical services arising in a Contracting State and paid to a resident of the other Contracting State may be taxed in that other Contracting State.
2. However, such royalties or fees for technical services may also be taxed in the Contracting State in which they arise, and according to the laws of that Contracting State, but if the recipient is the beneficial owner of the royalties or fees for technical services, the tax so charged shall not exceed 10 per cent of the gross amount of the royalties or fees for technical services.
3. The term "royalties" as used in this Article means payment of any kind received as a consideration for the use of, or the right to use, any copyright of literary, artistic or scientific work including cinematography films and films or tapes for radio or television broadcasting, any patent, trade mark, design or model, plan, secret formula or process, or for the use of, or the right to use, industrial, commercial or scientific equipment, or for information concerning industrial, commercial or scientific experience.
4. The term "fees for technical services" as used in this Article means any payment for the provision of services of managerial, technical or consultancy nature by a resident of a Contracting State in the other Contracting State, but does not include payment for activities mentioned in paragraph 2(k) of Article 5 and Article 15 of the Agreement.
5. The provisions of paragraphs 1 and 2 shall not apply if the beneficial owner of the royalties or fees for technical services, being a resident of a Contracting State, carries on business in the other Contracting State in which the royalties or fees for technical services arise, through a permanent establishment or Performs in that other contracting state independent Personal service from a fixed base situated therein or performs in that other contracting state independent personal service from a fixed base situated therein and the right, property or contract in respect of which the royalties or fees for technical services are paid is effectively connected with such permanent establishment or fixed base. In such case the provisions of Article 7 or Article 14, as the case may be, shall apply.
6. Royalties or fees for technical services shall be deemed to arise in a Contracting State when the payer is the Government of that Contracting State, a political subdivision, a local authority thereof or a resident of that Contracting State. Where, however, the person paying the royalties or fees for technical services, whether he is a resident of a Contracting State or not, has in a Contracting State a permanent establishment or a fixed base in connection with which the liability to pay the royalties or fees for technical services was incurred, and such royalties or fees for technical services are borne by such permanent establishment or fixed base, then such royalties or fees for technical services shall be deemed to arise in the Contracting State in which the permanent establishment or fixed base is situated.
7. Where, by reason of a special relationship between the payer and the beneficial owner or between both of them and some other person, the amount of the royalties or fees for technical services, having regard to the use, right or information for which they are paid, exceeds the amount which would have been agreed upon by the payer and the beneficial owner in the absence of such relationship, the provisions of this Article shall apply only to the last-mentioned amount. In such case, the excess part of the payments shall remain taxable according to the laws of each Contracting State, due regard being had to the other provisions of this Agreement.

Article 13 - Capital Gains

1. Gains derived by a resident of a Contracting State from the alienation of immovable property referred to in Article 6 and situated in the other Contracting State may be taxed in that other Contracting State.
2. Gains from the alienation of movable property forming part of business property of a permanent establishment which an enterprise of a Contracting State has in the other Contracting State or of movable property pertaining to a fixed base available to a resident of a Contracting State in the other Contracting State for the purpose of performing independent personal services, including such gains from the alienation of such a permanent establishment (alone or together with the whole enterprise) or of such a fixed base, may be taxed in that other Contracting State.
3. Gains from the alienation of ships or aircraft operated in international traffic or movable property pertaining to the operation of such ships or aircraft shall be taxable only in the Contracting State of which the alienator is a resident.
4. Gains from the alienation of shares of the capital stock of a company the property of which consists directly or indirectly principally have immovable property situated in a Contracting State may be taxed in that Contracting State.
5. Gains from the alienation of any property other than that referred to in the preceding paragraphs of this Article, arising in a Contracting State, may be taxed in that Contracting State.

Article 14 - Independent Personal Services

1. Income derived by a resident of a Contracting State in respect of professional services or other activities of an independent character shall be taxable only in that Contracting State except in one of the following circumstances, when such income may also be taxed in the other Contracting State:

   a. If he has a fixed base regularly available to him in the other Contracting State for the purpose of performing his activities; in that case, only so much of the income as is attributable to that fixed base may be taxed in that other Contracting State;
   b. if his stay in the other Contracting State is for a period or periods exceeding in the aggregate 183 days in the taxable year concerned; in that case, only so much of the income as is derived from his activities performed in that other Contracting State may be taxed in that other Contracting State.

2. The term "professional services" includes especially independent scientific, literary, artistic, educational or teaching activities as well as the independent activities of physicians, lawyers, engineers, architects, dentists and accountants.

Article 15 - Dependent Personal Services

1. Subject to the provisions of Articles 16, 18, 19, 20 and 21, salaries, wages and other similar remuneration derived by a resident of a Contracting State in respect of an employment shall be taxable only in that Contracting State unless the employment is exercised in the other Contracting State. If the employment is so exercised, such remuneration as is derived therefrom may be taxed in that other Contracting State.
2. Notwithstanding the provisions of paragraph 1, remuneration derived by resident of a Contracting State in respect of an employment exercised in the other Contracting State shall be taxable only in the first-mentioned State if:

   a. the recipient is present in the other Contracting State for a period or periods not exceeding in the aggregate 183 days in the taxable year concerned; and
   b. the remuneration is paid by, or on behalf of, an employer who is not a resident of the other Contracting State; and
   c. the remuneration is not borne by a permanent establishment or a fixed base which the employer has in the other Contracting State.

3. Notwithstanding the provisions of paragraphs 1 and 2 of this Article remuneration derived in respect of an employment exercised aboard a ship or aircraft operated by an enterprise which is a resident of a Contracting State in international traffic shall be taxable only in that Contracting State.

Article 16 - Directors' Fees

Directors' fees and other similar payments derived by a resident of a contracting state in his capacity as a member of the board of directors of a company which is resident of the other Contracting State may be taxed in that other Contracting State.

Article 17 - Artistes and Sports Persons

1. Notwithstanding the provisions of Articles 14 and 15, income derived by a resident of a Contracting State as an entertainer, such as a theatre, motion picture, radio or television artiste, or a musician, or as a sportsperson, from his personal activities and such exercised in the other Contracting State, may be taxed in that other Contracting State.
2. Where income in respect of personal activities exercised by an entertainer or sportsperson in his capacity as such accrues not to the entertainer or sportsperson himself but to another person, that income may, notwithstanding the provisions of Articles 7, 14 and 15, be taxed in the Contracting State in which the activities of the entertainer or sportsperson are exercised.
3. Notwithstanding the provisions of paragraphs 1 and 2, income derived by entertainers or sportspersons who are residents of a Contracting State from the activities exercised in the other Contracting State either as a part of cultural exchange between the Contracting States or supported wholly or substantially from the public funds in either of the Contracting States or political subdivisions or local authorities thereof shall be exempt from tax in that other Contracting State.

Article 18 – Pensions

1. Subject to the provisions of paragraph 2 of Article 19, pensions, annuity and other similar remuneration paid to a resident of a Contracting State in consideration of past employment shall be taxable only in that Contracting State.
2. Notwithstanding the provisions of paragraph 1, pensions, annuity paid and other similar payments made by the Government of a Contracting State or a political subdivision or a local authority thereof under a public welfare scheme of the social security system of that Contracting State shall be taxable only in that Contracting State.

Article 19 - Remuneration and Pensions in Respect of Government Services

1.

   a) Remuneration, other than pension, paid by the Government of a Contracting State or a political subdivision or a local authority thereof to an individual in respect of services rendered to the Government of that Contracting State or a political subdivision or a local authority thereof, in the discharge of functions of a governmental nature, shall be taxable only in that Contracting State.
   b) However, such remuneration shall be taxable only in the other Contracting State if the services are rendered in that other Contracting State and the individual is a resident of that other Contracting State who:

      I. is a national of that other Contracting States; or
      II. did not become a resident of that other Contracting State solely for the purpose of rendering the services.

2.

   a) Any pension paid by, or out of funds to which contributions are made by the Government of a Contracting State or a political subdivision or a local authority thereof to an individual in respect of services rendered to the Government of that Contracting State or a political subdivision or a local authority thereof shall be taxable only in that Contracting State. (b) However, such pension shall be taxable only in the other Contracting State if the individual is a resident of and a national of, that other Contracting State.

3. The provisions of Articles 15, 16, 17 and 18 shall apply to remuneration and pensions in respect of services rendered in connection with a business carried on by the Government of a Contracting State or a political subdivision or a local authority thereof.

Article 20 - Payments Received by Professors, Teachers and Research Scholars

1. An individual who is, or immediately before visiting a Contracting State was, a resident of the other Contracting State and is present in the first-mentioned Contracting State for the primary purpose of teaching, giving lectures or conducting research at a university, college, school or educational institution or scientific research institution approved by the Government of the first-mentioned Contracting State shall be exempt from tax in the first-mentioned Contracting State, for a period of three years from the date of his first arrival in the first-mentioned Contracting State, in respect of remuneration for such teaching, lectures or research.
2. This Article shall not apply to income from research if such research is undertaken primarily for the private benefit of a specific person or persons.

Article 21 - Payments Received by Students, Trainees and Apprentices

1. A student, business apprentice or trainee who is or was immediately before visiting a Contracting State a resident of the other Contracting State and who is present in the first-mentioned State solely for the purpose of his education, training shall be exempt from tax in that first-mentioned State on the following payments or income received or derived by him for the purpose of his maintenance, education or training:

   a. payments derived from sources outside that Contracting State for the purpose of his maintenance, education, study, research or training;
   b. grants, scholarships or awards supplied by the Government, or a scientific, educational, cultural or other tax-exempt organization; and
   c. income derived from personal services performed in that Contracting State for the purpose of maintenance.

2. The benefits of this Article shall extend only for such period of time as may be reasonable or customarily required to complete the education or training undertaken, but in no event shall any individual have the benefits of this Article, for more than five consecutive years from the date of his first arrival in that Contracting State.

Article 22 - Other Income

1. Items of income of a resident of a Contracting State, wherever arising, not dealt with in the foregoing Articles of this Agreement shall be taxable only in that Contracting State.
2. The provisions of paragraph 1 shall not apply to income, other than income from immovable property as defined in paragraph 2 of Article 6, if the recipient of such income, being a resident of a Contracting State, carries on business in the other Contracting State through a permanent establishment situated therein, or performs in that other Contracting State independent personal services from a fixed base situated

therein, and the right or property in respect of which the income is paid is effectively connected with such permanent establishment or fixed base. In such case the provisions of Article 7 or Article 14, as the case may be, shall apply.

3. Notwithstanding the provisions of paragraphs 1 and 2, items of income of a resident of a Contracting State not dealt with in the foregoing Articles of this Agreement and arising in the other Contracting State may be taxed in that other Contracting State.

Article 23 - Methods for the Elimination of Double Taxation

1. In China, double taxation shall be eliminated as follows:

   a. Where a resident of China derives income from India the amount of tax on that income payable in India in accordance with the provisions of this Agreement, may be credited against the Chinese tax imposed on that resident. The amount of credit, however, shall not exceed the amount of the Chinese tax on that income computed in accordance with the taxation laws and regulations of China.
   b. Where the income derived from India is a dividend paid by a company which is a resident of India to a company which is a resident of China and which owns not less than 10 per cent of the shares of the company paying the dividend, the credit shall take into account the tax paid to India by the company paying the dividend in respect of its income.

2. In India, double taxation shall be eliminated as follows:
   Where a resident of India derives income which, in accordance with the provisions of this Agreement may be taxed in China, India shall allow as a deduction from the tax on the income of that resident an amount equal to the income tax paid in China whether directly or by deduction. Such a deduction shall not, however, exceed that part of the income tax (as computed before the deduction is given) that is attributable, as the case may be, to the income that may be taxed in China.
3. The tax paid in a Contracting State mentioned in paragraphs 1 and 2 of this Article shall be deemed to include the tax which would have been payable but for the legal provisions concerning tax reduction, exemption or other tax incentives of the Contracting States for the promotion of economic development.

Article 24 - Non-discrimination

1. Nationals of a Contracting State shall not be subjected in the other Contracting State to any taxation or any requirement connected therewith, which is other or more burdensome than the taxation and connected requirements to which nationals of that other Contracting State in the same circumstances are or may be subjected.
2. The taxation on a permanent establishment which an enterprise of a Contracting State has in the other Contracting State shall not be less favorably levied in that other Contracting State than the taxation levied on enterprises of that other Contracting State carrying on the same activities in the same circumstances or under the same conditions.
3. Where a Contracting State charges the profits of a permanent establishment which an enterprise of the other Contracting State has in the first-mentioned Contracting State at a rate of tax which is different from that imposed on the profits of a similar enterprise of the first-mentioned Contracting State, it shall not be construed as discrimination under this Article.
4. Nothing contained in this Article shall be construed as obliging a Contracting State to grant to residents of the other Contracting State any personal allowances, reliefs and deductions for taxation purposes on account of civil status or family responsibilities which it grants to its own residents.
5. Except where the provisions of paragraph 1 of Article 9, paragraph 7 of Article 11, or paragraph 7 of Article 12, apply, interest, royalties and other disbursements paid by an

enterprise of a Contracting State to a resident of the other Contracting State shall, for the purpose of determining the taxable profits of such enterprise, be deductible under the same conditions as if they had been paid to a resident of the first-mentioned State subject to the provisions of domestic laws of that Contracting State.

6. Enterprises of a Contracting State, the capital of which is wholly or partly owned or controlled, directly or indirectly, by one or more residents of the other Contracting State, shall not be subjected in the first-mentioned State to any taxation or any requirement connected therewith which is other or more burdensome than the taxation and connected requirements to which other similar enterprises of the first-mentioned State are or may be subjected in the same circumstances and under the same conditions.
7. In this Article, the term "taxation" means taxes which are the subject of this Agreement.

Article 25 - Mutual Agreement Procedure

1. Where a person considers that the actions of one or both of the Contracting States result or will result for him in taxation not in accordance with the provisions of this Agreement, he may, irrespective of the remedies provided by the domestic law of those States, present his case to the competent authority of the Contracting State of which he is a resident or, if his case comes under paragraphs 1 of Article 24, to that of the Contracting State of which he is a national. The case must be presented within three years from the first notification of the action resulting in taxation not in accordance with the provisions of the Agreement.
2. The competent authority shall endeavor, if the objection appears to it to be justified and if it is not itself able to arrive at a satisfactory solution, to resolve the case by mutual agreement with the competent authority of the other Contracting State, with a view to the avoidance of taxation which is not in accordance with the provisions of this Agreement. Any agreement reached shall be implemented notwithstanding any time limits in the domestic law of the Contracting States.
3. The competent authorities of the Contracting States shall endeavor to resolve by mutual agreement any difficulties or doubts arising as to the interpretation or application of the Agreement. They may also consult together for the elimination of double taxation in cases not provided for in this Agreement.
4. The competent authorities of the Contracting States may communicate with each other directly for the purpose of reaching an agreement in the sense of paragraphs 2 and 3. When it seems advisable for reaching agreement, representatives of the competent authorities of the Contracting States may meet together for an oral exchange of opinions.

Article 26 - Exchange of Information

1. The competent authorities of the Contracting States shall exchange such information (including documents) as is necessary for carrying out the provisions of this Agreement or of the domestic laws of the Contracting States concerning taxes covered by the Agreement, insofar as the taxation thereunder is not contrary to this Agreement, in particular for the prevention of evasion of such taxes. The exchange of information is not restricted by Article 1. Any information received by a Contracting State shall be treated as secret and shall be disclosed only to persons or authorities (including Courts and administrative bodies) involved in the assessment of collection of the enforcement or prosecution in respect of, or the determination of appeals in relation to, the taxes covered by the Agreement. Such persons or authorities shall use the information only for such purposes. They may disclose the information in public Court proceedings or in judicial decisions.
2. In no case shall the provisions of paragraph 1 be construed so as to impose on a Contracting State the obligation:

   a. to carry out administrative measures at variance with the laws and administrative practice of that or of the other Contracting State;

b. to supply information or documents which is not obtainable under the laws or in the normal course of the administration of that or of the other Contracting State;
c. to supply information or documents which would disclose any trade, business, industrial, commercial or professional secret or trade process, or information, the disclosure of which would be contrary to public policy (order public).

Article 27 - Diplomatic Agents and Consular Officers

Nothing in this Agreement shall affect the fiscal privileges of diplomatic agents or consular officers under the general rules of international law or under the provisions of special agreements.

Article 28 - Entry Into Force

This Agreement shall enter into force on the thirtieth day after the date on which diplomatic notes indicating the completion of internal legal procedures necessary in each country for the entry into force of this Agreement have been exchanged. This Agreement shall have effect:

a. in China, in respect of income arising in any taxable year beginning on or after the first day of January next following the calendar year in which this Agreement enters into force;
b. in India, in respect of income arising in any previous year beginning on or after the first day of April next following the calendar year in which this Agreement enters into force.

Article 29 – Termination

This Agreement shall remain in force indefinitely but either of the Contracting States may, on or before the thirtieth day of June in any calendar year beginning after the expiration of a period of five years from the date of its entry into force, give written notice of termination to the other Contracting State through the diplomatic channels. In such event this Agreement shall cease to have effect:

a. in China, in respect of income arising in any taxable year beginning on or after the first day of January next following the calendar year in which the notice of termination is given;
b. in India, in respect of income arising in any previous year beginning on or after the first day of April next following the calendar year in which the notice is given.

In witness whereof, the undersigned, being duly authorized thereto, have signed the present Agreement. Done in duplicate at New Delhi on this eighteenth day of July one thousand nine hundred and ninety four in the Hindi, Chinese and English languages, with all three texts being equally authentic. In case of any divergence, the English text shall prevail.

Protocol

At the signing of the Agreement between the Government of the Republic of India and the Government of the People's Republic of China for the Avoidance of Double Taxation and the Prevention of Fiscal Evasion with respect to Taxes on Income (hereinafter referred to as "The Agreement") both sides have agreed upon the following provisions which form an integral part of the Agreement:

1. *With reference to paragraph (d) of Article 3:*
   It is understood that the term "tax" should not include any penalty imposed for non-compliance of the laws and regulations relating to the taxes to which this Agreement applies.

2. *With reference to Article 8, the exemption shall also include:*

   I. in China, the business tax;
   II. in India, any tax similar to the business tax in China which may be imposed in India after signing of the Agreement.

3. *With reference to Article 26:*
   The competent authorities of the Contracting States shall agree from time to time on the information or documents which shall be necessarily furnished on a routine basis.

In witness whereof, the undersigned, being duly authorized thereto, have signed the present Protocol.

Done in duplicate at New Delhi on this eighteenth day of July one thousand nine hundred and ninety four in the Hindi, Chinese and English languages, all three texts being authentic. In case of any divergence, the English text shall prevail.

9.2.3 Japan–China Treaty

The Government of the People's Republic of China and the Government of Japan, desiring to conclude an Agreement for the avoidance of double taxation and the prevention of fiscal evasion with respect to taxes on income, have agreed as follows:

Article 1 - Personal Scope

This Agreement shall apply to persons who are residents of one or both of the Contracting States.

Article 2 - Taxes Covered

1. The taxes to which this Agreement shall apply are:

   a) in the People's Republic of China:

      I) the individual income tax;
      II) the income tax concerning joint ventures using Chinese and foreign investment;
      III) the income tax concerning foreign enterprises; and
      IV) the local income tax (hereinafter referred to as "Chinese tax");

   b) in Japan:

      I) the income tax;
      II) the corporation tax; and
      III) the local inhabitant taxes (hereinafter referred to as "Japanese tax").

2. This Agreement shall also apply to any identical or substantially similar taxes which are imposed after the date of signature of this Agreement in addition to, or in place of, those referred to in paragraph 1. The competent authorities of the Contracting States shall notify each other of any substantial changes which have been made in their respective taxation laws within a reasonable period of time after such changes.

Article 3 - General Definitions

1. For the purposes of this Agreement, unless the context otherwise requires:

   a) the term "the People's Republic of China", when used in a geographical sense, means all the territory of the People's Republic of China, including its territorial sea, in which the laws relating to Chinese tax are in force, and all the area beyond its territorial sea, including the seabed and sub-soil thereof, over which the People's Republic of China has jurisdiction in accordance with international law and in which the laws relating to Chinese tax are in force;
   b) the term "Japan", when used in a geographical sense, means all the territory of Japan, including its territorial sea, in which the laws relating to Japanese tax are in force, and all the area beyond its territorial sea, including the seabed and subsoil thereof, over which Japan has jurisdiction in accordance with international law and in which the laws relating to Japanese tax are in force;
   c) the terms "a Contracting State" and "the other Contracting State" mean the People's Republic of China or Japan, as the context requires;
   d) the term "tax" means Chinese tax or Japanese tax, as the context requires;
   e) the term "person" includes an individual, a company and any other body of persons;
   f) the term "company" means any corporate or any entity which is treated as a body corporate for tax purposes;
   g) the terms "enterprise of a Contracting State" and "enterprise of the other Contracting State" mean, respectively, an enterprise carried on by a resident of a Contracting State and an enterprise carried on by a resident of the other Contracting State; h) the term "nationals" means all individuals possessing the nationality of either Contracting State and all juridical persons created or organized under the laws of that Contracting State and all organizations without juridical personality treated for the purposes of tax of that Contracting State as juridical persons created or organized under the laws of that Contracting State;
   h) the term "international traffic" means any transport by a ship or aircraft operated by an enterprise of a Contracting State, except when the ship or aircraft is operated solely between places in the other Contracting State;
   i) the term "competent authority" means, in the case of the People's Republic of China, the Ministry of Finance or its authorized representative and, in the case of Japan, the Minister of Finance or his authorized representative.

2. As regards the application of this Agreement by a Contracting State, any term not defined in this Agreement shall, unless the context otherwise requires, have the meaning which it has under the laws of that Contracting State concerning the taxes to which this Agreement applies.

Article 4 – Resident

1. For the purposes of this Agreement, the term "resident of a Contracting State" means any person who, under the laws of that Contracting State, is liable to tax therein by reason of his domicile, residence, place of head or main office or any other criterion of a similar nature.
2. Where by reason of the provisions of paragraph 1 an individual is a resident of both Contracting States, then the competent authorities of the Contracting States shall determine by mutual agreement the Contracting State of which that individual shall be deemed to be a resident for the purposes of this Agreement.
3. Where by reason of the provisions of paragraph 1 a person other than an individual is a resident of both Contracting States, then it shall be deemed to be a resident of the Contracting State in which its head or main office is situated.

Article 5 - Permanent Establishment

1. For the purposes of this Agreement, the term "permanent establishment" means affixed place of business through which the business of an enterprise is wholly or partly carried on.
2. The term "permanent establishment" includes especially:

   a) a place of management;
   b) a branch;
   c) an office;
   d) a factory;
   e) a workshop; and
   f) a mine, an oil or gas well, a quarry or any other place of extraction of natural resources.

3. A building site, a construction, assembly or installation project or supervisory activities in connection therewith, constitute a permanent establishment only if such site, project or activities continue for a period of more than six months.
4. Notwithstanding the provisions of paragraphs 1 to 3, the term "permanent establishment" shall be deemed not to include:

   a) the use of facilities solely for the purpose of storage, display or delivery of goods or merchandise belonging to the enterprise;
   b) the maintenance of a stock of goods or merchandise belonging to the enterprise solely for the purpose of storage, display or delivery;
   c) the maintenance of a stock of goods or merchandise belonging to the enterprise solely for the purpose of processing by another enterprise;
   d) the maintenance of a fixed place of business solely for the purpose of purchasing goods or merchandise, or of collecting information, for the enterprise;
   e) the maintenance of a fixed place of business solely for the purpose of carrying on, for the enterprise, any other activity of a preparatory or auxiliary character.

5. Contracting State shall be deemed to have a permanent establishment in the other Contracting State if it furnishes in that other Contracting State consultancy services through employees or other personnel–other than an agent of an independent status to whom the provisions of paragraph 7 apply–provided that such activities continue (for the same project or two or more connected projects) for a period or periods aggregating more than six months within any twelve-month period.
6. Notwithstanding the provisions of paragraphs 1 and 2, where a person–other than an agent of an independent status to whom the provisions of paragraph 7 apply–is acting in a Contracting State on behalf of an enterprise of the other Contracting State, that enterprise shall be deemed to have a permanent establishment in the first-mentioned Contracting State in respect of any activities which that person undertakes for the enterprise, if:

   a) that person has, and habitually exercises in the first-mentioned Contracting State, an authority to conclude contracts in the name of the enterprise, unless his activities are limited to those mentioned in paragraph 4 which, if exercised through a fixed place of business, would not make this fixed place of business a permanent establishment under the provisions of that paragraph; or
   b) that person regularly secures orders in the first-mentioned Contracting State wholly or almost wholly for the enterprise itself or for the enterprise and other enterprises which control or are controlled by that enterprise.

7. An enterprise of a Contracting State shall not be deemed to have a permanent establishment in the other Contracting State merely because it carries on business in that other

Contracting State through a broker, general commission agent or any other agent of an independent status, provided that such persons are acting in the ordinary course of their business.

8. The fact that a company which is a resident of a Contracting State controls or is controlled by a company which is a resident of the other Contracting State, or which carries on business in that other Contracting State (whether through a permanent establishment or otherwise), shall not of itself constitute either company a permanent establishment of the other.

Article 6 - Income From Immovable Property

1. Income derived by a resident of a Contracting State from immovable property situated in the other Contracting State may be taxed in that other Contracting State.
2. The term "immovable property" shall have the meaning which it has under the laws of the Contracting State in which the property in question is situated. The term shall in any case include property accessory to immovable property, livestock and equipment used in agriculture and forestry, rights to which the provisions of general law respecting landed property apply, usufruct of immovable property and rights to variable or fixed payments as consideration for the working of, or the right to work, mineral deposits, sources and other natural resources; ships and aircraft shall not be regarded as immovable property.
3. The provisions of paragraph 1 shall apply to income derived from the direct use, letting, or use in any other form of immovable property.
4. The provisions of paragraphs 1 and 3 shall also apply to the income from immovable property of an enterprise and to income from immovable property used for the performance of independent personal services.

Article 7 - Business Profits

1. The profits of an enterprise of a Contracting State shall be taxable only in that Contracting State unless the enterprise carries on business in the other Contracting State through a permanent establishment situated therein. If the enterprise carries on business as aforesaid, the profits of the enterprise may be taxed in that other Contracting State but only so much of them as is attributable to that permanent establishment.
2. Subject to the provisions of paragraph 3, where an enterprise of a Contracting State carries on business in the other Contracting State through a permanent establishment situated therein, there shall in each Contracting State be attributed to that permanent establishment the profits which it might be expected to make if it were a distinct and separate enterprise engaged in the same or similar activities under the same or similar conditions and dealing wholly independently with the enterprise of which it is a permanent establishment.
3. In determining the profits of a permanent establishment, there shall be allowed as deductions expenses which are incurred for the purposes of the permanent establishment, including executive and general administrative expenses so incurred, whether in the Contracting State in which the permanent establishment is situated or elsewhere.
4. Insofar as it has been customary in a Contracting State to determine the profits to be attributed to a permanent establishment on the basis of an apportionment of the total profits of the enterprise to its various parts, nothing in paragraph 2 shall preclude that Contracting State from determining the profits to be taxed by such an apportionment as may be customary; the method of apportionment adopted shall, however, be such that the result shall be in accordance with the principles contained in this Article.
5. No profits shall be attributed to a permanent establishment by reason of the mere purchase by that permanent establishment of goods or merchandise for the enterprise.
6. For the purposes of paragraphs 1 to 5, the profits to be attributed to the permanent establishment shall be determined by the same method year by year unless there is good and sufficient reason to the contrary.

7. Where profits include items of income which are dealt with separately in other Articles of this Agreement, then the provisions of those Articles shall not be affected by the provisions of this Article.

Article 8 - Shipping And Air Transport

1. Profits from the operation of ships or aircraft in international traffic carried on by an enterprise of a Contracting State shall be taxable only in that Contracting State.
2. In respect of the operation of ships or aircraft in international traffic carried on by an enterprise of a Contracting State, that enterprise, if an enterprise of the People's Republic of China, shall be exempt from the enterprise tax in Japan, and, if an enterprise of Japan, shall be exempt from any tax similar to the enterprise tax in Japan which is imposed in the People's Republic of China.
3. The provisions of paragraphs 1 and 2 shall also apply to profits from the participation in a pool, a joint business or an international operating agency.

Article 9 - Associated Enterprises

a) an enterprise of a Contracting State participates directly or indirectly in the management, control or capital of an enterprise of the other Contracting State, or
b) the same persons participate directly or indirectly in the management, control or capital of an enterprise of a Contracting State and an enterprise of the other Contracting State, and in either case conditions are made or imposed between the two enterprises in their commercial or financial relations which differ from those which would be made between independent enterprises, then any profits which would, but for those conditions, have accrued to one of the enterprises, but, by reason of those conditions, have not so accrued, may be included in the profits of that enterprise and taxed accordingly.

Article 10 – Dividends

1. Dividends paid by a company which is a resident of a Contracting State to a resident of the other Contracting State may be taxed in that other Contracting State.
2. However, such dividend may also be taxed in the Contracting State of which the company paying the dividends is a resident, and according to the laws of that Contracting State, but if the recipient is the beneficial owner of the dividends the tax so charged shall not exceed 10 per cent of the gross amount of the dividends. The provisions of this paragraph shall not affect the taxation of the company in respect of the profits out of which the dividends are paid.
3. The term "dividends" as used in this Article means income from shares or other rights, not being debt-claims, participating in profits, as well as income from other corporate rights which is subjected to the same taxation treatment as income from shares by the taxation laws of the Contracting State of which the company making the distribution is a resident.
4. The provisions of paragraphs 1 and 2 shall not apply if the beneficial owner of the dividends, being a resident of a Contracting State, carries on business in the other Contracting State of which the company paying the dividends is a resident, through a permanent establishment situated therein, or performs in that other Contracting State independent personal services from a fixed base situated therein, and the holding in respect of which the dividends are paid is effectively connected with such permanent establishment or fixed base. In such case the provisions of Article 7 or Article 14, as the case may be, shall apply.
5. Where a company which is a resident of a Contracting State derives profits or income from the other Contracting State, that other Contracting State may not impose any tax on the dividends paid by the company, except insofar as such dividends are paid to a resident of that other Contracting State or insofar as the holding in respect of which the dividends are paid is effectively connected with a permanent establishment or a fixed base situated in that other Contracting State, nor subject the company's undistributed

profits to a tax on the company's undistributed profits, even if the dividends paid or the undistributed profits consist wholly or partly of profits or income arising in that other Contracting State.

Article 11 - Interest

1. Interest arising in a Contracting State and paid to a resident of the other Contracting State may be taxed in that other Contracting State.
2. However, such interest may also be taxed in the Contracting State in which it arises, and according to the laws of that Contracting State, but if the recipient is the beneficial owner of the interest the tax so charged shall not exceed 10 per cent of the gross amount of the interest.
3. Notwithstanding the provisions of paragraph 2, interest arising in a Contracting State and derived by the Government of the other Contracting State, a local authority thereof, the Central Bank of that other Contracting State or any financial institution wholly owned by that Government, or by any resident of the other Contracting State with respect to debt-claims indirectly financed by the Government of that other Contracting State, a local authority thereof, the Central Bank of that other Contracting State or any financial institution wholly owned by that Government shall be exempt from tax in the first-mentioned Contracting State.
4. The term "interest" as used in this Article means income from debt-claims of every kind, whether or not secured by mortgage and whether or not carrying a right to participate in the debtor's profits, and in particular, income from Government securities and income from bonds or debentures, including premiums and prizes attaching to such securities, bonds or debentures.
5. The provisions of paragraphs 1, 2 and 3 shall not apply if the beneficial owner of the interest, being a resident of a Contracting State, carries on business in the other Contracting State in which the interest arises, through a permanent establishment situated therein, or performs in that other Contracting State independent personal services from a fixed base situated therein, and the debt-claim in respect of which the interest is paid is effectively connected with such permanent establishment or fixed base. In such case the provisions of Article 7 or Article 14, as the case may be, shall apply.
6. Interest shall be deemed to arise in a Contracting State when the payer is the Government of that Contracting State, a local authority thereof or a resident of that Contracting State. Where, however, the person paying the interest, whether he is a resident of a Contracting State or not, has in a Contracting State a permanent establishment or a fixed base in connection with which the indebtedness on which the interest is paid was incurred, and such interest is borne by such permanent establishment or fixed base, then such interest shall be deemed to arise in the Contracting State in which the permanent establishment or fixed base is situated.
7. Where, by reason of a special relationship between the payer and the beneficial owner or between both of them and some other person, the amount of the interest, having regard to the debt-claim for which it is paid, exceeds the amount which would have been agreed upon by the payer and the beneficial owner in the absence of such relationship, the provisions of this Article shall apply only to the last-mentioned amount. In such case, the excess part of the payments shall remain taxable according to the laws of each Contracting State, due regard being had to the other provisions of this Agreement.

Article 12 – Royalties

1. Royalties arising in a Contracting State and paid to a resident of the other Contracting State may be taxed in that other Contracting State.
2. However, such royalties may also be taxed in the Contracting State in which they arise, and according to the laws of that Contracting State, but if the recipient is the beneficial owner of the royalties the tax so charged shall not exceed 10 per cent of the gross amount of the royalties.

3. The term "royalties" as used in this Article means payments of any kind received as a consideration for the use of, or the right to use, any copyright of literary, artistic or scientific work including cinematograph films and films or tapes for radio or television broadcasting, any patent, trade mark, design or model, plan, secret formula or process, or for the use of, or the right to use, industrial, commercial or scientific equipment, or for information concerning industrial, commercial or scientific experience.
4. The provisions of paragraphs 1 and 2 shall not apply if the beneficial owner of the royalties, being a resident of a Contracting State, carries on business in the other Contracting State in which the royalties arise, through a permanent establishment situated therein, or performs in that other Contracting State independent personal services from a fixed base situated therein, and the right or property in respect of which the royalties are paid is effectively connected with such permanent establishment or fixed base. In such case the provisions of Article 7 or Article 14, as the case may be, shall apply.
5. Royalties shall be deemed to arise in a Contracting State when the payer is the Government of that Contracting State, a local authority thereof or a resident of that Contracting State. Where, however, the person paying the royalties, whether he is a resident of a Contracting State or not, has in a Contracting State a permanent establishment or a fixed base in connection with which the liability to pay the royalties was incurred, and such royalties are borne by such permanent establishment or fixed base, then such royalties shall be deemed to arise in the Contracting State in which the permanent establishment or fixed base is situated.
6. Where, by reason of a special relationship between the payer and the beneficial owner or between both of them and some other person, the amount of the royalties, having regard to the use, right or information for which they are paid, exceeds the amount which would have been agreed upon by the payer and the beneficial owner in the absence of such relationship, the provisions of this Article shall apply only to the last-mentioned amount. In such case, the excess part of the payments shall remain taxable according to the laws of each Contracting State, due regard being had to the other provisions of this Agreement.

Article 13 - Capital Gains

1. Gains derived by a resident of a Contracting State from the alienation of immovable property referred to in Article 6 and situated in the other Contracting State may be taxed in that other Contracting State.
2. Gains from the alienation of any property, other than immovable property, forming part of the business property of a permanent establishment which an enterprise of a Contracting State has in the other Contracting State or of any property, other than immovable property, pertaining to a fixed base available to a resident of a Contracting State in the other Contracting State for the purpose of performing independent personal services, including such gains from the alienation of such a permanent establishment (alone or together with the whole enterprise) or of such affixed base, may be taxed in that other Contracting State.
3. Gains derived by a resident of a Contracting State from the alienation of ships or aircraft operated in international traffic and any property, other than immovable property, pertaining to the operation of such ships or aircraft shall be taxable only in that Contracting State.
4. Gains derived by a resident of a Contracting State from the alienation of any property other than that referred to in paragraphs 1 to 3 and arising in the other Contracting State may be taxed in that other Contracting State.

Article 14 - Independent Personal Services

1. Income derived by a resident of a Contracting State in respect of professional services or other activities of an independent character shall be taxable only in that Contracting State unless he has a fixed base regularly available to him in the other Contracting State for the purpose of performing his activities or he is present in that other Contracting State for a period or periods exceeding in the aggregate 183 days in the calendar year concerned. If he has such a fixed base or remains in that other Contracting State for the aforesaid period or periods, the income may be taxed in that other Contracting State but only so much of it as is attributable to that fixed base or is derived in that other Contracting State during the aforesaid period or periods.
2. The term "professional services" includes, especially, independent scientific, literary, artistic, educational or teaching activities as well as the independent activities of physicians, lawyers, engineers, architects, dentists and accountants.

Article 15 - Dependent Personal Services

1. Subject to the provisions of Articles 16, 18, 19, 20 and 21, salaries, wages and other similar remuneration derived by a resident of a Contracting State in respect of an employment shall be taxable only in that Contracting State unless the employment is exercised in the other Contracting State. If the employment is so exercised, such remuneration as is derived therefrom may be taxed in that other Contracting State.
2. Notwithstanding the provisions of paragraph 1, remuneration derived by a resident of a Contracting State in respect of an employment exercised in the other Contracting State shall be taxable only in the first-mentioned Contracting State, if:

   a) the recipient is present in that other Contracting State for a period or periods not exceeding in the aggregate 183 days in the calendar year concerned; and
   b) the remuneration is paid by, or on behalf of, an employer who is not a resident of that other Contracting State; and
   c) the remuneration is not borne by a permanent establishment or a fixed base which the employer has in that other Contracting State.

3. Notwithstanding the provisions of paragraphs 1 and 2, remuneration in respect of an employment exercised aboard a ship or aircraft operated in international traffic by an enterprise of a Contracting State may be taxed in that Contracting State.

Article 16 - Directors' Fees

Directors 'fees and other similar payments derived by a resident of a Contracting State in his capacity as a member of the board of directors of a company which is a resident of the other Contracting State may be taxed in that other Contracting State.

Article 17 - Artistes And Athletes

1. Notwithstanding the provisions of Articles 14 and 15, income derived by an individual who is a resident of a Contracting State as an entertainer such as a theater, motion picture, radio or television artiste, and a musician, or as an athlete, from his personal activities as such exercised in the other Contracting State, may be taxed in that other Contracting State.
2. The income shall, however, be exempt from tax in that other Contracting State whose activities are exercised by an individual who is a resident of the first-mentioned Contracting State pursuant to a special program for cultural exchange agreed upon between the Governments of the Contracting States.
3. Where income in respect of personal activities exercised in a Contracting State by an entertainer or an athlete in his capacity as such accrues not to the entertainer or athlete himself but to another person who is a resident of the other Contracting State, that income may, notwithstanding the provisions of Articles 7, 14 and 15, be taxed in the

first-mentioned Contracting State. Such income shall, however, be exempt from tax in the first-mentioned Contracting State if such activities are exercised pursuant to a special program for cultural exchange agreed upon between the Governments of the Contracting States.

Article 18 - Pensions

Subject to the provisions of paragraph 2 of Article 19, pensions and other similar remuneration paid to a resident of a Contracting State in consideration of past employment shall be taxable only in that Contracting State.

Article 19 - Government Service

1.

a) Remuneration, other than pensions, paid by the Government of a Contracting State or a local authority thereof to an individual in respect of services rendered to the Government of that Contracting State or a local authority thereof, in the discharge of functions of a governmental nature, shall be taxable only in that Contracting State.
b) However, such remuneration shall be taxable only in the other Contracting State if the services are rendered in that other Contracting State and the individual is a resident of that other Contracting State who:

   i) is a national of that other Contracting State; or
   ii) did not become a resident of that other Contracting State solely for the purpose of rendering the services.

2.

a) Any pension paid by, or out of funds to which contributions are made by, the Government of a Contracting State or a local authority thereof to an individual in respect of services rendered to the Government of that Contracting State or a local authority thereof shall be taxable only in that Contracting State.
b) However, such pension shall be taxable only in the other Contracting State if the individual is a resident of, and a national of, that other Contracting State.

3. The provisions of Articles 15, 16, 17 and 18 shall apply to remuneration and pensions in respect of services rendered in connection with a business carried on by the Government of a Contracting State or a local authority thereof.

Article 20 - Teachers And Researchers

An individual who is, or immediately before visiting a Contracting State was, a resident of the other Contracting State and is temporarily present in the first-mentioned Contracting State for the primary purpose of teaching, giving lectures or conducting research at a university, college, school or other accredited educational institution in the first-mentioned Contracting State shall be exempt from tax in the first-mentioned Contracting State, for a period not exceeding three years from the date of his first arrival in the first-mentioned Contracting State, in respect of remuneration for such teaching, lectures or research.

Article 21 - Students And Trainees

Payments or income received for the purpose of his maintenance, education or training by a student, business apprentice or trainee who is present in a Contracting State solely for the purpose of his education, training or the acquisition of his special technical experience and who is, or immediately before being so present was, a resident of the other Contracting State shall be exempt from tax of the first-mentioned Contracting State.

Article 22 - Other Income

1. The income of a resident of a Contracting State not dealt with in the foregoing Articles of this Agreement and arising in the other Contracting State may be taxed in that other Contracting State.
2. However, items of income of a resident of a Contracting State, not dealt with in the foregoing Articles of this Agreement, and other than those referred to in paragraph1, shall be taxable only in that Contracting State.
3. The provisions of paragraphs 1 and 2 shall not apply to income, other than income from immovable property as defined in paragraph 2 of Article 6, if the recipient of such income who is a resident of a Contracting State, carries on business in the other Contracting State through a permanent establishment situated therein, or performs in that other Contracting State independent personal services from a fixed base situated therein, and the right or property in respect of which the income is paid is effectively connected with such permanent establishment or fixed base. In such case the provisions of Article 7 or Article 14, as the case may be, shall apply.

Article 23 - Methods For Elimination Of Double Taxation

1. In the People's Republic of China, double taxation shall be eliminated as follows:

   a) Where a resident of the People's Republic of China derives income from Japan, the amount of Japanese tax payable in respect of that income in accordance with the provisions of this Agreement shall be allowed as a credit against the Chinese tax imposed on that resident. The amount of credit, however, shall not exceed the amount of the Chinese tax computed as appropriate to that income in accordance with the taxation laws and regulations of the People's Republic of China.
   b) Where the income derived from Japan is a dividend paid by a company which is a resident of Japan to a company which is a resident of the People's Republic of China and which owns not less than 10 per cent of the shares of the company paying the dividend, the credit shall take into account the Japanese tax payable by the company paying the dividend in respect of its income.

2. Subject to the laws of Japan regarding the allowance as a credit against Japanese tax of tax payable in any country other than Japan:

   a) Where a resident of Japan derives income from the People's Republic of China and that income may be taxed in the People's Republic of China in accordance with the provisions of this Agreement, the amount of Chinese tax payable in respect of that income shall be allowed as a credit against the Japanese tax imposed on that resident. The amount of credit, however, shall not exceed that part of the Japanese tax which is appropriate to that income.
   b) Where the income derived from the People's Republic of China is a dividend paid by a company which is a resident of the People's Republic of China to a company which is a resident of Japan and which owns not less than 25 per cent either of the voting shares of the company paying the dividend, or of the total shares issued by that company, the credit shall take into account the Chinese tax payable by the company paying the dividend in respect of its income.

3. For the purposes of the credit referred to in sub-paragraph a) of paragraph 2, Chinese tax shall be deemed to have been paid:

   a) at the rate of 10 per cent in the case of dividends paid by a joint venture in the People's Republic of China and 20 per cent in the case of the other dividends, to which the provisions of paragraph 2 of Article 10 apply; and
   b) at the rate of 10 per cent in the case of interest to which the provisions of paragraph 2 of Article 11 apply; and

c) at the rate of 20 per cent in the case of royalties to which the provisions of paragraph 2 of Article 12 apply.

4. For the purposes of the credit referred to in paragraph 2, the term "Chinese tax payable" shall be deemed to include the amount of Chinese tax which would have been paid if the Chinese tax had not been exempted, reduced or refunded in accordance with:

   a) the provisions of Articles 5 and 6 of the Income Tax Law of the People's Republic of China Concerning Joint Ventures Using Chinese and Foreign Investment and the provisions of Article 3 of the Detailed Rules and Regulations for the Implementation of the Income Tax Law of the People's Republic of China Concerning Joint Ventures Using Chinese and Foreign Investment;
   b) the provisions of Articles 4 and 5 of the Income Tax Law of the People's Republic of China Concerning Foreign Enterprises; or
   c) any other similar special incentive measures designed to promote economic development in the People's Republic of China which may be introduced in the laws of the People's Republic of China after the date of signature of this Agreement, and which may be agreed upon by the Governments of the Contracting States.

Article 24 - Non-Discrimination

1. Nationals of a Contracting State shall not be subjected in the other Contracting State to any taxation or any requirement connected therewith which is other or more burdensome than the taxation and connected requirements to which nationals of that other Contracting State in the same circumstances are or may be subjected. The provisions of this paragraph shall, notwithstanding the provisions of Article 1, also apply to persons who are not residents of one or both of the Contracting States.
2. The taxation on a permanent establishment that an enterprise of a Contracting State has in the other Contracting State shall not be less favorably levied in that other Contracting State than the taxation levied on enterprises of that other Contracting State carrying on the same activities.
3. Except where the provisions of Article 9, paragraph 7 of Article 11, or paragraph6 of Article 12 apply, interest, royalties and other disbursements paid by an enterprise of a Contracting State to a resident of the other Contracting State shall, for the purpose of determining the taxable profits of such enterprise, be deductible under the same conditions as if they had been paid to a resident of the first-mentioned Contracting State.
4. Enterprises of a Contracting State, the capital of which is wholly or partly owned or controlled, directly or indirectly, by one or more residents of the other Contracting State, shall not be subjected in the first-mentioned Contracting State to any taxation or any requirement connected therewith which is other or more burdensome than the taxation and connected requirements to which other similar enterprises of the first-mentioned Contracting State are or may be subjected.
5. Nothing contained in this Article shall be construed as obliging a Contracting State to grant to residents of the other Contracting State any personal allowances, reliefs and reductions for tax purposes which are by law available only to residents of the first-mentioned Contracting State.

Article 25 - Mutual Agreement Procedure

1. Where a person considers that the actions of one or both of the Contracting States result or will result for him in taxation not in accordance with the provisions of this Agreement, he may, irrespective of the remedies provided by the domestic laws of those Contracting States, present his case to the competent authority of the Contracting State of which he is a resident or, if his case comes under paragraph 1 of Article 24, to that of the Contracting State of which he is a national. The case must be presented within three years from the first notification of the action resulting in taxation not in accordance with the provisions of this Agreement.

2. The competent authority shall endeavor, if the objection appears to it to be justified and if it is not itself able to arrive at a satisfactory solution, to resolve the case by mutual agreement with the competent authority of the other Contracting State, with a view to the avoidance of taxation which is not in accordance with the provisions of this Agreement. Any agreement reached shall be implemented notwithstanding any time limits in the domestic laws of the Contracting States.
3. The competent authorities of the Contracting States shall endeavor to resolve by mutual agreement any difficulties or doubts arising as to the interpretation or application of this Agreement. They may also consult together for the elimination of double taxation in cases not provided for in this Agreement.
4. The competent authorities of the Contracting States may communicate with each other directly for the purpose of reaching an agreement in the sense of paragraphs 2and 3. When it seems advisable for the purpose of reaching agreement, the competent authorities may meet together for an oral exchange of opinions.

Article 26 - Exchange Of Information

1. The competent authorities of the Contracting States shall exchange such information as is necessary for carrying out the provisions of this Agreement or of the domestic laws of the Contracting States concerning taxes covered by this Agreement insofar as the taxation thereunder is not contrary to the provisions of this Agreement, or for the prevention of fiscal evasion with respect to such taxes. The exchange of information is not restricted by Article 1. Any information so exchanged shall be treated as secret and shall be disclosed only to persons or authorities, including courts, involved in the assessment or collection of the taxes covered by this Agreement or the determination of appeals in relation thereto.
2. In no case shall the provisions of paragraph 1 be construed so as to impose on a Contracting State the obligation:

   a) to carry out administrative measures at variance with the laws and the administrative practice of that or of the other Contracting State;
   b) to supply information which is not obtainable under the laws or in the normal course of the administration of that or of the other Contracting State; or
   c) to supply information which would disclose any trade, business, industrial, commercial or professional secret or trade process, or information, the disclosure of which would be contrary to public policy.

Article 27 - Explanation To Tax Exemption, Reduction Or Other Allowance

Nothing in this Agreement shall be construed as restricting in any manner any tax exemption, reduction or other allowance which are or may hereafter be accorded in a Contracting State to the nationals or residents of the other Contracting State by the laws of the first-mentioned Contracting State or any agreement between the Governments of the Contracting States.

Article 28 - Diplomatic Agents And Consular Officials

Nothing in this Agreement shall affect the fiscal privileges of diplomatic agents or consular officers under the general rules of international law or under the provisions of special agreements.

Article 29 - Entry Into Force

1. This Agreement shall enter into force on the thirtieth day after the date on which diplomatic notes indicating the completion of internal legal procedures necessary in each country for the entry into force of this Agreement have been exchanged.

2. This Agreement shall have effect:

   a) in the People's Republic of China:

      i) as respects income derived during the taxable years beginning on or after the first day of January in the calendar year next following that in which this Agreement enters into force; and
      ii) as respects any tax similar to the enterprise tax in Japan referred to in paragraph 2 of Article 8 levied for the taxable years beginning on or after the first day of January in the calendar year next following that in which this Agreement enters into force;

   b) in Japan: As respects income derived during the taxable years beginning on or after the first day of January in the calendar year next following that in which this Agreement enters into force.

Article 30 - Termination

This Agreement shall continue in effect indefinitely but either of the Contracting States may, on or before the thirtieth day of June in any calendar year beginning after the expiration of a period of five years from the date of its entry into force, give to the other Contracting State, through the diplomatic channel, written notice of termination. In such event this Agreement shall cease to have effect:

a) in the People's Republic of China:

   i) as respects income derived during the taxable years beginning on or after the first day of January in the calendar year next following that in which the notice of termination is given; and
   ii) as respects any tax similar to the enterprise tax in Japan referred to in paragraph 2 of Article 8 levied for the taxable years beginning on or after the first day of January in the calendar year next following that in which the notice of termination is given;

b) in Japan: As respects income derived during the taxable years beginning on or after the first day of January in the calendar year next following that in which the notice of termination is given.

IN WITNESS WHEREOF the undersigned, duly authorized thereto by their respective Governments, have signed this Agreement. DONE at Beijing on the day of September 6, 1983, in duplicate in the Chinese, Japanese and English languages, all three texts being equally authentic. In case of any divergence of interpretations, the English text shall prevail.

9.2.4 Singapore–China Treaty

The Government of the People's Republic of China and the Government of the Republic of Singapore, desiring to conclude an Agreement for the Avoidance of Double Taxation and the Prevention of Fiscal Evasion with respect to Taxes on Income, have agreed as follows:

Article 1 - Persons Covered

This Agreement shall apply to persons who are residents of one or both of the Contracting States.

Article 2 - Taxes Covered

1. This Agreement shall apply to taxes on income imposed on behalf of a Contracting State or its local authorities, irrespective of the manner in which they are levied.
2. There shall be regarded as taxes on income all taxes imposed on total income or on elements of income, including taxes on gains from the alienation of movable or immovable property.
3. The existing taxes to which the Agreement shall apply are in particular:

   a) in China:

      I) the Individual Income Tax
      II) the Enterprise Income Tax (hereinafter referred to as "Chinese tax");

   b) in Singapore:

      I) the Income Tax (hereinafter referred to as "Singapore tax").

4. The Agreement shall apply also to any identical or substantially similar taxes which are imposed after the date of signature of the Agreement in addition to, or in place of, the existing taxes. The competent authorities of the Contracting States shall notify each other of any significant changes which have been made in their respective taxation laws.

Article 3 - General Definitions

1. For the purposes of this Agreement, unless the context otherwise requires:

   a) the term "China" means the People's Republic of China, and when used in geographical sense, means all the territory of the People's Republic of China, including its territorial sea, in which the Chinese laws relating to taxation apply, and any area beyond its territorial sea, within which the People's Republic of China has sovereign rights of exploration for and exploitation of resources of the sea-bed and its sub-soil and superjacent water resources in accordance with international law;
   b) the term "Singapore" means the Republic of Singapore and when used in a geographical sense, the term "Singapore" includes the territorial waters of Singapore and any area extending beyond the limits of the territorial waters of Singapore, and the sea-bed and subsoil of any such area, which has been or may hereafter be designated under the laws of Singapore and in accordance with international law as an area over which Singapore has sovereign rights for the purposes of exploring and exploiting the natural resources, whether living or nonliving;
   c) the terms "a Contracting State" and "the other Contracting State" mean China or Singapore as the context requires;
   d) the term "person" includes an individual, a company and any other body of persons;
   e) the term "company" means any corporate or any entity that is treated as a body corporate for tax purposes;
   f) the terms "enterprise of a Contracting State" and "enterprise of the other Contracting State" mean respectively an enterprise carried on by a resident of a Contracting State and an enterprise carried on by a resident of the other Contracting State;
   g) the term "international traffic" means any transport by a ship or aircraft operated by an enterprise of a Contracting State, except when the ship or aircraft is operated solely between places in the other Contracting State;
   h) the term "competent authority" means:

      (i) in the case of China, the State Administration of Taxation or its authorized representative; and
      (ii) in the case of Singapore, the Minister for Finance or his authorized representative;

i) the term "national" means:

(i) any individual possessing the nationality of a Contracting State;
(ii) any legal person, partnership or association deriving its status as such from the laws in force in a Contracting State.

2. As regards the application of the Agreement at any time by a Contracting State, any term not defined therein shall, unless the context otherwise requires, have the meaning that it has at that time under the law of that State for the purposes of the taxes to which the Agreement applies, any meaning under the applicable tax laws of that State prevailing over a meaning given to the term under other laws of that State.

Article 4 - Resident

1. For the purposes of this Agreement, the term "resident of a Contracting State" means any person who, under the laws of that State, is liable to tax therein by reason of his domicile, residence, place of management, place of head office, place of incorporation or any other criterion of a similar nature, and also includes that State, a local authority or statutory body thereof.
2. Where by reason of the provisions of paragraph 1 an individual is a resident of both Contracting States, then his status shall be determined as follows:

a) he shall be deemed to be a resident only of the State in which he has a permanent home available to him; if he has a permanent home available to him in both States, he shall be deemed to be a resident of the State with which his personal and economic relations are closer (center of vital interests);
b) if the State in which he has his center of vital interests cannot be determined, or if he has not a permanent home available to him in either State, he shall be deemed to be a resident only of the State in which he has an habitual abode;
c) if he has a habitual abode in both States or in neither of them, he shall be deemed to be a resident only of the State of which he is a national;
d) in any other case, the competent authorities of the Contracting States shall settle the Question by mutual agreement.

3. Where by reason of the provisions of paragraph 1 a person other than an individual is a resident of both Contracting States, then it shall be deemed to be a resident only of the State in which its place of effective management is situated. If its place of effective management cannot be determined, the competent authorities of the Contracting States shall settle the question by mutual agreement.

Article 5 - Permanent Establishment

1. For the purposes of this Agreement, the term "permanent establishment" means a fixed place of business through which the business of an enterprise is wholly or partly carried on.
2. The term "permanent establishment" includes especially:

a) a place of management;
b) a branch;
c) an office;
d) a factory;
e) a workshop; and
f) a mine, an oil or gas well, a quarry or any other place of extraction of natural resources.

3. The term “permanent establishment” likewise encompasses:

   a) a building site, a construction, assembly or installation project or supervisory activities in connection therewith, but only where such site, project or activities continue for a period of more than 6 months;
   b) the furnishing of services, including consultancy services, by an enterprise through employees or other personnel engaged by the enterprise for such purpose, but only if such activities of that nature continue (for the same or a connected project) within a Contracting State for a period or periods aggregating more than 6 months within any twelve-month period.

4. Notwithstanding the preceding provisions of this Article, the term “permanent establishment” shall be deemed not to include:

   a) the use of facilities solely for the purpose of storage, display or delivery of goods or merchandise belonging to the enterprise;
   b) the maintenance of a stock of goods or merchandise belonging to the enterprise solely for the purpose of storage, display or delivery;
   c) the maintenance of a stock of goods or merchandise belonging to the enterprise solely for the purpose of processing by another enterprise;
   d) the maintenance of a fixed place of business solely for the purpose of purchasing goods or merchandise or of collecting information, for the enterprise;
   e) the maintenance of a fixed place of business solely for the purpose of carrying on, for the enterprise, any other activity of a preparatory or auxiliary character;
   f) the maintenance of a fixed place of business solely for any combination of activities mentioned in sub-paragraphs a) to e), provided that the overall activity of the fixed place of business resulting from this combination is of a preparatory or auxiliary character.

5. Notwithstanding the provisions of paragraphs 1 and 2, where a person - other than an agent of an independent status to whom paragraph 6 applies - is acting in a Contracting State on behalf of an enterprise of the other Contracting State, has and habitually exercises an authority to conclude contracts in the name of the enterprise, that enterprise shall be deemed to have a permanent establishment in the first-mentioned Contracting State in respect of any activities which that person undertakes for the enterprise, unless the activities of such person are limited to those mentioned in paragraph 4 which, if exercised through a fixed place of business, would not make this fixed place of business a permanent establishment under the provisions of that paragraph.
6. An enterprise of a Contracting State shall not be deemed to have a permanent establishment in the other Contracting State merely because it carries on business in that other State through a broker, general commission agent or any other agent of an independent status, provided that such persons are acting in the ordinary course of their business. However, when the activities of such an agent are devoted wholly or almost wholly on behalf of that enterprise, and conditions are made or imposed between that enterprise and the agent in their commercial and financial relations which differ from those which would have been made between independent enterprises, he will not be considered an agent of an independent status within the meaning of this paragraph.
7. The fact that a company which is a resident of a Contracting State controls or is controlled by a company which is a resident of the other Contracting State, or which carries shall not of itself constitute either company a permanent establishment of the other.

Article 6 - Income From Immovable Property

1. Income derived by a resident of a Contracting State from immovable property (including income from agriculture or forestry) situated in the other Contracting State may be taxed in that other State.
2. The term "immovable property" shall have the meaning which it has under the law of the Contracting State in which the property in question is situated. The term shall in any case include property accessory to immovable property, livestock and equipment used in agriculture and forestry, rights to which the provisions of general law respecting landed property apply, usufruct of immovable property and rights to variable or fixed payments as consideration for the working of, or the right to work, mineral deposits, sources and other natural resources; ships and aircraft shall not be regarded as immovable property.
3. The provisions of paragraph 1 shall apply to income derived from the direct use, letting, or use in any other form of immovable property.
4. The provisions of paragraphs 1 and 3 shall also apply to the income from immovable property of an enterprise and to income from immovable property used for the performance of independent personal services.

Article 7 - Business Profits

1. The profits of an enterprise of a Contracting State shall be taxable only in that State unless the enterprise carries on business in the other Contracting State through a permanent establishment situated therein. If the enterprise carries on business as aforesaid, the profits of the enterprise maybe taxed in the other State but only so much of them as is attributable to that permanent establishment.
2. Subject to the provisions of paragraph 3, where an enterprise of a Contracting State carries on business in the other Contracting State through a permanent establishment situated therein, there shall in each Contracting State be attributed to that permanent establishment the profits which it might be expected to make if it were a distinct and separate enterprise engaged in the same or similar activities under the same or similar conditions and dealing wholly independently with the enterprise of which it is a permanent establishment.
3. In determining the profits of a permanent establishment, there shall be allowed as deductions expenses which are incurred for the purposes of the permanent establishment, including executive and general administrative expenses so incurred, whether in the State in which the permanent establishment is situated or elsewhere.
4. Insofar as it has been customary in a Contracting State to determine the profits to be attributed to a permanent establishment on the basis of an apportionment of the total profits of the enterprise to its various parts, nothing in paragraph 2 shall preclude that Contracting State from determining the profits to be taxed by such an apportionment as may be customary. The method of apportionment adopted shall, however, be such that the result shall be in accordance with the principle contained in this Article.
5. No profits shall be attributed to a permanent establishment by reason of the mere purchase by that permanent establishment of goods or merchandise for the enterprise.
6. For the purposes of the preceding paragraphs, the profits to be attributed to the permanent establishment shall be determined by the same method year by year unless there is good and sufficient reason to the contrary.
7. Where profits include items of income which are dealt with separately in other Articles of this Agreement, then the provisions of those Articles shall not be affected by the provisions of this Article.

Article 8 - Shipping And Air Transport

1. Profits derived by an enterprise of a Contracting State from the operation of ships or aircraft in international traffic shall be taxable only in that State.
2. The provisions of paragraph 1 shall also apply to profits from the participation in a pool, a joint business or an international operating agency.

3. Interest derived by an enterprise of a Contracting State from its deposits of moneys incidental to and connected with its operations of ships or aircraft in international traffic shall be regarded as profits derived from the operation of such ships or aircraft.
4. For the purposes of this Article, profits from the operation of ships or aircraft in international traffic shall include:

   a) profits from the rental on a bareboat basis of ships or aircraft; and
   b) profits from the use, maintenance or rental of containers (including trailers and related equipment for the transport of containers), used for the transport of goods or merchandise;

Where such rental or such use, maintenance or rental, as the case may be, is incidental to the operation of ships or aircraft in international traffic.

Article 9 - Associated Enterprises

1. Where:

   a) an enterprise of a Contracting State participates directly or indirectly in the management, control or capital of an enterprise of the other Contracting State, or
   b) the same persons participate directly or indirectly in the management, control or capital of an enterprise of a Contracting State and an enterprise of the other Contracting State, and in either case conditions are made or imposed between the two enterprises in their commercial or financial relations which differ from those which would be made between independent enterprises, then any profits which would, but for those conditions, have accrued to one of the enterprises, but, by reason of those conditions, have not so accrued, may be included in the profits of that enterprise and taxed accordingly.

2. Where a Contracting State includes in the profits of an enterprise of that State – and taxes accordingly – profits on which an enterprise of the other Contracting State has been charged to tax in that other State and the profits so included are profits which would have accrued to the enterprise of the first-mentioned State if the conditions made between the two enterprises had been those which would have been made between independent enterprises, then that other State shall make an appropriate adjustment to the amount of the tax charged therein on those profits. In determining such adjustment, due regard shall be had to the other provisions of this Agreement and the competent authorities of the Contracting States shall if necessary consult each other.

Article 10 - Dividends

1. Dividends paid by a company which is a resident of a Contracting State to a resident of the other Contracting State may be taxed in that other State.
2. However, such dividends may also be taxed in the Contracting State of which the company paying the dividends is a resident and according to the laws of that State, but if the beneficial owner of the dividends is a resident of the other Contracting State, the tax so charged shall not exceed:

   a) 5 per cent of the gross amount of the dividends if the beneficial owner is a company (other than a partnership) which holds directly at least 25 per cent of the capital of the company paying the dividends;
   b) 10 per cent of the gross amount of the dividends in all other cases. The competent authorities of the Contracting States shall by mutual agreement settle the mode of application of these limitations.

This paragraph shall not affect the taxation of the company in respect of the profits out of which the dividends are paid.

3. The term "dividends" as used in this Article means income from shares or other rights, not being debt-claims, participating in profits, as well as income from other corporate rights which is subjected to the same taxation treatment as income from shares by the laws of the State of which the company making the distribution is a resident.
4. The provisions of paragraphs 1 and 2 shall not apply if the beneficial owner of the dividends, being a resident of a Contracting State, carries on business in the other Contracting State of which the company paying the dividends is a resident, through a permanent establishment situated therein, or performs in that other State independent personal services from a fixed base situated therein, and the holding in respect of which the dividends are paid is effectively connected with such permanent establishment or fixed base. In such case the provisions of Article 7 or Article 14, as the case may be, shall apply.
5. Where a company which is a resident of a Contracting State derives profits or income from the other Contracting State, that other State may not impose any tax on the dividends paid by the company, except insofar as such dividends are paid to a resident of that other State or insofar as the holding in respect of which the dividends are paid is effectively connected with a permanent establishment or a fixed base situated in that other State, nor subject the company's undistributed profits to a tax on undistributed profits, even if the dividends paid or the undistributed profits consist wholly or partly of profits or income arising in such other State.
6. The provisions of this Article shall not apply if it was the main purpose of any which the dividend is paid to take advantage of this Article by means of that creation or assignment.

Article 11 - Interest

1. Interest arising in a Contracting State and paid to a resident of the other Contracting State may be taxed in that other State.
2. However, such interest may also be taxed in the Contracting State in which it arises and according to the laws of that State, but if the beneficial owner of the interest is a resident of the other Contracting State, the tax so charged shall not exceed:

   a) 7 per cent of the gross amount of the interest if it is received by any bank or financial institution;
   b) 10 per cent of the gross amount of the interest in all other cases. The competent authorities of the Contracting States shall by mutual Agreement settle the mode of application of this limitation.

3. Notwithstanding the provisions of paragraph 2, interest derived from a Contracting State is exempt from tax in that State, if the beneficial owner is:

   a) in the case of China:

      i) the Government of the People's Republic of China and any local authority thereof;
      ii) the China Development Bank;
      iii) the Agricultural Development Bank of China;
      iv) the Export–import Bank of China;
      v) the National Council for Social Security Fund;
      vi) the China Export & Credit Insurance Corporation; and
      vii) any institution wholly owned by the Government of China as may be agreed from time to time between the competent authorities of the Contracting States.

   b) in the case of Singapore:

      i) the Government of the Republic of Singapore;
      ii) the Monetary Authority of Singapore;

iii) the Government of Singapore Investment Corporation Pte Ltd;
iv) a statutory body; and
v) any institution wholly owned by the Government of Singapore as may be agreed from time to time between the competent authorities of the Contracting States.

4. The term "interest" as used in this Article means income from debt-claims of every kind, whether or not secured by mortgage and whether or not carrying a right to participate in the debtor's profits, and in particular, income from government securities and income from bonds or debentures, including premiums and prizes attaching to such securities, bonds or debentures. Penalty charges for late payment shall not be regarded as interest for the purpose of this Article.
5. The provisions of paragraphs 1 and 2 shall not apply if the beneficial owner of the interest, being a resident of a Contracting State, carries on business in the other Contracting State in which the interest arises, through a permanent establishment situated therein, or performs in that other State independent personal services from a fixed base situated therein, and the debt-claim in respect of which the interest is paid is effectively connected with such permanent establishment or fixed base. In such case the provisions of Article 7 or Article 14, as the case may be, shall apply.
6. Interest shall be deemed to arise in a Contracting State when the payer is a resident of that State. Where, however, the person paying the interest, whether he is a resident of a Contracting State or not, has in a Contracting State a permanent establishment or a fixed base in connection with which the indebtedness on which the interest is paid was incurred, and such interest is borne by such permanent establishment or fixed base, then such interest shall be deemed to arise in the State in which the permanent establishment or fixed base is situated.
7. Where, by reason of a special relationship between the payer and the beneficial owner or between both of them and some other person, the amount of the interest, having regard to the debt claim for which it is paid, exceeds the amount which would have been agreed upon by the payer and the beneficial owner in the absence of such relationship, the provisions of this Article shall apply only to the last-mentioned amount. In such case, the excess part of the payments shall remain taxable according to the laws of each Contracting State, due regard being had to the other provisions of this Agreement.
8. The provisions of this Article shall not apply if it was the main purpose of any person concerned with the creation or assignment of the debt-claim in respect of which the interest is paid to take advantage of this Article by means of that creation or assignment.

Article 12 - Royalties

1. Royalties arising in a Contracting State and paid to a resident of the other Contracting State may be taxed in that other State.
2. However, such royalties may also be taxed in the Contracting State in which they arise and according to the laws of that State, but if the beneficial owner of the royalties is a resident of the other Contracting State, the tax so charged shall not exceed 10 per cent of the gross amount of the royalties. The competent authorities of the Contracting States shall by mutual agreement settle the mode of application of this limitation.
3. The term "royalties" as used in this Article means payments of any kind received as a consideration for the use of, or the right to use, any copyright of literary, artistic or scientific work including cinematograph films, or films or tapes for radio or television broadcasting, any computer software, patent, trade mark, design or model, plan, secret formula or process, or for the use of, or the right to use, industrial, commercial or scientific equipment or for information concerning industrial, commercial or scientific experience.

4. The provisions of paragraphs 1 and 2 shall not apply if the beneficial owner of the royalties, being a resident of a Contracting State, carries on business in the other Contracting State in which the royalties arise, through a permanent establishment situated therein, or performs in that other State independent personal services from a fixed base situated therein, and the right or property in respect of which the royalties are paid is effectively connected with such permanent establishment or fixed base. In such case, the provisions of Article 7 or Article 14, as the case may be, shall apply.
5. Royalties shall be deemed to arise in a Contracting State when the payer is a resident of that State. Where, however, the person paying the royalties, whether he is a resident of a Contracting State or not, has in a Contracting State a permanent establishment or a fixed base in connection with which the liability to pay the royalties was incurred, and such royalties are borne by such permanent establishment or fixed base, then such royalties shall be deemed to arise in the State in which the permanent establishment or fixed base is situated.
6. Where, by reason of a special relationship between the payer and the beneficial owner or between both of them and some other person, the amount of the royalties, having regard to the use, right or information for which they are paid, exceeds the amount which would have been agreed upon by the payer and the beneficial owner in the absence of such relationship, the provisions of this Article shall apply only to the last-mentioned amount. In such case, the excess part of the payments shall remain taxable according to the laws of each Contracting State, due regard being had to the other provisions of this Agreement.
7. The provisions of this Article shall not apply if it was the main purpose of any person concerned with the creation or assignment of rights in respect of which the royalties are paid to take advantage of this Article by means of that creation or assignment.

Article 13 - Capital Gains

1. Gains derived by a resident of a Contracting State from the alienation of immovable property referred to in Article 6 and situated in the other Contracting State may be taxed in that other State.
2. Gains from the alienation of movable property forming part of the business property of a permanent establishment which an enterprise of a Contracting State has in the other Contracting State or of movable property pertaining to a fixed base available to a resident of a Contracting State in the other Contracting State for the purpose of performing independent personal services, including such gains from the alienation of such a permanent establishment (alone or with the whole enterprise) or of such fixed base, may be taxed in that other State.
3. Gains derived by a resident of a Contracting State from the alienation of ships or aircraft operated in international traffic, or movable property pertaining to the operation of such ships or aircraft, shall be taxable only in that State.
4. Gains derived by a resident of a Contracting State from the alienation of shares deriving more than 50 per cent of their value directly or indirectly from immovable property situated in the other Contracting State may be taxed in that other State.
5. Subject to paragraph 4, gains derived by a resident of a Contracting State from the alienation of shares, participation, or other rights in the capital of a company or other legal person which is a resident of the other Contracting State may be taxed in that other Contracting State if the recipient of the gains, at any time during the twelve-month period preceding such alienation, had a participation, directly or indirectly, of at least 25 per cent in the capital of that company or other legal person.
6. Gains from the alienation of any property other than that referred to in the preceding paragraphs of this Article shall be taxable only in the Contracting State of which the alienator is a resident.

Article 14 - Independent Personal Services

1. Income derived by an individual who is a resident of a Contracting State from the performance of professional services or other activities of an independent character shall be taxable only in that State unless:

   a) he has a fixed base regularly available to him in the other Contracting State for the purpose of performing his activities; in that case, only so much of the income as is attributable to that fixed base may be taxed in that other Contracting State; or
   b) his stay in the other Contracting State is for a period or periods amounting to or exceeding in the aggregate 183 days within any twelve-month period; in that case, only so much of the income as is derived from his activities performed in that other State may be taxed in that other State.

2. The term "professional services" includes especially independent scientific, literary, artistic, educational or teaching activities as well as the independent activities of physicians, lawyers, engineers, architects, dentists and accountants.

Article 15 - Dependent Personal Services

1. Subject to the provisions of Articles 16, 18 and 19, salaries, wages and other similar remuneration derived by a resident of a Contracting State in respect of an employment shall be taxable only in that State unless the employment is exercised in the other Contracting State. If the employment is so exercised, such remuneration as is derived therefrom may be taxed in that other State.
2. Notwithstanding the provisions of paragraph 1, remuneration derived by a resident of a Contracting State in respect of an employment exercised in the other Contracting State shall be taxable only in the first-mentioned State if:

   a) the recipient is present in the other State for a period or periods not exceeding in the aggregate 183 days within any twelve-month period; and
   b) the remuneration is paid by, or on behalf of, an employer who is not a resident of the other State; and
   c) the remuneration is not borne by a permanent establishment or a fixed base which the employer has in the other State.

3. Notwithstanding the preceding provisions of this Article, remuneration derived in respect of an employment exercised aboard a ship or aircraft operated in international traffic by an enterprise of a Contracting State, shall be taxable only in that State.

Article 16 - Directors' Fees

Directors' fees and other similar payments derived by a resident of a Contracting State in his capacity as a member of the board of directors of a company which is a resident of the other Contracting State may be taxed in that other State.

Article 17 - Artistes And Sportsmen

1. Notwithstanding the provisions of Articles 14 and 15, income derived by a resident of a Contracting State as an entertainer, such as a theatre, motion picture, radio or television artiste, or a musician, or as a sportsman, from his personal activities as such exercised in the other Contracting State, may be taxed in that other State.
2. Where income in respect of personal activities exercised by an entertainer or a sportsman in his capacity as such accrues not to the entertainer or sportsman himself but to another person, that income may, notwithstanding the provisions of Articles 7, 14 and 15, be taxed in the Contracting State in which the activities of the entertainer or sportsman are exercised.

Article 18 - Pensions

Subject to the provisions of paragraph 2 of Article 19, pensions and other similar remuneration paid to a resident of a Contracting State in consideration of past employment shall be taxable only in that State.

Article 19 - Government Service

1.

a) Salaries, wages and other similar remuneration, other than a pension, paid by a Contracting State or a local authority or statutory body thereof to an individual in respect of services rendered to that State or authority or body shall be taxable only in that State.

b) However, such salaries, wages and other similar remuneration shall be taxable only in the other Contracting State if the services are rendered in that State and the individual is a resident of that State who:

i) is a national of that State; or

ii) did not become a resident of that State solely for the purpose of rendering the services.

2.

a) Any pension paid by, or out of funds created by, a Contracting State or a local authority or statutory body thereof to an individual in respect of services rendered to that State or authority or body shall be taxable only in that State.

b) However, such pension shall be taxable only in the other Contracting State if the individual's a resident of, and a national of, that State.

3. The provisions of Articles 15, 16, 17 and 18 shall apply to salaries, wages and other similar remuneration, and to pensions, in respect of services rendered in connection with a business carried on by a Contracting State or a local authority or statutory body thereof.

Article 20 - Students And Trainees

Payments which a student or business apprentice who is or was immediately before visiting a Contracting State a resident of the other Contracting State and who is present in the first mentioned State solely for the purpose of his education or training receives for the purpose of his maintenance, education or training shall not be taxed in that State, provided that such payments arise from sources outside that State.

Article 21 - Other Income

Items of income not dealt with in the foregoing Articles of this Agreement and arising in a Contracting State may be taxed in that State.

Article 22 - Elimination Of Double Taxation

1. In China, double taxation shall be eliminated as follows:

a) Where a resident of China derives income from Singapore the amount of tax on that income payable in Singapore in accordance with the provisions of this Agreement, may be credited against the Chinese tax imposed on that resident.
The amount of the credit, however, shall not exceed the amount of the Chinese tax on that income computed in accordance with the taxation laws and regulations of China.

b) Where the income derived from Singapore is a dividend paid by a company which is a resident of Singapore to a company which is a resident of China and which owns not less than 10 per cent of the shares of the company paying the dividend, the credit shall take into account the tax paid to Singapore by the company paying the dividend in respect of its income.

2. In Singapore, double taxation shall be avoided as follows: Where a resident of Singapore derives income from China which, in accordance with the provisions of this Agreement, may be taxed in China, Singapore shall, subject to its laws regarding the allowance as a credit against Singapore tax of tax payable in any country other than Singapore, allow the Chinese tax paid, whether directly or by deduction, as accredit against the Singapore tax payable on the income of that resident. Where such income is a dividend paid by a company which is a resident of China to a resident of Singapore which is a company owning directly or indirectly not less than 10 per cent of the share capital of the first-mentioned company, the credit shall take into account the Chinese tax paid by that company on the portion of its profits out of which the dividend is paid.
3. For the purposes of the credit referred to in paragraph 2 of this Article, Chinese tax payable shall be deemed to include the amount of Chinese tax which would have been paid if the Chinese tax had not been exempted, reduced or refunded in accordance with the Enterprise Income Tax Law of the People's Republic of China and the Detailed Rules and Regulations for the Implementation of such Law.

Article 23 - Non-Discrimination

1. Nationals of a Contracting State shall not be subjected in the other Contracting State to any taxation or any requirement connected therewith which is other or more burdensome than the taxation and connected requirements to which nationals of that other Contracting State in the same circumstances, in particular with respect to residence, are or may be subjected.
2. The taxation on a permanent establishment which an enterprise of a Contracting State has in the other Contracting State shall not be less favorably levied in that other Contracting State than the taxation levied on enterprises of that other Contracting State carrying on the same activities.
3. Nothing in this Article shall be construed as obliging a Contracting State to grant to:

   a) residents of the other Contracting State any personal allowances, reliefs and reductions for tax purposes which it grants to its own residents, or
   b) nationals of the other Contracting State those personal allowances, reliefs and reductions for tax purposes which it grants to its own nationals who are not resident in that Contracting State or to such other persons as may be specified in the taxation laws of that Contracting State.

4. Enterprises of a Contracting State, the capital of which is wholly or partly owned or controlled, directly or indirectly, by one or more residents of the other Contracting State, shall not be subjected in the first-mentioned State to any taxation or any requirement connected therewith which is other or more burdensome than the taxation and connected requirements to which other similar enterprises of the first-mentioned State are or may be subjected.
5. Where a Contracting State grants tax incentives to its nationals designed to promote social or economic development in accordance with its national policy and criteria, it shall not be construed as discrimination under this Article.6. In this Article, the term "taxation" means taxes which are the subject of this Agreement.

Article 24 - Mutual Agreement Procedure

1. Where a person considers that the actions of one or both of the Contracting States result or will result for him in taxation not in accordance with the provisions of this Agreement, he may, irrespective of the remedies provided by the domestic law of those States, present his case to the competent authority of the Contracting State of which he is a resident or, if his case comes under paragraph 1 of Article 23, to that of the Contracting

State of which he is a national. The case must be presented within 3 years from the first notification of the action resulting in taxation not in accordance with the provisions of the Agreement.

2. The competent authority shall endeavor, if the objection appears to it to be justified and if it is not itself able to arrive at a satisfactory solution, to resolve the case by mutual agreement with the competent authority of the other Contracting State, with a view to the avoidance of taxation which is not in accordance with the Agreement. Any agreement reached shall be implemented notwithstanding any time limits in the domestic law of the Contracting States.
3. The competent authorities of the Contracting States shall endeavor to resolve by mutual agreement any difficulties or doubts arising as to the interpretation or application of the Agreement. They may also consult together for the elimination of double taxation in cases not provided for in the Agreement.
4. The competent authorities of the Contracting States may communicate with each other directly for the purpose of reaching an agreement in the sense of the preceding paragraphs.

Article 25 - Exchange Of Information

1. The competent authorities of the Contracting States shall exchange such information as is foreseeably relevant for carrying out the provisions of this Agreement or to the administration or enforcement of the domestic laws concerning taxes covered by the Agreement imposed on behalf of the Contracting States or their local authorities, insofar as the taxation thereunder is not contrary to the Agreement.
2. Any information received by a Contracting State shall be treated as secret in the same manner as information obtained under the domestic laws of that State and shall be disclosed only to persons or authorities (including courts and administrative bodies) concerned with the assessment or collection of, the enforcement or prosecution in respect of, or the determination of appeals in relation to the taxes referred to in paragraph 1. Such persons or authorities shall use the information only for such purposes. They may disclose the information in public court proceedings or in judicial decisions.
3. In no case shall the provisions of paragraphs 1 and 2 be construed so as to impose on a Contracting State the obligation:

   a) to carry out administrative measures at variance with the laws and administrative practice of that or of the other Contracting State;
   b) to supply information which is not obtainable under the laws or in the normal course of the administration of that or of the other Contracting State;
   c) to supply information which would disclose any trade, business, industrial, commercial or professional secret or trade process, or information, the disclosure of which would be contrary to public policy (order public).

Article 26 - Miscellaneous Rule

Nothing in this Agreement shall prejudice the right of each Contracting State to apply its domestic laws and measures concerning the prevention of tax avoidance, whether or not described as such, insofar as they do not give rise to taxation contrary to the Agreement.

Article 27 - Members Of Diplomatic Missions And Consular Posts

Nothing in this Agreement shall affect the fiscal privileges of members of diplomatic missions or consular posts under the general rules of international law or under the provisions of special agreements.

Article 28 - Entry Into Force

1. Each of the Contracting States shall notify to the other the completion of the procedures required by its law for the bringing into force of this Agreement.
2. The Agreement shall enter into force on the date of the later of these notifications and its provisions shall have effect:

   a) in China: In respect of income derived during the taxable years beginning on or after t he first day of January next following that in which this Agreement enters into force.
   b) in Singapore: in respect of tax chargeable for any year of assessment beginning on or after 1January in the second calendar year following the year in which the Agreement enters into force.

3. The Agreement between the People's Republic of China and the Republic of Singapore for the Avoidance of Double Taxation and the Prevention of Fiscal Evasion with respect to Taxes on Income signed on 18th April 1986 shall cease to have effect for all cases covered by this Agreement as from the date on which the provisions of this Agreement commence to have effect.

Article 29 - Termination

This Agreement shall remain in force until terminated by a Contracting State. Either Contracting State may terminate the Agreement, through diplomatic channels, by giving notice of termination at least six months before the end of any calendar year after the expiration of a period of five years from the date of its entry into force. In such event, the Agreement shall cease to have effect:

a) in China: in respect of income derived during the taxable years beginning on or after the first day of January in the calendar year next following that in which the notice of termination is given.
b) in Singapore: in respect of tax chargeable for any year of assessment beginning on or after 1January in the second calendar year following the year in which the notice is given.

IN WITNESS WHEREOF the undersigned, duly authorized thereto, have signed this Agreement. DONE at Singapore on this 11th day of July 2007 in duplicate in the Chinese and English languages, both texts being equally authentic.

Protocol

At the moment of signing the Agreement between the Government of the People's Republic of China and the Government of the Republic of Singapore for the Avoidance of Double Taxation and the Prevention of Fiscal Evasion with respect to Taxes on Income (hereinafter referred to as "the Agreement"), both sides have agreed upon the following provisions which shall Forman integral part of the Agreement.

1. With respect to Article 3 (General Definitions) The term "body of persons" in paragraph 1(d) includes a trust established in a Contracting State if the domestic law of that Contracting State regards the trust as a tax resident of that State.
2. With respect to Article 8 (Shipping and Air Transport)

   a) Residents of Singapore carrying on the operation of ships or aircraft in international traffic shall be exempt from Business Tax or any other similar tax imposed on the gross receipts in China; and
   b) For residents of China carrying on the operation of ships or aircraft in international traffic, supplies of international transportation shall be zero-rated in terms of the Goods and Services Tax or any other similar tax and the input tax attributable to such supplies shall be creditable in full amount in Singapore.

3. With respect to Article 12 (Royalties) For the application of the percentage rate referred to in Paragraph 2 there shall be taken as the taxable base of the royalties paid for the use of or the right to use any industrial, commercial or scientific equipment, 60 percent of the gross amount of these payments.

IN WITNESS WHEREOF the undersigned, duly authorized thereto, have signed this Protocol. DONE at Singapore on this 11th day of July 2007 in duplicate in the Chinese and English languages, both texts being equally authentic.

9.3 European Area

9.3.1 China–European Area Bilateral Agreement's History

9.3.1.1 China–France Bilateral Agreements' History and Evolution

On May 7, 2012 the French president met Chinese president Hu Jintao at the G-20 Mexico Summit. This later followed a series of exchanges that changed the scenario in a century that will be largely characterized by the interactions between Washington, Brussels, and Beijing.

François Hollande showed an interest in enforcing the Sino–French cooperation and pushing forward economic links between the two countries. The Sino–French trade represented in 2011 only 40 % of the Sino–German trade, whose amount reached 144 billion Euros—1/3 of the total EU–China trade.

During the last decades, France and China have worked on bilateral relations to intensify communication and coordination on topics such as global governance, the G-20, the Iranian nuclear issue, the Korean nuclear issue, Darfur, and other major global/regional hot-spot issues.

Economic cooperation and trade flourished, the bilateral trade picked up steadily, and two-way investment further increased; furthermore, the two sides signed a host of intergovernmental agreements and important commercial documents on energy conservation, environmental protection, aviation, nuclear energy, telecommunications, new energy and other areas exhibited through the China–France investment promotion fair. Bilateral cultural and people-to-people exchanges progressed and strengthened through exchanges and cooperation in cultural heritage protection, artistic creation, cultural management, cultural industry, and other realms. Many joint programs between top-class Chinese and French universities were explored, established, and strengthened.

9.3.1.2 China–Germany Bilateral Agreements' History and Evolution

German and China have cemented a strong relation in a broad range of fields. China is now the world's second largest economy, and Germany is the best performing country in the indebted eurozone. There is a strong potential in China's huge market for a country with its strong high-tech industries as Germany. Furthermore, China can move up the value chain through partnerships with German companies.

The two sides maintained close high-level contacts and continued exchanges with cooperation between parliaments, political parties, and localities in science, education, culture, law, military, and other fields. The two countries had frequent high-level exchanges on bilateral ties, the Iranian nuclear issue, climate change, and other related issues. These hot topics have been discussed and deeply analyzed many times during the various meetings between the delegations of PRC and Germany. Views on the global economic and financial situation, as well as closely connected topics such as the RMB exchange rate, have been exchanged with particular concern. Afterwards a joint press communiqué on advancing China–Germany strategic partnership had been released, and the two parties agreed to set up a government consultation mechanism. In this first China–Germany joint communiqué, the two sides, as briefly expressed before, gave their bilateral ties the new status of "strategic partnership" but, most of all, agreed to upgrade their strategic dialogue and forge a partnership on energy and the environment. They proposed measures for stepping up military, economic, trade, energy, environmental, financial, cultural, people-to-people cooperation and cooperation in other fields. The German side affirmed its active support for an early EU recognition of China's full market economy status and it readiness to work for a smooth conclusion of the China–EU Partnership and Cooperation Agreement. In addition, the two sides signed ten governmental cooperation documents and commercial contracts.

In recent times, business ties between the two countries surpassed the level prior to the international financial crisis and contributed significantly to the economic stability and growth of their respective regions and the world at large. China eventually became Germany's largest non-EU trading partner with additional commercial agreements signed.

Finally, cooperation in science, education, culture, law, military, and local exchanges are proceeding smoothly between the two.

A high point in political relations in 2011 was the first round of Sino–German intergovernmental consultations. At the invitation of Federal Chancellor Angela Merkel, Chinese Prime Minister Wen Jiabao traveled to Berlin in June, accompanied by 13 ministers. Wen met with Federal Chancellor Merkel for detailed talks. Numerous agreements and memorandums of understanding are aimed at further intensifying cooperation between the two countries.

From first to fourth of February 2012, Federal Chancellor Merkel visited Beijing and the southern Chinese city of Guangzhou and met for talks with Chinese leaders. The visit kicked off a year of events marking the 40th anniversary of the establishment of diplomatic relations between the Federal Republic of Germany and the People's Republic of China.

9.3.1.3 China–Great Britain & Northern Ireland Bilateral Agreements' History

The United Kingdom, of Great Britain and Northern Ireland, recognized the People's Republic of China in 1950. The two sides reached an agreement to exchange state of affairs in 1954 and signed the "Joint Communiqué on the Agreement on the Exchange of Ambassadors" in 1972. In 1984, the two governments signed "The Joint Declaration on the Question of Hong Kong," thus ushering in a period of sound development in Sino–British relations, evidenced by exchanges of important visits and many agreements signed for cooperation in various fields. The bilateral relations, however, suffered a serious setback resulting from the UK's sanctions against China after 1989, and it was not until the latter half of the year in 1994 that any sign of improvement could be seen. Then in 1997, Prime Minister Tony Blair decided to transfer the government of Hong Kong to China, and this event improved the developing comprehensive Sino–British relations. In 1998, the two countries issued the "Joint Statement" announcing officially the establishment of their comprehensive partnership. All these high-level contacts gave further impetus to the development of bilateral relations. Presently, close contacts and frequent exchange of visits at a high level are maintained between the two countries; there is also dynamic exchange and cooperation at all levels in the fields of politics, trade, economy, culture, and military.

In particular, in recent years, it has been registered as a steady growth of trade volume with UK now becoming the second largest trade partner of China and the major European investor in the Chinese territory. On education and culture, different agreements have been signed since 1979, and in the last 15 years, many Programs of Cultural Exchanges and joint project between universities of the two countries have been established. In addition, from 1979, over 20 agreements or memorandums have been signed by relevant scientific-technological departments or institutions of the two countries, covering many different areas such as basic research, environmental protection, health, agriculture, meteorology, space, and aviation. Regarding military exchange, in 1986, China and UK signed officially the "Understanding Memorandum on Co-operation on Defense Equipment."

Trade between the UK and China is also growing. Last year, total exports in goods and services to China increased by 18 %. In the first quarter of 2012, in comparison with the same period in 2011, they have increased by a further 12 %. While those increases are impressive, there is opportunity to do much more. The share of the UK's total exports that go to China has increased to 3 % but is growing day by day, especially in services, where the UK excels. In 2010, the Prime Minister and Premier Wen agreed to a bilateral trade target of $100 billion and a goal of 250 more Chinese investment projects in the UK by 2015, and we must make sure those targets are reached, if not exceeded.

9.3.1.4 China–Luxembourg Bilateral Agreements' History and Evolution

The ties between China and Luxembourg have progressed smoothly since the two countries established diplomatic ties over 40 years ago. Particularly, in recent years, both sides have witnessed frequent exchanges of high-level visits and remarkable achievements in mutually beneficial cooperation. The two countries have also maintained sound delegations in multilateral affairs, with Luxembourg's government adhering to the one-China policy and actively developing relations with China. Even Grand Duke Henri and Luxembourg's royal family have always been committed to bilateral friendship with China and have made important contributions to relations between the two countries.

China values the friendly cooperation with Luxembourg and would like to maintain the good momentum of high-level visits and enhance dialogue at various levels, as well as communication and coordination on major international and regional issues. Both sides are expanding mutually beneficial cooperation and encouraging their companies to strengthen two-way investment. Efforts are also made to deepen bilateral cultural and educational exchanges, enrich cooperation connotations, and well implement bilateral agreement on cultural cooperation. Luxembourg is working hard to promote Chinese–EU relations, and China is ready to join Luxembourg and other EU countries to push for Chinese and EU comprehensive strategic partnership.

The two countries enjoy a sincere friendship and have conducted fruitful cooperation on trade, finance, iron and steel, satellite communications, tourism, culture, and education in recent years. China is an important partner for Luxembourg, as evidenced by the latter's readiness to expand and deepen mutually beneficial cooperation with China in all areas. Chinese–Luxembourgian agreements in the areas of trade, finance, and education have recently been signed.

In 2010, steady progress was made in the development of relations with vigorous exchanges and cooperation in various fields. New progress was made in economic cooperation and trade, with China becoming Luxembourg's second largest trading partner outside the EU and largest trading partner in Asia. Exchanges in culture, education, and other areas were also vigorous. Quite a few Luxembourg art groups staged performances in China during the Shanghai World Expo. Joint university programs between the two countries have been strengthened as well.

On the morning of May 23, 2012, Wu Bangguo, chairman of the Standing Committee of China's National People's Congress (NPC), who is on an official goodwill visit to Luxembourg, met with Prime Minister Jean-Claude Juncker at the prime minister's office. Both sides had an in-depth exchange of views and reached broad consensus on bilateral relations, pragmatic cooperation, China–EU ties, and other issues in a friendly and candid atmosphere.

The two countries have a lot of common interests and are starting to collaborate. Both sides should handle differences and entrust and expand consensus. The two nations, as Wu said, "*should especially make a point of strengthening coordination in the improvement of laws and regulations, operations and management and human resources training.*" He also suggested the "*two countries' central banks establish exchanges in the future.*"

9.3.1.5 China–Netherlands Bilateral Agreements' History and Evolution

Both countries agreed to promote relations and to develop their cooperation in trade, tourism, culture, and modern agriculture. The pledge came out of a meeting between top political advisor Jia Qinglin and Dutch Foreign Minister Uri Rosenthal, who visited China on October 8 and 9 of 2012. Bilateral relations have witnessed significant development since their establishment 40 years ago and are facing new opportunities in the future, said Jia, chairman of the National Committee of the Chinese People's Political Consultative Conference (CPPCC), the country's top political advisory body. He said China is ready to further enhance political mutual trust with the Netherlands, take each other's core interests and major concerns into consideration, expand comprehensive trade relations, and conduct closer cooperation in tourism, education, and culture. Jia said the two sides should prioritize the development of people-to-people and cultural exchanges and push China–Netherlands relations to a new high. Rosenthal said the establishment of relations 40 years ago laid an important foundation for their development today. He reaffirmed Netherlands' adherence to the one-China policy and respect for China's sovereignty and territorial integrity. The minister also called on the two countries to strengthen cooperation in trade, energy, logistics, and modern agriculture so as to promote bilateral relations. The two sides also exchanged views on the current situation in Europe and overall China–Europe relations. Jia said strengthening the comprehensive strategic relationship between China and Europe is important for world peace and the stable growth of the global economy. He said China and Europe should make joint efforts to promote the sound and stable development of their relations.

Economic cooperation and trade ensured rapid development momentum with trade volume between the two countries growing continually in recent years. The Netherlands remained China's second largest trading partner in the EU for the eighth consecutive year. Bilateral cooperation was successful in water resources management, new energy development, agriculture, energy conservation, and environmental protection, and two-way investment expanded greatly. Steady progress was made in education, science, technology and culture. Joint school programs are expanding in size with Dutch people showing a greater interest in learning the Chinese language. The Program Strategic Scientific Alliances (PSA) and Joint Scientific Thematic Research Program (JSTP) between China and the Netherlands are also advancing steadily. Moreover, the two countries are enjoying even closer cooperation in counter-piracy and international peacekeeping.

9.3.1.6 China–Russia Bilateral Agreements' History and Evolution

Putin visited China last June 2012 to discuss about the enlargement of the cooperation between Russia and China in various fields. Since Russia and China signed the Treaty on Good-Neighborliness, Friendship and Cooperation in 2001, the two countries have witnessed many breakthroughs in the development of their relations.

The two countries explored different ways to promote their economic relations, conduct joint border inspections and rational ways to protect their borders. This was especially prevalent in 2011, when the two countries initiated strategic cooperation in the energy sector, launched reciprocal National Years and Years of Languages, and was in close coordination regarding international affairs.

Since the leaders of the two countries decided to upgrade their relationship, both China and Russia have made concerted efforts to reinforce their mutual trust and strategic partnership.

Diplomatic relations between China and Russia began more than 60 years ago with contracts between the two countries yearly totaling to over billions of dollars. In 1991, Moscow and Beijing entered into an initial agreement on strategic cooperation, in 2001, signed a treaty of good neighborliness and friendly cooperation, and in 2008, at least apparently, resolved the vexed question of defining the borders. Today, from a purely commercial point of view, the partnership between the two countries is changing. In 2008, trade reached 56.83 billion dollars and China is the third largest trading partner of Russia, while Russia is the eleventh for China.

On the political front, the two countries base their relation on the principle of "non-alliance, non-rivalry and non-hostility towards third countries." Thus, Moscow and Beijing, both permanent members of UN Security Council, are committed to cooperate on international issues to the extent to which their national interest is compatible: this is the case of Iran, Afghanistan, and North Korea. Both countries have an interest in the success of the stabilization effort promoted by the United States.

However, economy is the most relevant field of agreements between China and Russia. The two countries share important lines of credit and continuously define relevant financing deals. Regarding infrastructure, in Tianjin, a port city located east of Beijing, Russia and China built up a refinery joint venture and managed together 300 to 500 filling stations. In any case, the most important agreement between the two countries is related to the supplies of Russian gas to China. Gazprom, the Russian monopoly, negotiates every year with China to define the supply amount and the relative prices. Among the international issues, China and Russia continue to have a substantial uniformity of views against the Iranian and North Korean nuclear situation and the turmoil in Afghanistan. Both Moscow and Beijing disagree to impose new sanctions against Tehran or Pyongyang, insisting on the need of staying on the path of negotiation.

The implications of these bilateral agreements reveal a not obvious desire for collaboration and mutual trust. The reason for this strong partnership is mutually beneficial; Russia, hard hit by the global financial crisis, is facing a sharp decline in consumption in Europe and is increasingly looking to Asia-Pacific markets, where instead the demand is growing. For its part, China needs to diversify its sources of supply, and Russian energy resources are probably its best decision. The two superpowers need each other despite the great differences of their economies. On the one hand, there is Beijing's liquidity and financial resources, and on the other hand, there exists Moscow's oil and gas. The deals are closed in the energetic field serving the needs of both countries: Russian economic and financial needs paired with Chinese energetic needs.

9.3.1.7 China–Spain Bilateral Agreements' History and Evolution

China and Spain decided to expand their cooperation in trade and strategic partnership. The pledge was made in May 24th 2012, during a meeting between two top legislators, Wu Bangguo and Mariano Rajoy.

During the meeting, Wu, chairman of the Standing Committee of China's National People's Congress (NPC), made three-point proposal about their collaboration:

> First "*the two countries should scale up two-way investment and trade. Active and effective measures are needed to bring into full play the role of cooperation mechanisms. China, encourages its enterprises to import competitive and marketable products from Spain, such as wine and olive oil, so as to promote a more balanced trade and facilitate trade and investment*" Wu said.
>
> Second, "*the two countries should tap the potential of cooperation in emerging fields, such as renewable energy. China is making efforts to optimize its energy mix by implementing policies to promote the development of renewable energy, adding that Spain is a world leader in developing wind power and solar power. China is willing to learn from Spain's experiences in power generation management and to introduce cutting-edge technologies and equipment.*" he said.
>
> Third, "*they should strengthen people-to-people and cultural exchanges. Both China and Spain enjoy ancient civilizations and the two peoples are attracted by each other's history and culture*" Wu said.

Wu expressed hope that Spain and China could reinforce promotional campaigns and make better conditions to cooperate in culture, education, sports, and tourism. Rajoy, said Spain attaches great importance to developing friendly ties with China.

During the meeting, Rajoy thanked China for the aid offered to his country during the debt crisis: support to the Spanish government, belief in its ability and conditions to tide over temporary difficulty, and readiness to deepen practical cooperation with Spain. China, as from Wu's point of view, will support Europe's effort to overcome the current difficulties.

Parliamentary exchanges between the two sides have been very close with the special committees of the two sides enjoying sound cooperation. The government departments of the two countries engaged in frequent dialogue and contacts in particular ministries of China and Spain, exchanging views on the international economic and financial situation (further strengthening of bilateral cooperation).

Close consultation and dialogue, as well as cooperation on major international and regional issues, have always been the heart of the relationship between these countries. A key role has been the advancement of Chinese and EU relations during the Spanish Presidency of the EU in the first half of 2010.

Bilateral economic, technological, and investment cooperation maintained a good momentum in the last few years. In December 2010, the 22nd meeting of the Chinese and Spanish Joint Economic and Trade Commission was held in Beijing. Cultural and people-to-people exchanges continued to expand. In April 2010, several educational activities were sponsored by China and Spain, including the third Chinese and Spanish University Presidents Forum, the opening ceremony and art performance for the "Chinese Language Year," and China–Spain cultural dialogue. Vice Education Minister Hao Ping and Minister of Education Angel Gabilondo attended the opening ceremony of the "Chinese Language Year" on April 12. In November, the "2010 China Tibetan Culture Week" was held in Madrid and Valencia.

9.3.1.8 China–Switzerland Bilateral Agreements' History and Evolution

In July 11th 2012, Swiss Economics Minister Johann Schneider-Ammann said, "*There are still many problems and challenges, but I'm very confident that we can find a solution before the end of the yea*r," with the hope that Switzerland and China can sign a free trade agreement soon. The economics minister's entourage includes 25 captains of industry, a dozen officials, and several journalists. In Beijing, the Swiss organized the Sino–Swiss Economic Forum, which brought together 300 Swiss and Chinese business people. "*The Swiss mission has a strong symbolic aspect, allowing us to get to get to know our partners better. It is crucial to develop a positive relationship*," said Stéphane Graber of the Swiss-Chinese Chamber of Commerce.

Labor, human rights, and development in China were included in the speech that Schneider-Ammann had with Chinese officials. Furthermore, Christian Etter, Switzerland's chief negotiator, insisted that any free trade agreement should include an exception clause to prevent the entry of products into Switzerland from prisons or labor camps.

From 2012, the bilateral relationship between the two countries enjoyed sound development with cooperative efforts in their politics, economy, education, science and technology, culture, and other fields. China and Switzerland enjoyed close high-level exchanges and economic cooperation with trade. During President Doris Leuthard's visit to China, the *Memorandum of Understanding Between the Ministry of Commerce of the People's Republic of China and the Federal Department of Economic Affairs of the Swiss Confederation on the Conclusion of the Joint Feasibility Study for a China–Switzerland Free Trade Agreement* was signed.

The two countries had dynamic exchanges and cooperation in the educational, cultural, and military fields between localities. From September 16 to December

Table 9.19 European Union imports (Product Grouping from China, 2012)

	2007		2009		2011	
Product groups	Millions Euro	%	Millions Euro	%	Millions Euro	%
Primary products	9,207.8	4.0	6,586.2	3.1	10,466.7	3.6
Agricultural products	5,180.0	2.2	4,860.0	2.3	6,731.1	2.3
Fuels and mining goods	4,027.8	1.7	1,726.2	0.8	3,735.6	1.3
Manufactures	222,074.8	95.5	206,619.0	96.5	278,682.4	95.4
Iron and steel	8,495.8	3.7	1,844.8	0.9	4,742.0	1.6
Chemicals	7,535.8	3.2	7,939.0	3.7	12,955.5	4.4
Semi-manufactures	20,296.2	8.7	16,655.6	7.8	22,837.2	7.8
Machinery	107,363.3	46.2	101,496.5	47.4	143,432.1	49.1
Office equipment	70,346.2	30.2	66,587.7	31.1	91,872.2	31.5
Transport equipment	5,894.9	2.5	7,104.4	3.3	10,305.3	3.5
Other machinery	31,120.3	13.4	27,804.5	13.0	41,254.6	14.1
Textiles	5,443.7	2.3	5,045.0	2.4	7,151.9	2.4
Clothing	23,711.3	10.2	27,388.5	12.8	31,876.8	10.9
Other manufactures	49,228.8	21.2	46,249.7	21.6	55,686.8	19.1
Other products	495.1	0.2	721.0	0.3	932.7	0.3
Total	232,628.1	100	214,147.7	100	292,070.9	100

Source: Eurostat, 2012

7, 2010, "The Cultural Landscape Arts Festival- China as Guest of Honor" was staged in Basle (Switzerland), and from November 24 to December 24, "Experience China in Geneva" was hosted. Other important events and visits of prominent and distinguished people were organized between both Switzerland and China. Furthermore, by the end of 2010, five sister state/province or city pairs had been formed between the two countries (Tables 9.19, 9.20, 9.21, 9.22, and 9.23).

9.3.2 France–China Treaty

The Government of the People's Republic of China and the Government of the French Republic, desiring to conclude an Agreement for the avoidance of double taxation and the prevention of fiscal evasion with respect to taxes on income, have agreed as follows:

Article 1 - Personal Scope

This Agreement shall apply to persons who are residents of one or both of the Contracting States.

Article 2 - Taxes Covered

1. This Agreement shall apply to taxes on income imposed on behalf of a Contracting State or of its local authorities, irrespective of the manner in which they are levied.

Table 9.20 European Union Export (Product Grouping to China, 2012)

	2007		2009		2011	
Product groups	Millions Euro	%	Millions Euro	%	Millions Euro	%
Primary products	8,415.0	11.7	9,657.3	11.7	18,089.9	13.3
Agricultural products	3,255.0	4.5	3,858.4	4.7	8,019.1	5.9
Fuels and mining goods	5,160.0	7.2	5,798.9	7.0	10,070.8	7.4
Manufactures	61,737.5	86.0	70,895.9	86.1	115,965.7	85.1
Iron and steel	2,495.3	3.5	2,131.9	2.6	2,204.2	1.6
Chemicals	7,403.8	10.3	10,097.9	12.3	14,798.5	10.9
Semi-manufactures	4,019.7	5.6	4,221.1	5.1	6,333.3	4.6
Machinery	42,639.3	59.4	48,284.8	58.7	82,020.2	60.2
Office equipment	5,010.5	7.0	4,497.7	5.5	4,935.8	3.6
Transport equipment	12,808.7	17.8	14,569.3	17.7	33,535.4	24.6
Other machinery	24,150.7	33.6	28,489.2	34.6	42,972.8	31.5
Textiles	701.7	1.0	666.8	0.8	965.6	0.7
Clothing	201.8	0.3	301.1	0.4	627.8	0.5
Other manufactures	4,254.9	5.9	5,119.8	6.2	8,962.9	6.6
Other products	768.8	1.1	948.4	1.2	1,107.7	0.8
Total	71,787.7	100	82,311.8	100	136,216.9	100

Source: Eurostat, 2012

Table 9.21 EU trade with China from 2007 to 2012 (millions of Euro)

Period	Imports	Variation (%, y-o-y)	Share of total EU imports (%)	Exports	Variation (%, y-o-y)	Share of total EU exports (%)	Balance	Trade
2007	232,628	19.4	16.1	71,788	12.7	5.8	**−160,840**	**304,416**
2008	247,856	6.5	15.7	78,245	9.0	5.9	**−169,611**	**326,102**
2009	214,236	−13.6	17.4	82,320	5.2	7.5	**−131,916**	**296,555**
2010	282,522	31.9	18.5	113,269	37.6	8.3	**−169,253**	**395,791**
2011	293,281	3.8	17.1	136,343	20.4	8.7	**−156,938**	**429,624**
2011 Q1	71,419	–	16.8	32,527	–	8.7	**−38,892**	**103,946**
2011 Q2	69,382	–	16.2	33,156	–	8.7	**−36,226**	**102,538**
2011 Q3	77,824	–	18.0	34,011	–	8.7	**−43,813**	**111,836**
2011 Q4	74,656	–	17.3	36,648	–	8.9	**−38,007**	**111,304**
2012 Q1	69,956	−2.0	15.5	35,850	10.2	8.8	**−34,106**	**105,806**
2012 Q2	70,487	1.6	16.0	36,879	11.2	8.7	**−33,608**	**107,366**
2012 Q3	76,900	−1.2	17.1	35,448	4.2	8.3	**−41,452**	**112,348**
2012 Q4	–	–	–	–	–	–	**–**	**–**

Source: European Commission, 2012

2. There shall be regarded as taxes on income all taxes imposed on total income or on elements of income, including taxes on gains from the alienation of movable or immovable property, as well as taxes on capital appreciation.

Table 9.22 EU's trade with main partners extra EU 27 (millions of Euro) 2011

The major import partners				The major export partners			
1	**China**	**293,281.3**	**17.1 %**	1	US	263,638.5	16.9 %
2	Russia	199,092.9	11.6 %	2	Switzerland	139,510.3	9.0 %
3	US	190,911.0	11.1 %	**3**	**China**	**136,343.0**	**8.7 %**
4	Norway	93,766.5	5.5 %	4	Russia	108,313.4	7.0 %
5	Switzerland	91,837.6	5.3 %	5	Turkey	72,977.2	4.7 %
6	Japan	69,145.3	4.0 %	6	Japan	49,004.9	3.1 %
7	Turkey	48,059.7	2.8 %	7	Norway	46,661.6	3.0 %
8	India	39,587.9	2.3 %	8	India	40,545.8	2.6 %
9	Brazil	38,909.4	2.3 %	9	Brazil	35,739.9	2.3 %
10	South Korea	36,107.6	2.1 %	10	Arab Emirates	33,300.8	2.1 %

Source: European Commission, 2012

Table 9.23 China's trade with main partners extra EU 27 (millions of Euro) 2011

The major import partners				The major export partners			
1	**EU 27**	**159,312.8**	**13.1 %**	**1**	**EU 27**	**268,700.0**	**19.1 %**
2	Japan	146,647.1	12.0 %	2	US	245,044.9	17.4 %
3	South Korea	121,952.9	10.0 %	**3**	Hong Kong	201,792.3	14.4 %
4	US	89,887.6	7.4 %	4	Japan	111,103.6	7.9 %
5	Australia	61,046.8	5.0 %	5	South Korea	62,551.6	4.4 %
6	Malaysia	46,780.8	3.8 %	6	India	38,084.5	2.7 %
7	Brazil	39,714.0	2.8 %	7	Russia	29,332.3	2.1 %
8	Saudi Arabia	37,372.6	3.1 %	8	Singapore	26,625.5	1.9 %
9	Russia	29,451.1	2.4 %	9	Australia	25,576.3	1.8 %
10	Thailand	29,448.5	2.4 %	10	Brazil	24,028.3	1.7 %

Source: European Commission, 2012

3. The existing taxes to which the Agreement shall apply are:

   a) In the People's Republic of China:

      I) the individual income tax;
      II) the income tax concerning joint ventures with Chinese and foreign investment;
      III) the income tax concerning foreign enterprises;
      IV) the local income tax; including any withholding taxes and any prepayments with respect to the aforesaid taxes (hereinafter referred to as "Chinese tax");

   b) In the French Republic:

      I) the tax on income (imptsur le revenu);
      II) the tax on companies (imptsur les sociétés), including any withholding taxes and any prepayments with respect to the aforesaid taxes (hereinafter referred to as "French tax").

4. The Agreement shall apply also to any taxes which are identical or substantially similar to the taxes mentioned in paragraph 3 of this Article and which are imposed after the date of signature of the Agreement in addition to, or in place of, the existing taxes. If opportune, the competent authorities of the Contracting States shall notify each other of changes which have been made in their respective taxation laws.

Article 3 - General Definitions

1. For the purposes of this Agreement, unless the context otherwise requires:

   a) the term "a Contracting State" and "the other Contracting State" mean the People's Republic of China or the French Republic, as the context requires;
   b) the term "tax" means Chinese tax or French tax, as the context requires;
   c) the term "person" includes an individual, a company and any other body of persons;
   d) the term "company" means any corporate or any entity which is treated as a body corporate for tax purposes;
   e) the terms "enterprise of a Contracting State" and "enterprise of the other Contracting State" mean respectively an enterprise carried on by a resident of a Contracting State and an enterprise carried on by a resident of the other Contracting State;
   f) the term "nationals" means all individuals possessing the nationality of a Contracting State and all legal entities constituted in accordance with the law in force in a Contracting State, as well as any person which is not a body corporate but which is treated as a body corporate under the laws of that Contracting State for tax purposes;
   g) the term "competent authority" means:

      i) in the case of the People's Republic of China, the Ministry of Finance or its authorized representative;
      ii) in the case of the French Republic, the Minister of the Budget or his authorized representative.

2. As regards the application of the Agreement by a Contracting State any term not defined therein shall, unless the context otherwise requires, have the meaning which it has under the law of that State concerning the taxes to which the Agreement applies.

Article 4 – Resident

1. For the purposes of this Agreement, the term "resident of a Contracting State" means any person who, under the laws of that State, is liable to tax therein by reason of his domicile, residence, place of head office or any other criterion of a similar nature.
2. Where by reason of the provisions of paragraph 1 an individual is a resident of both Contracting States, the competent authorities of the Contracting States shall settle by mutual agreement the State where such person is a resident.
3. Where by reason of the provisions of paragraph 1 a person other than an individual is a resident of both Contracting States, then it shall be deemed to be a resident of the Contracting State in which its place of head office is situated.

Article 5 - Permanent Establishment

1. For the purposes of this Agreement, the term "permanent establishment" means affixed place of business through which the business of an enterprise is wholly or partly carried on.
2. The term "permanent establishment" includes especially:

   a) a place of management;
   b) a branch;
   c) an office;
   d) a factory;
   e) a workshop; and
   f) a mine, an oil or gas well, a quarry or any other place of extraction of natural resources.

3. The term "permanent establishment" shall also include:
   a) a building site or installation or assembly project, but only if it lasts for more than 6 months;
   b) the furnishing of services, including consultancy services, by an enterprise through employees or other personnel engaged by the enterprise for such purposes, but only where such activities continue (for the same or a connected project) within the country for a period or periods aggregating more than six months within any twelve-month period.
4. Notwithstanding the provisions of paragraphs 1 to 3, the term "permanent establishment" shall be deemed not to include:
   a) the use of facilities solely for the purpose of storage, display or delivery of goods or merchandise belonging to the enterprise;
   b) the maintenance of a stock of goods or merchandise belonging to the enterprise solely for the purpose of storage, display or delivery;
   c) the maintenance of a stock of goods or merchandise belonging to the enterprise solely for the purpose of processing by another enterprise;
   d) the maintenance of a fixed place of business solely for the purpose of purchasing goods or merchandise or of collecting information, for the enterprise;
   e) the maintenance of a fixed place of business solely for the purpose of carrying on, for the enterprise, any other activity of a preparatory or auxiliary character.
5. Notwithstanding the provisions of paragraphs 1 and 2, where a person, other than an agent of an independent status to whom paragraph 6 applies, is acting in a Contracting State on behalf of an enterprise of the other Contracting State and has, and habitually exercises, in the first-mentioned Contracting State an authority to conclude contracts in the name of the enterprise, that enterprise shall be deemed to have a permanent establishment in that State in respect of any activities which that person undertakes for the enterprise, unless the activities of such a person are limited to those mentioned in paragraph 4 which, if exercised through a fixed place of business a permanent establishment under the provisions of that paragraph.
6. An enterprise of a Contracting State shall not be deemed to have a permanent establishment in the other Contracting State merely because it carries on business in that other State through a broker, general commission agent or any other agent of an independent status, provided that such a person is acting in the ordinary course of his business. However, when the activities of such an agent are devoted wholly or almost wholly on behalf of that enterprise, he shall not be considered an agent of an independent status within the meaning of this paragraph.
7. The fact that a company which is a resident of a Contracting State controls or is controlled by a company which is a resident of the other Contracting State, or which carries on business in that other State (whether through a permanent establishment or otherwise), shall not of itself constitute either company a permanent establishment of the other.

Article 6 - Income From Immovable Property

1. Income derived by a resident of a Contracting State from immovable property situated in the other Contracting State may be taxed in that other State.
2. The term "immovable property" shall have the meaning which it has under the law of the Contracting State in which the property in question is situated. The term shall in any case include property accessory to immovable property, livestock and equipment used in agriculture and forestry, rights to which the provisions of general law respecting landed property apply, usufruct of immovable property and rights to variable or fixed payments

as consideration for the working of, or the right to work, mineral deposits, sources and other natural resources; ships and aircraft shall not be regarded as immovable property.
3. The provisions of paragraph 1 shall apply to income derived from the direct use, letting, or use in any other form of immovable property.
4. The provisions of paragraphs 1 and 3 shall also apply to the income from immovable property of an enterprise and to income from immovable property used for the performance of independent personal services.

Article 7 - Business Profits

1. The profits of an enterprise of a Contracting State shall be taxable only in that State unless the enterprise carries on business in the other Contracting State through a permanent establishment situated therein. If the enterprise carries on business as aforesaid, the profits of the enterprise may be taxed in the other State but only so much of them as is attributable to that permanent establishment.
2. Subject to the provisions of paragraph 3, where an enterprise of a Contracting State carries on business in the other Contracting State through a permanent establishment situated therein, there shall in each Contracting State be attributed to that permanent establishment the profits which it might be expected to make if it were a distinct and separate enterprise engaged in the same or similar activities under the same or similar conditions and dealing wholly independently with the enterprise of which it is a permanent establishment.
3. In the determination of the profits of a permanent establishment, there shall be allowed as deductions expenses which are incurred for the purposes of the business of the permanent establishment including executive and general administrative expenses so incurred, whether in the Contracting State in which the permanent establishment is situated or elsewhere. However, no such deduction shall be allowed in respect of amounts, if any, paid (otherwise than towards reimbursement of actual expenses) by the permanent establishment to the head office of the enterprise or any of its other offices, by way of royalties, fees or other similar payments in return for the use of patents or other rights, or by way of commission, for specific services performed or for management, or, except in the case of a banking enterprise, by way of interest on moneys lent to the permanent establishment. Likewise, no account shall be taken, in the determination of the profits of a permanent establishment, of amounts charged (otherwise than towards reimbursement of actual expenses) by the permanent establishment to the head office of the enterprise or any of its other offices, by way of royalties, fees or other similar payments, or by way of commission for specific services performed or for management, or, except in the case of a banking enterprise, by way of interest on moneys lent to the head office of the enterprise or any of its other offices.
4. Insofar as it has been customary in a Contracting State to determine the profits to be attributed to a permanent establishment on the basis of an apportionment of the total profits of the enterprise to its various parts, nothing in paragraph 2 shall preclude that State from determining the profits to be taxed by such an apportionment as maybe customary; the method of apportionment adopted shall, however, be such that the result shall be in accordance with the principles contained in this Article.
5. No profits shall be attributed to a permanent establishment by reason of the mere purchase by that permanent establishment of goods or merchandise for the enterprise.
6. For the purposes of paragraphs 1 to 5, the profits to be attributed to the permanent establishment shall be determined by the same method year by year unless there is good and sufficient reason to the contrary.
7. Where profits include items of income which are dealt with separately in other Articles of this Agreement, then the provisions of those Articles shall not be affected by the provisions of this Article.

Article 8 - Associated Enterprises

Where:

a) an enterprise of a Contracting State participates directly or indirectly in the management, control or capital of an enterprise of the other Contracting State, or
b) the same persons participate directly or indirectly in the management, control or capital of an enterprise of a Contracting State and an enterprise of the other Contracting State, and in either case the commercial or financial relations between the two enterprises differ from those which would be made between independent enterprises, then any profits which would, but for those conditions, have accrued to one of the enterprises, but, by reason of those conditions, have not so accrued, may be included in the profits of that enterprise and taxed accordingly.

Article 9 – Dividends

1. Dividends paid by a company which is a resident of a Contracting State to a resident of the other Contracting State may be taxed in that other State.
2. However, such dividends may also be taxed in the Contracting State of which the company paying the dividends is a resident and according to the laws of that State, but if the recipient is the beneficial owner of the dividends the tax so charged shall in any case not exceed 10 per cent of the gross amount of the dividends.

This paragraph shall not affect the taxation of the company in respect of the profits out of which the dividends are paid.

3. The term "dividends" as used in this Article means income from shares or other rights, not being debt-claims, participating in profits as well as other income which is subjected to the same taxation treatment as income from shares by the laws of the Contracting State of which the company making the distribution is a resident.
4. The provisions of paragraphs 1 and 2 shall not apply if the beneficial owner of the dividends, being a resident of a Contracting State, carries on business in the other Contracting State of which the company paying the dividends is a resident, through a permanent establishment situated therein, or performs in that other State independent personal services from a fixed base situated therein and the holding in respect of which the dividends are paid is effectively connected with such permanent establishment or fixed base. In such case the provisions of Article 7 or Article 13, as the case may be, shall apply.
5. A resident of China who receives dividends paid by a company which is a resident of France may claim a refund of the prepayment (précompte) relating to those French dividends. Such refund may be taxed in France in accordance with the provisions of paragraph 2.
6. Where a company which is a resident of a Contracting State derives profits or income from the other Contracting State, that other State may not impose any tax on the dividends paid by the company, except insofar as such dividends are paid to a resident of that other State or insofar as the holding in respect of which the dividends are paid is effectively connected with a permanent establishment or a fixed base situated in that other State, nor subject the company's undistributed profits to a tax on the company's undistributed profits, even if the dividends paid or the undistributed profits consist wholly or partly of profits or income arising in such other State.

Article 10 - Interest

1. Interest arising in a Contracting State and paid to a resident of the other Contracting State may be taxed in that other State.
2. However, such interest may also be taxed in the Contracting State in which it arises and according to the laws of that State, but if the recipient is the beneficial owner of the

interest the tax so charged shall not exceed 10 per cent of the gross amount of the interest.

3. Notwithstanding the provisions of paragraph 2, interest derived from a Contracting State is exempt from tax in that State, if it is paid:

   a) in the case of the People's Republic of China:

      i) to the Government of the People's Republic of China;
      ii) to the People's Bank of China;
      iii) on a loan directly or indirectly financed or guaranteed by the Bank of China or the Chinese International Trust and Investment Company (CITIC);
      iv) to a financial establishment appointed by the Government of the People's Republic of China and mutually agreed upon by the competent authorities of the two Contracting States;

   b) in the case of the French Republic:

      i) to the Government of the French Republic;
      ii) to the Bank of France;
      iii) on a loan, directly or indirectly financed or guaranteed by the French Bank for Foreign Trade or by the French Foreign Trade Insurance Company;
      iv) to a financial establishment appointed by the Government of the French Republic and mutually agreed upon by the competent authorities of the two Contracting States.

4. The term "interest" as used in this Article means income from debt-claims of every kind, whether or not secured by mortgage and whether or not carrying a right to participate in the debtor's profits, and in particular, income from government securities and income from bonds or debentures, including premiums and prizes attaching to such securities, bonds or debentures.
5. The provisions of paragraphs 1, 2 and 3 shall not apply if the beneficial owner of the interest, being a resident of a Contracting State, carries on business in the other Contracting State in which the interest arises, through a permanent establishment situated therein, or performs in that other State independent personal services from affixed base situated therein, and the debt-claim in respect of which the interest is paid is effectively connected with such permanent establishment or fixed base. In such case the provisions of Article 7 or Article 13, as the case may be, shall apply.
6. Interest shall be deemed to arise in a Contracting State when the payer is that State itself, a local authority or a resident of that State. Where, however, the person paying the interest, whether he is a resident of a Contracting State or not, has in a Contracting State a permanent establishment or a fixed base in connection with which the indebtedness on which the interest is paid was incurred, and such interest is borne by such permanent establishment or fixed base, then such interest shall be deemed to arise in the Contracting State in which the permanent establishment or fixed base is situated.
7. Where, by reason of a special relationship between the payer and the beneficial owner or between both of them and some other person, the amount of the interest, having regard to the debt-claim for which it is paid, exceeds the amount which would have been agreed upon by the payer and the beneficial owner in the absence of such relationship, the provisions of this Article shall apply only to the last-mentioned amount. In such case, the excess part of the payments shall remain taxable according to the laws of each Contracting State, due regard being had to the other provisions of this Agreement.

Article 11 – Royalties

1. Royalties arising in a Contracting State and paid to a resident of the other Contracting State shall be taxable only in that other State.
2. However, such royalties may also be taxed in the Contracting State in which they arise and according to the laws of that State, but if the recipient is the beneficial owner of the royalties, the tax so charged shall not exceed 10 per cent of the gross amount of the royalties.
3. The term "royalties" as used in this Article means payments of any kind received as a consideration for the use of, or the right to use, any copyright of literary, artistic or scientific work including cinematograph films and films and tapes recorded for broadcasting or television, any patent, know-how, trade mark, design or model plan, secret formula or process, or for the use of, or the right to use, industrial, commercial, or scientific equipment, or for information concerning industrial, commercial or scientific experience.
4. The provisions of paragraphs 1 and 2 shall not apply if the beneficial owner of the royalties, being a resident of a Contracting State, carries on business in the other Contracting State in which the royalties arise, through a permanent establishment situated therein, or performs in that other State independent personal services from affixed base situated therein, and the right or property in respect of which the royalties are paid is effectively connected with such permanent establishment or fixed base. In such case the provisions of Article 7 or Article 13, as the case may be, shall apply.
5. Royalties shall be deemed to arise in a Contracting State when the payer is the Government of that State itself, a local authority or a resident of that Contracting State. Where, however, the person paying the royalties, whether he is a resident of a Contracting State or not, has in a State a permanent establishment or a fixed base in connection with which the obligation to pay the royalties was incurred, and those royalties are borne by that permanent establishment or fixed base, then such royalties shall be deemed to arise in the Contracting State in which the permanent establishment or fixed base is situated.
6. Where, by reason of a special relationship between the payer and the beneficial owner or between both of them and some other person, the amount of the royalties, having regard to the use, right or information for which they are paid, exceeds the amount which would have been agreed upon by the payer and the beneficial owner in the absence of such relationship, the provisions of this Article shall apply only to the last-mentioned amount. In such case, the excess part of the payments shall remain taxable according to the laws of each Contracting State, due regard being had to the other provisions of this Agreement.

Article 12 - Capital Gains

1. Gains derived by a resident of a Contracting State from the alienation of immovable property referred to in Article 6 and situated in the other Contracting State may be taxed in that other Contracting State.
2. Gains from the alienation of movable property forming part of the business property of a permanent establishment which an enterprise of a Contracting State has in the other Contracting State or of movable property pertaining to a fixed base available to a resident of a Contracting State in the other Contracting State for the purpose of performing independent personal services, including such gains from the alienation of such a permanent establishment (alone or with the whole enterprise) or of such a fixed base, may be taxed in that other Contracting State.
3. Gains from the alienation of ships or aircraft operated in international traffic and movable property pertaining to the operation of such ships or aircraft which are received by a resident of a Contracting State may only be taxed in that State.

4. Gains from the alienation of shares in the capital of a company, the assets of which consist mainly, directly or indirectly, of immovable property situated in a Contracting State, may be taxed in that Contracting State.
5. Gains derived from the alienation of shares, other than those mentioned in paragraph 4 and which represent a participation of 25 per cent in a company which is a resident of a Contracting State, may be taxed in that Contracting State.
6. Gains which a resident of a Contracting State derives from the alienation of any property other than that mentioned in paragraphs 1 to 5 above, may be taxed in the other Contracting State, if those gains are derived therefrom.

Article 13 - Independent Personal Services

1. Income derived by a resident of a Contracting State in respect of professional services or other activities of an independent character shall be taxable only in that Contracting State; however, such income may also be taxed in the other Contracting State in the following circumstances:

   a) if he has a fixed base regularly available to him in the other Contracting State for the purpose of performing his activities; in such case so much of the income as is attributable to that fixed base may be taxed in that other Contracting State; or
   b) if his stay in the other Contracting State is for a period or periods exceeding in the aggregate 183 days in the calendar year concerned; in such case only so much of the income as is derived from the activities performed in that other Contracting State may be taxed in that other State.

2. The term "professional services" includes especially independent scientific, literary, artistic, educational or teaching activities as well as the independent activities of physicians, lawyers, engineers, architects, dentists and accountants.

Article 14 - Dependent Personal Services

1. Subject to the provisions of Articles 15, 17, 18, 19 and 20, salaries, wages and other similar remuneration derived by a resident of a Contracting State in respect of an employment shall be taxable only in that Contracting State unless the employment is exercised in the other Contracting State. If the employment is so exercised, such remuneration as is derived therefrom may be taxed in that other Contracting State.
2. Notwithstanding the provisions of paragraph 1, remuneration derived by a resident of a Contracting State in respect of an employment exercised in the other Contracting State shall be taxable only in the first-mentioned State: if the three following conditions are simultaneously met:

   a) the recipient is present in the other Contracting State for a period or periods not exceeding in the aggregate 183 days in the calendar year concerned; and
   b) the remuneration is paid by, or on behalf of, an employer who is not a resident of the other State; and
   c) the remuneration is not borne by a permanent establishment or a fixed base which the employer has in the other Contracting State.

3. Notwithstanding the provisions of paragraphs 1 and 2, remuneration derived in respect of an employment exercised aboard a ship or aircraft operated in international traffic by an enterprise of a Contracting State may be taxed in that Contracting State.

Article 15 - Directors' Fees

Directors' fees and other similar payments derived by a resident of a Contracting State in his capacity as a member of the board of directors of a company which is a resident of the other Contracting State may be taxed in that other State.

Article 16 - Artistes And Athletes

1. Notwithstanding the provisions of Articles 13 and 14, income derived by a resident of a Contracting State as an entertainer, such as a theatre, motion picture, radio or television artiste, or a musician, or as an athlete, from his personal activities as such exercised in the other Contracting State, may be taxed in that other Contracting State.
2. Where income in respect of personal activities exercised by an entertainer or an athlete in his capacity as such accrues not to the entertainer or athlete himself but to another person, that income may, notwithstanding the provisions of Articles 7, 13 and14, be taxed in the Contracting State in which the activities of the entertainer or athlete are exercised.
3. Notwithstanding the provisions of paragraphs 1 and 2, income derived from activities of an entertainer or an athlete who is a resident of a Contracting State, exercised in the other Contracting State within the framework of a cultural exchange program between the Governments of both Contracting States, shall not be taxed in that other Contracting State.

Article 17 - Pensions

1. Subject to the provisions of paragraph 2 of Article 18, pensions and other similar remuneration paid to a resident of a Contracting State in consideration of past employment shall be taxable only in that Contracting State.
2. Notwithstanding the provisions of paragraph 1, pensions and other payments made by a Contracting State or a local authority thereof under its social security legislation shall be taxable only in that Contracting State.

Article 18 – Government Service

1.

   a) Remuneration, other than a pension, paid by the Government of a Contracting State or a local authority thereof to any individual in respect of services rendered to that State or authority shall be taxable only in that State.
   b) However, such remuneration shall be taxable only in the other Contracting State if the services are rendered in that Contracting State and the individual is a resident of that Contracting State who:

      i) is a national of that other Contracting State; or
      ii) did not become a resident of that other State solely for the purpose of performing the services.

2.

   a) Any pension paid by, or out of funds created by the Government of a Contracting State or a local authority thereof to an individual in respect of services rendered to that State or authority shall be taxable only in that Contracting State.
   b) However, such pension shall be taxable only in the other Contracting State if the individual is a resident of, and a national of, that other Contracting State.

3. The provisions of Articles 14, 15, 16 and 17 shall apply to remuneration and pensions in respect of services rendered in connection with a business carried on by the Government of a Contracting State or a local authority thereof.

Article 19 - Professors And Researchers

Remuneration which an individual who is or was immediately before visiting a Contracting State a resident of the other Contracting State, and who is present in the first-mentioned State solely for the purpose of teaching, giving lectures or engaging in research in a university, institute, school, or teaching institution or research institution recognized by the Government of that State, receives for such services shall be exempt from tax in that State for a period not exceeding, in total, three years, as from the date of his first arrival in that State.

Article 20 - Students And Trainees

Payments which a student, a business apprentice or a trainee who is or was immediately before visiting a Contracting State a resident of the other Contracting State, and who is present in the first-mentioned Contracting State solely for the purpose of his education or training, receives for the purpose of his maintenance, education or training, shall be exempt from tax in that State.

Article 21 - Other Income

1. Items of income of a resident of a Contracting State not dealt with in the foregoing Articles of this Agreement and arising in the other Contracting State maybe taxed in that other Contracting State.
2. However, items of income of a resident of a Contracting State, wherever arising, other than those mentioned in paragraph 1, which are not dealt with in the foregoing Articles of this Agreement, shall be taxable only in that Contracting State.
3. The provisions of paragraphs 1 and 2 shall not apply to income, other than income from immovable property as defined in paragraph 2 of Article 6, if the recipient of such income, being a resident of a Contracting State, carries on business in the other Contracting State through a permanent establishment situated therein, or performs in that other State independent personal services from a fixed base situated therein, and the right or property in respect of which the income is paid is effectively connected with such permanent establishment or fixed base. In such case the provisions of Article 7 or Article 13, as the case may be, shall apply.

Article 22 - Methods For Elimination Of Double Taxation

Double taxation shall be avoided in the two Contracting States as follows:

1. In the case of the People's Republic of China:

   a) where a resident of China derives income from France, the tax levied in accordance with this Agreement in France on income, may be deducted from the Chinese tax payable by that resident of China, but the amount of the deduction shall not exceed the amount of Chinese tax on that income, calculated in accordance with the tax laws and regulations in the People's Republic of China;
   b) where the income consists of dividends paid by a company that is a resident of France to a company which is a resident of China and which owns more than 10% of the shares of the company paying the dividends, then, for the deduction from Chinese tax, the French tax paid by the company paying the dividends which corresponds to those dividends must be taken into account.

2. In the case of the French Republic:

   a) income other than that referred to in sub-paragraph b) below shall be exempt from the French taxes mentioned in sub-paragraph b) of paragraph 3 of Article 2, when such income is taxable in China under this Agreement;
   b) income referred to in Articles 9, 10, 11, 12, 15 and 16 derived from China shall be taxable in France, in accordance with the provisions of those Articles, on their gross amount. Residents of France will be entitled to a tax credit in France corresponding to the amount of Chinese tax levied on such income, but which shall not exceed the amount of French tax pertaining on such income;
   c) for the purposes of sub-paragraph b) and in the case of the items of income referred to in Articles 9, 10 and 11, the amount of Chinese tax levied shall be deemed to be equal to:

i) 10 per cent of the gross amount of the dividends paid by Chinese companies with mixed capital, 20 per cent of other dividends;
ii) 10 per cent of the gross amount of the interest;
iii) 20 per cent of the gross amount of the royalties.

d) notwithstanding the provisions of sub-paragraphs (a) and (b), French tax is computable on income taxable in France by virtue of this Agreement, at rates appropriate to the total of income taxable in accordance with French law.

Article 23 - Non-Discrimination

1. Nationals of a Contracting State shall not be subjected in the other Contracting State to any taxation or any requirement connected therewith, which is other or more burdensome than the taxation and connected requirements to which nationals of that other State in the same circumstances are or may be subjected. This provision shall notwithstanding the provisions of Article 1, also apply to persons who are not residents of one or both of the Contracting States.
2. The taxation on a permanent establishment which an enterprise of a Contracting State has in the other Contracting State shall not be less favorably levied in that other State than the taxation levied on enterprises of that other State carrying on the same activities. This provision shall not be construed as obliging a Contracting State to grant to residents of the other Contracting State any personal allowances, reliefs and reductions for taxation purposes on account of civil status or family responsibilities which it grants to its own residents.
3. Except where the provisions of Article 8, paragraph 7 of Article 10 or paragraph6 of Article 11, apply, interest, royalties and other disbursements paid by an enterprise of a Contracting State to a resident of the other Contracting State shall, for the purpose of determining the taxable profits of such enterprise, be deductible under the same conditions as if they had been paid to a resident of the first-mentioned State.
4. Enterprises of a Contracting State, the capital of which is wholly or partly owned or controlled, directly or indirectly, by one or more residents of the other Contracting State, shall not be subjected in the first-mentioned Contracting State to any taxation or any requirement connected therewith which is other or more burdensome than the taxation and connected requirements to which other similar enterprises of that first-mentioned State are or may be subjected.
5. The provisions of this Article shall, notwithstanding the provisions of Article 2, apply to taxes of every kind and description.

Article 24 - Mutual Agreement Procedure

1. Where a person considers that the actions of one or both of the Contracting States result or will result for him in taxation not in accordance with the provisions of this Agreement, he may, irrespective of the remedies provided by the domestic law of those States, present his case to the competent authority of the Contracting State of which he is a resident or, if his case comes under paragraph 1 of Article 23, to that of the Contracting State of which he is a national. The case must be presented within three years from the first notification of the action resulting in taxation not in accordance with the provisions of the Agreement.
2. The competent authority shall endeavor, if the objection appears to it to be justified and if it is not itself able to arrive at a satisfactory solution, to resolve the case by mutual agreement with the competent authority of the other Contracting State, with a view to the avoidance of taxation not in accordance with the Agreement. Any agreement reached shall be implemented notwithstanding any time limits in the domestic laws of the Contracting States.
3. The competent authorities of the Contracting States shall endeavor to resolve by mutual agreement any difficulties or doubts arising as to the interpretation or application of the

Agreement. They may also consult together for the elimination of double taxation in cases not provided for in the Agreement.
4. The competent authorities of the two Contracting States may communicate with each other directly for the purpose of reaching an agreement in the sense of paragraphs 2 and 3. To facilitate an agreement, the competent authorities of the two Contracting States may endeavor to reach an agreement through an oral exchange of opinions.

Article 25 - Exchange Of Information

1. The competent authorities of the Contracting States shall exchange such information as is necessary for carrying out the provisions of this Agreement or of the domestic laws of the Contracting States concerning taxes covered by the Agreement insofar as the taxation thereunder is not contrary to the Agreement and, in particular, for the prevention of tax evasion. The exchange of information is not restricted by Article 1. Any information received by a Contracting State shall be treated as secret and shall be disclosed only to persons or authorities, including courts and administrative bodies, involved in the assessment or collection of, or the determination of appeals in relation to, the taxes covered by the Agreement. Such persons or authorities shall use the information only for such purposes. But they may disclose the information in public court proceedings or in judicial decisions.
2. In no case shall the provisions of paragraph 1 be construed so as to impose on a Contracting State the obligation:

a) to carry out administrative measures at variance with the laws or the administrative practice of that or of the other Contracting State;
b) to supply information which is not obtainable under the laws or in the normal course of the administration of that or of the other Contracting State;
c) to supply information which would disclose any trade, business, industrial, commercial or professional secret or trade process, or information, the disclosure of which would be contrary to public policy (*order public*).

Article 26 - Diplomats

Nothing in this Agreement shall affect the fiscal privileges of diplomatic agents or consular officers under the general rules of international law or under the provisions of special agreements.

Article 27 - Scope Of Territorial Application

This Agreement shall apply:

a) in the case of the People's Republic of China, to the entire territory of the People's Republic of China in which the Chinese tax legislation is effectively applied, including the territorial sea and the areas adjacent thereto, over which the People's Republic of China may, in accordance with international law, exercise sovereign rights for the purpose of exploration and exploitation of the natural resources of the sea bed and sub-soil, and of the waters above the sea bed and sub-soil;
b) in the case of the French Republic, to all departments and territories of the French Republic in which the French tax legislation with respect to the taxes referred to in this Agreement effectively applies, including the territorial sea and areas adjacent thereto, over which the French Republic may, in accordance with international law, exercise sovereign rights for the purpose of exploration and exploitation of the natural resources of the sea bed and sub-soil, and of the waters above the sea bed and sub-soil.

Article 28 - Entry Into Force

The two Contracting States shall notify each other in writing through diplomatic channels that the procedures required by their respective laws for the bringing into force of this Agreement have been completed. This Agreement shall enter into force on the 30th day after the date of the later of the notifications. It shall have effect on income arising as from

1 January or on income pertaining to accounting periods beginning in the course of the year following that in which the Agreement enters into force.

Article 29 - Termination

This Agreement shall continue in effect indefinitely. However, five years after the date of entry into force, each of the Contracting States may give notice through diplomatic channels, before 1 July, of termination of this Agreement at the end of that calendar year.

In such event, the Agreement shall apply for the last time to income arising as from 1 January, or on income pertaining to accounting periods ending during the year following that in which such notice is given.

IN WITNESS WHEREOF the undersigned, duly authorized thereto, have signed this Agreement. DONE in duplicate in Paris on 30 May 1984, in the Chinese and French languages, both texts being equally authentic.

9.3.3 Germany–China Treaty

The People's Republic of China and the Federal Republic of Germany, desiring to further their economic relations and to avoid double taxation of income, as well as to eliminate tax evasion, have, following amicable negotiations by the representatives of each Government, agreed as follows:

Article 1 - Personal Scope

This Agreement shall apply to persons who are residents of one or both of the Contracting States.

Article 2 - Taxes Covered

1. This Agreement shall apply to taxes on income and on capital imposed on behalf of a Contracting State, irrespective of the manner in which they are levied.
2. There shall be regarded as taxes on income and on capital all taxes imposed on total income, on total capital, or on elements of income or of capital, including taxes on gains from the alienation of movable or immovable property, as well as taxes on capital appreciation.
3. The existing taxes to which the Agreement shall apply are:

   a) in the People's Republic of China:

      I) the individual income tax;
      II) the income tax concerning joint ventures with Chinese and foreign investment;
      III) the income tax concerning foreign enterprises; and
      IV) the local income tax (hereinafter referred to as "Chinese tax");

   b) in the Federal Republic of Germany:

      I) the individual income tax (die Einkommensteuer);
      II) the corporate income tax (die Korperschaftsteuer);
      III) the capital tax (die Vermgensteuer); and
      IV) the trade tax (die Gewerbesteuer, hereinafter referred to as "German tax").

4. The Agreement shall apply also to any identical or substantially similar taxes which are imposed after the date of signature of the Agreement in addition to, or in place of, the existing taxes. Within reasonable periods of time, the competent authorities of the Contracting States shall notify each other of changes which have been made in their respective taxation laws.

Article 3 - General Definitions

1. For the purposes of this Agreement, unless the context otherwise requires:
   a) the terms "a Contracting State" and "the other Contracting State" mean, as the context requires, the People's Republic of China or the Federal Republic of Germany, and when used in a geographical sense, the territory in which the tax laws of the relevant Contracting State are in force, including the territorial sea and areas beyond the territorial sea within which the relevant Contracting State may, in accordance with international law, exercise the right of exploration for and exploitation of the natural resources of the seabed and its subsoil;
   b) the term "person" includes an individual, a company and any other body of persons;
   c) the term "company" means any corporate or any entity which is treated as a body corporate for tax purposes;
   d) the terms "enterprise of a Contracting State" and "enterprise of the other Contracting State" mean respectively an enterprise carried on by a resident of a Contracting State and an enterprise carried on by a resident of the other Contracting State;
   e) the term "national" means an individual who under the laws of a Contracting State possesses the nationality of that Contracting State, as well as a legal person, partnership and association deriving its status as such from the laws in force in a Contracting State;
   f) the term "international traffic" means any transport by a ship or aircraft operated by an enterprise which has its place of head office in a Contracting State, except when the ship or aircraft is operated solely between places in the other Contracting State;
   g) the term "competent authority" means in the case of the People's Republic of China the Ministry of Finance or its authorized representative and in the case of the Federal Republic of Germany the Federal Ministry of Finance.

2. As regards the application of the Agreement by a Contracting State any term not defined therein shall, unless the context otherwise requires, have the meaning which it has under the law of that State concerning the taxes to which the Agreement applies.

Article 4 – Resident

1. For the purposes of this Agreement, the term "resident of a Contracting State" means any person who, under the laws of that State, is liable to tax therein by reason of his domicile, residence, place of head office or any other criterion of a similar nature.
2. Where by reason of the provisions of paragraph 1 an individual is a resident of both Contracting States, then his status shall be determined as follows:

   a) he shall be deemed to be a resident of the State in which he has a permanent home available to him; if he has a permanent home available to him in both States; he shall be deemed to be a resident of the State with which his personal and economic relations are closer (center of vital interests);
   b) if the State in which he has his center of vital interests cannot be determined, or if he has not a permanent home available to him in either State, he shall be deemed to be a resident of the State in which he has an habitual abode;
   c) if he has an habitual abode in both States or in neither of them, he shall be deemed to be a resident of the State of which he is a national;
   d) if he is a national of both States or of neither of them, the competent authorities of the Contracting States shall settle the question by mutual agreement.

3. Where by reason of the provisions of paragraph 1 a person other than an individual is a resident of both Contracting States, then it shall be deemed to be a resident of the State in which its place of head office is situated.

Article 5 - Permanent Establishment

1. For the purposes of this Agreement, the term "permanent establishment" means affixed place of business through which the business of an enterprise is wholly or partly carried on.
2. The term "permanent establishment" includes especially:

   a) a place of management;
   b) a branch;
   c) an office;
   d) a factory;
   e) a workshop; and
   f) a mine, an oil or gas well, a quarry or any other place of extraction of natural resources.

3. The term "permanent establishment" shall also include:

   a) a building site or assembly project or any supervising activities connected therewith, if the construction, assembly or supervising activities last for more than 6 months;
   b) the furnishing of services, including consultancy services, by an enterprise of a Contracting State through its employees or other personnel, when the activities in the other Contracting State (for the same or a connected project) continue for a period or periods aggregating more than 6 months within any 12-month period.

4. Notwithstanding paragraphs 1 to 3 of this Article, the term "permanent establishment" shall be deemed not to include:

   a) the use of facilities solely for the purpose of storage, display or delivery of goods or merchandise belonging to the enterprise;
   b) the maintenance of a stock of goods or merchandise belonging to the enterprise solely for the purpose of storage, display or delivery;
   c) the maintenance of a stock of goods or merchandise belonging to the enterprise solely for the purpose of processing by another enterprise;
   d) the maintenance of a fixed place of business solely for the purpose of purchasing goods or merchandise or of collecting information, for the enterprise;
   e) the maintenance of a fixed place of business solely for the purpose of carrying on, for the enterprise, any other activity of a preparatory or auxiliary character;
   f) the maintenance of a fixed place of business solely for any combination of activities mentioned in sub-paragraphs a) to e), provided that the overall activity of the fixed place of business resulting from this combination is of a preparatory or auxiliary character.

5. Notwithstanding the provisions of paragraphs 1 and 2, where a person—other than an agent of an independent status to whom paragraph 6 applies—is acting on behalf of an enterprise and has, and habitually exercises in a Contracting State an authority to conclude contracts in the name of the enterprise, that enterprise shall be deemed to have a permanent establishment in that State in respect of any activities which that person undertakes for the enterprise, unless the activities of such person are limited to those mentioned in paragraph 4 which, if exercised through a fixed place of business, would not make this fixed place of business a permanent establishment under the provisions of that paragraph.
6. An enterprise shall not be deemed to have a permanent establishment in a Contracting State merely because it carries on business in that State through a broker, general

commission agent or any other agent of an independent status, provided that such persons are acting in the ordinary course of their business.

7. The fact that a company which is a resident of a Contracting State controls or is controlled by a company which is a resident of the other Contracting State, or which carries on business in that other State (whether through a permanent establishment or otherwise), shall not of itself constitute either company a permanent establishment of the other.

Article 6 - Income From Immovable Property

1. Income derived by a resident of a Contracting State from immovable property situated in the other Contracting State may be taxed in that other State.
2. The term "immovable property" shall have the meaning which it has under the law of the Contracting State in which the property is situated. The term shall in any case include property accessory to immovable property, livestock and equipment used in agricultural and forestry, rights to which the provisions of general law respecting landed property apply, usufruct of immovable property and rights to variable or fixed payments as consideration for the working of, or the right to work, mineral deposits, sources and other natural resources; ships and aircraft shall not be regarded as immovable property.
3. The provisions of paragraph 1 shall apply to income derived from the direct use, letting, leasing, or use in any other form of immovable property.
4. The provisions of paragraphs 1 and 3 shall also apply to the income from immovable property of an enterprise and to income from immovable property used for the performance of independent personal services.

Article 7 - Business Profits

1. The profits of an enterprise of a Contracting State shall be taxable only in that State unless the enterprise carries on business in the other Contracting State through a permanent establishment situated therein. If the enterprise carries on business as aforesaid, the profits of the enterprise may be taxed in the other State but only so much of them as is attributable to that permanent establishment.
2. Subject to the provisions of paragraph 3, where an enterprise of a Contracting State carries on business in the other Contracting State through a permanent establishment situated therein, there shall in each Contracting State be attributed to that permanent establishment the profits which it might be expected to make if it were a distinct and separate enterprise engaged in the same or similar activities under the same or similar conditions and dealing wholly independently with the enterprise of which it is a permanent establishment.
3. In determining the profits of a permanent establishment, there shall be allowed as deductions expenses which are incurred for the purposes of the permanent establishment, including executive and general administrative expenses so incurred, whether in the State in which the permanent establishment is situated or elsewhere.
4. Insofar as it has been customary in a Contracting State to determine the profits to be attributed to a permanent establishment on the basis of an apportionment of the total profits of the enterprise to its various parts, nothing in paragraph 2 shall preclude that Contracting State from determining the profits to be taxed by such an apportionment as may be customary; the method of apportionment adopted shall, however, be such that the result shall be in accordance with the principles contained in this Article.
5. No profits shall be attributed to a permanent establishment by reason of the mere purchase by that permanent establishment of goods or merchandise for the enterprise.
6. For the purposes of paragraphs 1 to 5, the profits to be attributed to the permanent establishment shall be determined by the same method year by year unless there is good and sufficient reason to the contrary.

7. Where profits include items of income which are dealt with in other Articles of this Agreement, then the provisions of those Articles shall not be affected by the provisions of this Article.

Article 8 - Shipping And Air Transport

1. Profits from the operation of ships or aircraft in international traffic shall be taxable only in the Contracting State in which the place of head office of the enterprise is situated.
2. If the place of head office of a shipping enterprise is aboard a ship, then it shall be deemed to be situated in the Contracting State in which the home harbor of the ship is situated, or, if there is no such home harbor, in the Contracting State of which the operator of the ship is a resident.
3. The provisions of paragraph 1 shall also apply to profits from the participation in a pool, a joint business or an international operating agency.

Article 9 - Associated Enterprises

Where:

a) an enterprise of a Contracting State participates directly or indirectly in the management, control or capital of an enterprise of the other Contracting State, or
b) the same persons participate directly or indirectly in the management, control or capital of an enterprise of a Contracting State and an enterprise of the other Contracting State; and in either case conditions are made or imposed between the two enterprises in their commercial or financial relations which differ from those which would be made between independent enterprises, then any profits which would, but for those conditions, have accrued to one of the enterprises, but, by reason of those conditions, have not so accrued, may be included in the profits of that enterprise and taxed accordingly.

Article 10 - Dividends

1. Dividends paid by a company which is a resident of a Contracting State to resident of the other Contracting State may be taxed in that other State.
2. However, such dividends may also be taxed in the Contracting State of which the company paying the dividends is a resident and according to the laws of that State, but if the recipient is the beneficial owner of the dividends the tax so charged shall not exceed 10 per cent of the gross amount of the dividends.

This paragraph shall not affect the taxation of the company in respect of the profits out of which the dividends are paid.

3. The term "dividends" as used in this Article means income from shares, mining shares, founders' shares or other rights, not being debt-claims, participating in profits, as well as income from other corporate rights which is subjected to the same taxation treatment as income from shares by the laws of the State of which the company making the distribution is a resident.
4. The provisions of paragraphs 1 and 2 shall not apply if the beneficial owner, being a resident of a Contracting State, carries on business in the other Contracting State of which the company paying the dividends is a resident, through a permanent establishment situated therein, or performs in that other State independent personal services from a fixed base situated therein and the holding in respect of which the dividends are paid is effectively connected with such permanent establishment or fixed base. In such case the provisions of Article 7 or Article 14, as the case may be, shall apply.
5. Where a company which is a resident of a Contracting State derives profits or income from the other Contracting State, that other State may not impose any tax on the dividends paid by the company, except insofar as such dividends are paid to a resident of that other State or insofar as the holding in respect of which the dividends are paid is effectively connected with a permanent establishment or a fixed base situated in that other State, nor subject the company's undistributed profits to a tax on undistributed

profits, even if the dividends paid or the undistributed profits consist wholly or partly of profits or income arising in such other State.

Article 11 – Interest

1. Interest arising in a Contracting State and paid to a resident of the other Contracting State may be taxed in that other State.
2. However, such interest may also be taxed in the Contracting State in which it arises and according to the laws of that State. But if the recipient is the beneficial owner of the interest the tax so charged shall not exceed 10 per cent of the gross amount of the interest.
3. Notwithstanding the provisions of paragraph 2, interest derived from the Federal Republic of Germany is exempt from German tax, if paid:

   a)

      i) to the Government of the People's Republic of China;
      ii) to the People's Bank of China, the Agricultural Bank of China, the People's Construction Bank of China, the Investment Bank of China or the Industrial and Commercial Bank of China;
      iii) on a loan directly guaranteed or financed by the Bank of China or the Chinese International Trust and Investment Company; or
      iv) to public credit institution of the Government of the People's Republic of China, if the competent authorities of both States have mutually agreed thereto;

   b) derived from the People's Republic of China is exempt from Chinese tax, if paid:

      i) to the Government of the Federal Republic of Germany;
      ii) to the Deutsche Bundesbank, the Kredietanstaltfür Wiederaufbau or the Deutsche Finanzierungs gesellschaftfür Beteiligungen in Entwicklungslndern (the German Federal Bank, the Credit Institute for Reconstruction, or the German Finance Company for Investment in Developing Countries);
      iii) on a loan, directly guaranteed or financed by Hermes; or
      iv) to a public credit institution of the Federal Government, if the competent authorities of both States have agreed thereto.

4. The term "interest" as used in this Article means income from debt-claims of every kind, whether or not secured by mortgage and whether or not carrying a right to participate in the debtor's profits, and in particular, income from government securities and income from bonds or debentures, including premiums and prizes attaching to such securities, bonds or debentures. Penalty charges for late payment shall not be regarded as interest for the purpose of this Article.
5. The provisions of paragraphs 1 to 3 shall not apply if the beneficial owner of the interest being a resident of a Contracting State, carries on business in the other Contracting State in which the interest arises, through a permanent establishment situated therein, or performs in that other State independent personal services from affixed base situated therein, and the debt-claim in respect of which the interest is paid is effectively connected with such permanent establishment or fixed base. In such case the provisions of Article 7 or Article 14, as the case may be, shall apply.
6. Interest shall be deemed to arise in a Contracting State when the payer is that State itself, a local authority or a resident of that State. Where, however, the person paying the interest, whether he is a resident of a Contracting State or not, has in a Contracting State a permanent establishment or a fixed base in connection with which the indebtedness on which the interest is paid was incurred, and such interest is borne by such permanent establishment or fixed base, then such interest shall be deemed to arise in the State in which the permanent establishment or fixed base is situated.

7. Where, by reason of a special relationship between the payer and the beneficial owner or between both of them and some other person, the amount of the interest, having regard to the debt-claim for which it is paid, exceeds the amount which would have been agreed upon by the payer and the beneficial owner in the absence or such relationship, the provisions of this Article shall apply only to the last-mentioned amount. In such case, the excess part of the payments shall remain taxable according to the laws of each Contracting State, due regard being had to the other provisions of this Agreement.

Article 12 - Royalties

1. Royalties arising in a Contracting State and paid to a resident of the other Contracting State may be taxed in that other State.
2. However, such royalties may also be taxed in the Contracting State in which they arise and according to the laws of that State, but if the recipient is the beneficial owner of the royalties, the tax so charged shall not exceed 10 per cent of the gross amount of the royalties.
3. The term "royalties" as used in this Article means payments of any kind received as a consideration for the use of, or the right to use, any copyright of literary, artistic or scientific work including cinematograph films and films or tapes for broadcasting or television, any patent, trade mark, design or model, plan, secret formula or process, or for the use of, or the right to use, industrial, commercial, or scientific equipment, or for information concerning industrial, commercial or scientific experience.
4. The provisions of paragraphs 1 and 2 shall not apply if the beneficial owner of the royalties, being a resident of a Contracting State, carries on business in the other Contracting State in which the royalties arise, through a permanent establishment situated therein, or performs in that other State independent personal services from affixed base situated therein, and the right or property in respect of which the royalties are paid is effectively connected with such permanent establishment or fixed base. In such case the provisions of Article 7 or Article 14, as the case may be, shall apply.
5. Royalties shall be deemed to arise in a Contracting State when the payer is the Government of that State itself, a local authority or a resident of that Contracting State. Where, however, the person paying the royalties, whether he is a resident of a Contracting State or not, has in a Contracting State a permanent establishment or affixed base in connection with which the obligation to pay the royalties was incurred, and those royalties are borne by that permanent establishment or fixed base, then such royalties shall be deemed to arise in the Contracting State in which the permanent establishment or fixed base is situated.
6. Where, by reason of a special relationship between the payer and the beneficial owner or between both of them and some other person, the amount of the royalties, having regard to the use, right or information for which they are paid, exceeds the amount which would have been agreed upon by the payer and the beneficial owner in the absence of such relationship, the provisions of this Article shall apply only to the last-mentioned amount. In such case, the excess part of the payments shall remain taxable according to the laws of each Contracting State, due regard being had to the other provisions of this Agreement.

Article 13 - Capital Gains

1. Gains derived by a resident of a Contracting State from the alienation of immovable property referred to in Article 6 and situated in the other Contracting State may be taxed in that other State.
2. Gains from the alienation of movable property forming part of the business property of a permanent establishment which an enterprise of a Contracting State has in the other Contracting State or of movable property pertaining to a fixed base available to a resident of a Contracting State in the other Contracting State for the purpose of performing independent personal services, including such gains from the alienation of

such a permanent establishment (alone or with the whole enterprise) or of such a fixed base, may be taxed in that other State.

3. Gains from the alienation of ships or aircraft operated in international traffic, or movable property pertaining to the operation of such ships, aircraft or boats, shall be taxable only in the Contracting State in which the place of head office of the enterprise is situated.
4. Gains derived by a resident of a Contracting State from the alienation of any property other than that referred to in paragraphs 1 to 3 and which is situated in the other Contracting State, may be taxed in that other State.

Article 14 - Independent Personal Services

1. Income derived by a resident of a Contracting State in respect of professional services or other activities of an independent character shall be taxable only in that State. However, such income may also be taxed in the other Contracting State:
   a) if he has a fixed base regularly available to him in the other Contracting State for the purpose of performing his activities but only so much of the income as is attributable to that fixed base; or
   b) if his stay in the other Contracting State is for a period or periods, in the aggregate, more than 183 days in the calendar year concerned, only so much of the income as is derived from the activities in that other State.
2. The term "professional services" includes especially independent scientific, literary, artistic, educational or teaching activities as well as the independent activities of physicians, lawyers, engineers, architects, dentists and accountants.

Article 15 - Dependent Personal Services

1. Subject to the provisions of Articles 16, 18, 19, 20 and 21, salaries, wages and other similar remuneration derived by a resident of a Contracting State in respect of an employment shall be taxable only in that State unless the employment is exercised in the other Contracting State. If the employment is so exercised, such remuneration as is derived therefrom may be taxed in that other State.
2. Notwithstanding the provisions of paragraph 1, remuneration derived by a resident of a Contracting State in respect of an employment exercised in the other Contracting State shall be taxable only in the first-mentioned State if:
   a) the recipient is present in the other State for a period or periods not exceeding in the aggregate 183 days in the calendar year concerned; and
   b) the remuneration is paid by, or on behalf of, an employer who is not a resident of the other State; and
   c) the remuneration is not borne by a permanent establishment or a fixed base which the employer has in the other State.
3. Notwithstanding the preceding provisions of this Article, remuneration derived in respect of an employment exercised aboard a ship or aircraft operated in international traffic, may be taxed in the Contracting State in which the place of head office of the enterprise is situated.

Article 16 - Directors' Fees

Directors' fees and other similar payments derived by a resident of a Contracting State in his capacity as a member of the board of directors of a company which is a resident of the other Contracting State may be taxed in that other State.

Article 17 - Artistes And Athletes

1. Notwithstanding the provisions of Articles 14 and 15, income derived by a resident of a Contracting State as an entertainer, such as a theatre, motion picture, radio or television artiste, or a musician, or as an athlete, from his personal activities as such exercised in the other Contracting State, may be taxed in that other State.

2. Where income in respect of personal activities exercised by an entertainer or an athlete in his capacity as such accrues not to the entertainer or athlete himself but to another person, that income may, notwithstanding the provisions of Articles 7, 14 and15, be taxed in the Contracting State in which the activities of the entertainer or athlete are exercised.
3. Notwithstanding the provisions of paragraphs 1 and 2, income derived by an entertainer or athlete who is resident in a Contracting State from activities exercised in the other Contracting State within the framework of a cultural exchange program agreed upon by the Governments of both Contracting States shall not be taxed in that other State.

Article 18 - Pensions

Subject to the provisions of paragraph 2 of Article 19, pensions and other similar remuneration paid to a resident of a Contracting State in consideration of past employment shall be taxable only in that State.

Article 19 - Government Service

1.
   a) Remuneration, other than a pension, paid by a Contracting State or a local authority or organ thereof to an individual in respect of services rendered to that State, authority or organ shall be taxable only in that State.
   b) However, such remuneration shall be taxable only in the other Contracting State if the services are rendered in that other State and the individual is a resident of that other State who:
      i) is a national of that other State; or
      ii) did not become a resident of that other State solely for the purpose of rendering the services.
2.
   a) Any pension paid by a Contracting State or a local authority or organ thereof to an individual in respect of services rendered to that State or authority or organ shall be taxable only in that State.
   b) However, such pension shall be taxable only in the other Contracting State if the individual is a resident of, and a national of, that other State.
3. The provisions of Articles 15, 16, 17 and 18 shall apply to remuneration and pensions in respect of services rendered in connection with a business carried on by a Contracting State or a local authority or organ thereof.

Article 20 - Professors And Researchers

1. A professor or researcher who is, or was immediately before visiting the other a Contracting State, a resident of a Contracting State and who is present in the first-mentioned Contracting State for a period not exceeding three years for the purpose of advanced study to research or for the purpose of teaching at a university, college, school or any other educational or research institution shall be exempt from tax in the other Contracting State in respect of remuneration derived from such activities.
2. The provisions of paragraph 1 shall not apply to income from research, if this research is not in the public interest but primarily for the private benefit of a certain person or persons.

Article 21 - Students And Trainees

A student, business apprentice or trainee who is a resident of a Contracting State or was, immediately before visiting the other Contracting State, a resident of the first-mentioned

State and who is present in the other State solely for the purpose of his education or training, shall be exempt from tax in that other State on:

a) all payments made by persons outside the other State for the purpose of his maintenance, or training; and
b) all scholarships, allowances or maintenance payments paid by governmental, charitable, scientific, cultural or educational organizations for the purpose of his maintenance, education or training; and
c) income from personal services performed in the other Contracting State during in the aggregate not more than 5 years and in an amount not exceeding 6,000 DM or its equivalent in Chinese currency RMB per calendar year, for the purpose of supplementing his income for his maintenance, education or training.

Article 22 - Other Income

1. Items of income of a resident of a Contracting State, wherever arising, not dealt with in the foregoing Articles of this Agreement shall be taxable only in that State.
2. The provisions of paragraph 1 shall not apply to income, other than income from immovable property as defined in paragraph 2 of Article 6, if the recipient of such income, being a resident of a Contracting State, carries on business in the other Contracting State through a permanent establishment situated therein, or performs in that other State independent personal services from a fixed base situated therein, and the right or property in respect of which the income is paid is effectively connected with such permanent establishment or fixed base. In such case the provisions of Article 7 or Article 14, as the case may be, shall apply.
3. Notwithstanding the provisions of paragraphs 1 and 2, items of income of a resident of a Contracting State which are not covered under the preceding Articles of this Agreement may be taxed in the other Contracting State, if they are arising in that other State.

Article 23 - Capital

1. Capital represented by immovable property referred to in Article 6, owned by a resident of a Contracting State and situated in the other Contracting State, may be taxed in that other State.
2. Capital represented by movable property forming part of the business property of a permanent establishment which an enterprise of a Contracting State has in the other Contracting State or by movable property pertaining to a fixed base available to a resident of a Contracting State in the other Contracting State for the purpose of performing independent personal services, may be taxed in that other State.
3. Capital represented by ships or aircraft operated in international traffic, and by movable property pertaining to the operation of such ships or aircraft, shall be taxable only in the Contracting State in which the place of head office of the enterprise is situated.
4. All other elements of capital of a resident of a Contracting State shall be taxable only in that State.

Article 24 - Methods For Elimination Of Double Taxation

1. For a resident of the People's Republic of China double taxation shall be eliminated as follows:

    a) the German tax levied in accordance with the provisions of this Agreement on income derived from the Federal Republic of Germany shall be allowed as a credit against the Chinese tax to be paid by that resident in the People's Republic of China. The amount of German tax to be credited, however, shall not exceed the amount of Chinese tax computed with respect to such income in accordance with the tax regulations of the People's Republic of China;
    b) where the income consists of dividends paid by a company which is a resident of the Federal Republic of Germany to a company which is a resident of the People's

Republic of China and which owns at least 10 per cent of the capital of the first-mentioned company the tax paid by the first-mentioned company may be credited against the tax imposed by the People's Republic of China, to the extent it can be attributed to such

2. For a resident of the Federal Republic of Germany double taxation shall be eliminated as follows:

   a) Unless the provisions of subparagraph (b) apply, there shall be excluded from the basis upon which German tax is imposed any item of income arising in the People's Republic of China and any item of capital situated within the People's Republic of China which, according to this Agreement, may be taxed in the People's Republic of China. The Federal Republic of Germany, however, retains the right to take into account in the determination of its rate of tax the items of income and capital so excluded.

      In the case of dividends the foregoing provisions shall apply only to such dividends as are paid to a company (not including partnerships) being a resident of the Federal Republic of Germany by a company being a resident of the People's Republic of China at least 10 per cent of the capital of which is owned directly by the German company. For the purposes of taxes on capital there shall also be excluded from the basis upon which German tax is imposed any shareholding, the dividends from which, if paid, would be excluded according to the immediately foregoing sentence from the basis upon which German tax is imposed.

   b) Subject to the provisions of German tax law regarding credit for foreign tax, a credit shall be allowed against German individual income and corporate income tax payable in respect of the following items of income arising in the People's Republic of China, the Chinese tax paid under Chinese laws and in accordance with this Agreement on:

      i) dividends not dealt with in subparagraph a);
      ii) interest;
      iii) royalties;
      iv) income to which paragraph 4 of Article 13 applies;
      v) remuneration to which Article 16 applies;
      vi) income to which Article 17 applies;
      vii) income to which paragraph 3 of Article 22 applies.

   c) For the purpose of subparagraph b) the Chinese credited shall be deemed to be tax to be:

      i) in the case of dividends referred to in sub-paragraph b) under i): 10percent of the gross amount of dividends;
      ii) in the case of interest and royalties referred to in sub-paragraph b)under ii) and
      iii) 15 per cent of the gross amount of such payments.

Article 25 - Non-Discrimination

1. Nationals of a Contracting State shall not be subjected in the other Contracting State to any taxation or any requirement connected therewith, which is other or more burdensome than the taxation and connected requirements to which nationals of that other State in the same circumstances are or may be subjected. This provision shall, notwithstanding the provisions of Article 1, also apply to persons who are not residents of a Contracting State.
2. The taxation on a permanent establishment which an enterprise of a Contracting State has in the other Contracting State shall not be less favorably levied in that other State than the taxation levied on enterprises of that other State carrying on the same activities. This provision shall not be construed as obliging a Contracting State to grant to residents

of the other Contracting State any personal allowances, reliefs and reductions for taxation purposes on account of civil status or family responsibilities which it grants exclusively to its own residents.

3. Except where the provisions of Article 9, paragraph 7 of Article 11 or paragraph6 of Article 12 apply, interest, royalties and other disbursements paid by an enterprise of a Contracting State to a resident of the other Contracting State shall, for the purpose of determining the taxable profits of such enterprise, be deductible under the same conditions as if they had been paid to a resident of the first-mentioned State. Similarly, any debts of an enterprise of a Contracting State to a resident of the other Contracting State shall, for the purpose of determining the taxable capital of such enterprise, be deductible under the same conditions as if they had been contracted to a resident of the first-mentioned State.
4. Enterprises of a Contracting State, the capital of which is wholly or partly owned or controlled, directly or indirectly, by one or more residents of the other Contracting State, shall not be subjected in the first-mentioned State to any taxation or any requirement connected therewith which is other or more burdensome than the taxation and connected requirements to which other similar enterprises of that first-mentioned State are or may be subjected.
5. The provisions of this Article shall, notwithstanding the provisions of Article 2, apply to taxes of every kind and description.

Article 26 - Mutual Agreement Procedure

1. Where a person considers that the actions of one or both of the Contracting States result or will result for him in taxation not in accordance with the provisions of this Agreement, he may, irrespective of the remedies provided by the domestic law of those States, present his case to the competent authority of the Contracting State of which he is a resident or, if his case comes under paragraph 1 of Article 25, to that of the Contracting State of which he is a national. The case must be presented within three years from the first notification of the action resulting in taxation not in accordance with the provisions of the Agreement.
2. The competent authority shall endeavor, if the objection appears to it to be justified and if it is not itself able to arrive at a satisfactory solution, to resolve the case by mutual agreement with the competent authority of the other Contracting State, with a view to the avoidance of taxation not in accordance with the Agreement. Any agreement reached shall be implemented notwithstanding any time limits in the domestic law of the Contracting States.
3. The competent authorities of the Contracting States shall endeavor to resolve by mutual agreement any difficulties or doubts arising as to the interpretation or application of the Agreement. They may also consult together for the elimination of double taxation in cases not provided for in the Agreement.
4. The competent authorities of the Contracting States may communicate with each other directly for the purpose of reaching an agreement in the sense of the preceding paragraphs.

Article 27 - Exchange Of Information

1. The competent authorities of the Contracting States shall exchange such information as is necessary for carrying out the provisions of this Agreement. Any information received by a Contracting State shall be treated as secret in the same manner as information obtained under the domestic laws of that State and shall be disclosed only to persons or authorities (including courts and administrative bodies) involved in the assessment or collection of, the enforcement or prosecution in respect of, or the determination of appeals in relation to, the taxes covered by the Agreement. Such persons or authorities

shall use the information only for such purposes. They may disclose the information in public court proceedings or in judicial decisions.

2. In no case shall the provisions of paragraph 1 be construed so as to impose on a Contracting State the obligation:

   a) to carry out administrative measures at variance with the laws and administrative practice of that or of the other Contracting State;
   b) to supply information which is not obtainable under the laws or in the normal course of the administration of that or of the other Contracting State;
   c) to supply information which would disclose any trade, business, industrial, commercial or professional secret or trade process, or information, the disclosure of which would be contrary to public policy (*order public*).

Article 28 - Diplomatic Agents And Consular Officers

Nothing in this Agreement shall affect the fiscal privileges of diplomatic Agents or consular officers under the general rules of international law or under the provisions of special agreements.

Article 29 - Berlin Clause

This Agreement shall also apply to Berlin (West) in accordance with the procedure agreed upon.

Article 30 - Entry Into Force

This Agreement shall enter into force on the thirtieth day following the date on which each of the two Governments has notified the other that the procedures required by its law for the bringing into force of this Agreement have been completed.

The Agreement shall have effect:

a) on taxes withheld at the source on dividends paid on or after January 1st 1985;
b) on taxes withheld at source on interest or royalties paid on or after July 1st 1985;
c) on other taxes, for any tax year beginning on or after January 1st 1985.

Article 31 - Termination

This Agreement shall continue in effect indefinitely but either Contracting State may, on or before the thirtieth day of June in any calendar year beginning after the expiration of a period of five years from the date of its entry into force, give to the other Contracting State, through diplomatic channels, written notice of termination; in such case the

Agreement shall cease to have effect:

a) on taxes withheld at source on dividends, interest and royalties paid on or after 1 January of the year following that in which the notice is given;
b) on other taxes, for any tax year beginning on or after 1 January of the year following that in which the notice is given.

DONE in duplicate at Bonn this 10th day of June 1985, in the Chinese and German languages, both texts being equally authentic.

9.3.4 Great Britain and Northern Ireland–China Treaty

The Government of the People's Republic of China and the Government of the United Kingdom of Great Britain and Northern Ireland, desiring to conclude an Agreement for the reciprocal avoidance of double taxation and the prevention of fiscal evasion with respect to taxes on income and capital gains, have agreed as follows:

Article 1 - Personal Scope

This Agreement shall apply to persons who are residents of one or both of the Contracting States.

Article 2 - Taxes Covered

1. The existing taxes to which this Agreement applies are:

   a) in the People's Republic of China:

      I) the individual income tax;
      II) the income tax (including the additional local income tax) concerning joint ventures with Chinese and foreign investment; and
      III) the income tax (including the local income tax) concerning foreign enterprises (hereinafter referred to as "Chinese tax");

   b) in the United Kingdom of Great Britain and Northern Ireland:

      I) the income tax;
      II) the corporation tax; and
      III) the capital gains tax (hereinafter referred to as "United Kingdom tax").

2. This Agreement shall also apply to any identical or substantially similar taxes which are imposed by either Contracting State after the date of signature of this Agreement in addition to, or in place of, the taxes referred to in paragraph 1) of this Article. The competent authorities of the Contracting States shall notify each other of any changes which are made in their respective taxation laws.

Article 3 - General Definitions

1. In this Agreement, unless the context otherwise requires:

   a) the term "China" means the People's Republic of China, including all the territory and the territorial sea of the People's Republic of China, in which the laws relating to Chinese tax are in force, and all the area beyond its territorial sea, and the sea bed and sub-soil thereof, over which the People's Republic of China has jurisdiction in accordance with international law and in which the laws relating to Chinese tax are in force;
   b) the term "United Kingdom" means Great Britain and Northern Ireland, including any area outside the territorial sea of the United Kingdom which in accordance with international law has been or may hereafter be designated, under the laws of the United Kingdom concerning the Continental Shelf, as an area within which the rights of the United Kingdom with respect to the seabed and sub-soil and their natural Resources may be exercised;
   c) the terms "a Contracting State" and "the other Contracting State" mean China or the United Kingdom as the context requires;
   d) the term "national" means:

      i) in relation to China any individual who under the law in China possesses Chinese nationality; and any legal person, partnership or other body of persons deriving its status as such from the law in force in China;
      ii) in relation to the United Kingdom, any individual who has under the law in the United Kingdom the status of United Kingdom national, provided he has the right of abode in the United Kingdom; and any legal person, partnership, association or other entity deriving its status as such from the law in force in the United Kingdom;

e) the term "person" means an individual, a company and any other body of persons;
f) the term "company" means any corporate or any entity which is treated as a body corporate for tax purposes;
g) the terms "enterprise of a Contracting State" and "enterprise of the other Contracting State" mean respectively an enterprise carried on by a resident of a Contracting State and an enterprise carried on by a resident of the other Contracting State;
h) the term "international traffic" means any transport by a ship or aircraft operated by an enterprise which has its place of effective management of the business in a Contracting State, except when the ship or aircraft is operated solely between places in the other Contracting State;
i) the term "competent authority" means, in the case of China, the General Taxation Bureau of the Ministry of Finance or its authorized representatives, and in the case of the United Kingdom, the Board of Inland Revenue or their authorized representatives.

2. As regards the application of this Agreement by a Contracting State any term not otherwise defined shall, unless the context otherwise requires, have the meaning which it has under the law of that Contracting State relating to the taxes to which this Agreement applies.

Article 4 - Resident

1. For the purposes of this Agreement, the term "resident of a Contracting State" means any person who, under the law of that State, is liable to tax therein by reason of his domicile, residence, place of head office, place of effective management or any other criterion of a similar nature.
2. Where by reason of the provisions of paragraph 1) of this Article an individual is a resident of both Contracting States, then his status shall be determined in accordance with the following rules:

   a) he shall be deemed to be a resident of the State in which he has a permanent home available to him; if he has a permanent home available to him in both States, he shall be deemed to be a resident of the State with which his personal and economic relations are closer (center of vital interests);
   b) if the State in which he has his center of vital interests cannot be determined, or if he has not a permanent home available to him in either State, he shall be deemed to be a resident of the State in which he has an habitual abode;
   c) if he has a habitual abode in both States or in neither of them, he shall be deemed to be a resident of the State of which he is national;
   d) if he is a national of both States or of neither of them, the competent authorities of the Contracting States shall settle the question by mutual agreement.

3. Where by reason of the provisions of paragraph 1) of this Article a person other than an individual is a resident of both Contracting States, then it shall be deemed to be a resident of the State in which the place of effective management of its business is situated. However, where such a person has the place of effective management of its business in one of the Contracting States and the place of head office of its business in the other Contracting State, then the competent authorities of the Contracting State shall determine by mutual agreement the State of which the company shall be deemed to be a resident for the purposes of this Agreement.

Article 5 - Permanent Establishment

1. For the purposes of this Agreement, the term "permanent establishment" means affixed place of business through which the business of an enterprise is wholly or partly carried on.

2. The term "permanent establishment" includes especially:

   a) a place of management;
   b) a branch;
   c) an office;
   d) a factory;
   e) a workshop;
   f) a mine, an oil or gas well, a quarry or any other place of extraction of natural resources; and
   g) an installation or structure used for the exploration or exploitation of natural resources.

3. A building site or a construction, installation or assembly project constitutes a permanent establishment only if it lasts more than six months.
4. Notwithstanding the provisions of paragraphs 1) to 3) of this Article, the term "permanent establishment" shall be deemed not to include:

   a) the use of facilities solely for the purpose of storage, display or delivery of goods or merchandise belonging to the enterprise;
   b) the maintenance of a stock of goods or merchandise belonging to the enterprise solely for the purpose of storage, display or delivery;
   c) the maintenance of a stock of goods or merchandise belonging to the enterprise solely for the purpose of processing by another enterprise:
   d) the maintenance of a fixed place of business solely for the purpose of purchasing goods or merchandise, or of collecting information, for the enterprise;
   e) the maintenance of a fixed place of business solely for the purpose of carrying on, for the enterprise, any other activity of a preparatory or auxiliary character;
   f) the maintenance of a fixed place of business solely for any combination of activities mentioned in sub-paragraphs a) to e) of this paragraph provided that the overall activity of the fixed place of business resulting from this combination is of a preparatory or auxiliary character.

5. Notwithstanding the provisions of paragraphs 1) and 2) of this Article, where a person, other than an agent of an independent status to whom paragraph 6) of this Article applies, is acting in a Contracting State on behalf of an enterprise of the other Contracting State and has, and habitually exercises, in the first-mentioned Contracting State an authority to conclude contracts in the name of the enterprise, that enterprise shall be deemed to have a permanent establishment in the first-mentioned Contracting State in respect of any activities which that person undertakes for the enterprise, unless the activities of such a person are limited to those mentioned in paragraph 4) of this Article which, if exercised through a fixed place of business, would not make that fixed place of business a permanent establishment under the provisions of that paragraph.
6. An enterprise of a Contracting State shall not be deemed to have a permanent establishment in the other Contracting State merely because it carries on business in that other State through a broker, general commission agent or any other agent of an independent status, provided that such a person is acting in the ordinary course of his business. However, when the activities of such an agent are devoted wholly or almost wholly on behalf of that enterprise, he shall not be considered an agent of an independent status within the meaning of this paragraph.
7. The fact that a company which is a resident of a Contracting State controls or is controlled by a company which is a resident of the other Contracting State, or which carries on business in that other State (whether through a permanent establishment or otherwise), shall not of itself constitute either company a permanent establishment of the other.

Article 6 - Income From Immovable Property

1. Income derived by a resident of a Contracting State from immovable property (including income from agriculture or forestry) situated in the other Contracting State may be taxed in that other State.
2. The term "immovable property" shall have the meaning which it has under the law of the Contracting State in which the property in question is situated. The term shall in any case include property accessory to immovable property, livestock and equipment used in agriculture and forestry, rights to which the provisions of general law respecting landed property apply, usufruct of immovable property and rights to variable or fixed payments as consideration for the working of, or the right to work, mineral deposits, sources and other natural resources; ships and aircraft shall not be regarded as immovable property.
3. The provisions of paragraph 1) of this Article shall apply to income derived from the direct use, letting, or use in any other form of immovable property.
4. The provisions of paragraphs 1) and 3) of this Article shall also apply to the income from immovable property of an enterprise and to income from immovable property used for the performance of independent personal services.

Article 7 - Business Profits

1. The profits of an enterprise of a Contracting State shall be taxable only in that State unless the enterprise carries on business in the other Contracting State through a permanent establishment situated therein. If the enterprise carries on business as aforesaid, the profits of the enterprise may be taxed in the other State but only so much of them as is attributable to that permanent establishment.
2. Subject to the provisions of paragraph 3) of this Article, where an enterprise of a Contracting State carries on business in the other Contracting State through a permanent establishment situated therein, there shall in each Contracting State be attributed to that permanent establishment the profits which it might be expected to make if it were a distinct and separate enterprise engaged in the same or similar activities under the same or similar conditions and dealing wholly independently with the enterprise of which it is a permanent establishment.
3. In the determination of the profits of a permanent establishment, there shall be allowed as deductions expenses which are incurred for the purposes of the business of the permanent establishment including executive and general administrative expenses so incurred, whether in the State in which the permanent establishment is situated or elsewhere. However, no such deduction shall be allowed in respect of amounts, if any, paid (otherwise than towards reimbursement of actual expenses) by the permanent establishment to the head office of the enterprise or any of its other offices, by way of royalties, fees or other similar payments in return for the use of patents or other rights, or by way of commission, for specific services performed or for management, or by way of fees for technical services, or, except in the case of a banking enterprise, by way of interest on moneys lent to the permanent establishment. Likewise, no account shall be taken, in the determination of the profits of a permanent establishment, of amounts charged (otherwise than towards reimbursement of actual expenses) by the permanent establishment to the head office of the enterprise or any of its other offices, by way of royalties, fees or other similar payments in return for the use of patents or other rights, or by way of commission for specific services performed or for management, or by way of8fees for technical services, or, except in the case of a banking enterprise, by way of interest on moneys lent to the head office of the enterprise or any of its other offices.
4. No profits shall be attributed to a permanent establishment by reason of the mere purchase by that permanent establishment of goods or merchandise for the enterprise.
5. Where profits include items of income which are dealt with separately in other Articles of this Agreement, then the provisions of those Articles shall not be affected by the provisions of this Article.

Article 8 - Shipping And Air Transport

1. Profits from the operation of ships or aircraft in international traffic shall be taxable only in the Contracting State in which the place of effective management of the business of the enterprise is situated.
2. If the place of effective management of the business of a shipping enterprise is aboard a ship, then it shall be deemed to be situated in the Contracting State in which the home harbor of the ship is situated, or, if there is no such home harbor, in the Contracting State of which the operator of the ship is a resident.
3. The provisions of this Article shall also apply to profits derived from participation in a pool, a joint business or an international operating agency.

Article 9 - Associated Enterprises

Where:

a) an enterprise of a Contracting State participates directly or indirectly in the management, control or capital of an enterprise of the other Contracting State; or
b) the same persons participate directly or indirectly in the management, control or capital of an enterprise of a Contracting State and an enterprise of the other Contracting State; and in either case conditions are made or imposed between the two enterprises in their commercial or financial relations which differ from those which would be made between independent enterprises, then any profits which would, but for those conditions, have accrued to one of the enterprises, but, by reason of those conditions, have not so accrued, may be included in the profits of that enterprise and taxed accordingly.

Article 10 - Dividends

1. Dividends derived from a company which is a resident of a Contracting State by a resident of the other Contracting State may be taxed in that other State.
2. However, such dividends may also be taxed in the Contracting State of which the company paying the dividends is a resident and according to the law of that State, but if the beneficial owner of the dividends is a resident of the other Contracting State the tax so charged shall not exceed 10 per cent of the gross amount of the dividends.
3. The term "dividends" as used in this Article shall have the meaning which it has under the taxation law of the Contracting State of which the company paying the dividend is a resident and shall include any item which is treated under that law as a dividend or distribution.
4. The provisions of paragraph 2) of this Article shall not affect the taxation of the company in respect of the profits out of which the dividends are paid.
5. The provisions of paragraphs 1) and 2) of this Article shall not apply if the beneficial owner of the dividends, being a resident of a Contracting State, carries on business in the other Contracting State of which the company paying the dividends is a resident, through a permanent establishment situated therein, or performs in that other State independent personal services from a fixed base situated therein, and the holding in respect of which the dividends are paid is effectively connected with such permanent establishment or fixed base. In such case, the provisions of Article 7 or Article 15, as the case may be, shall apply.
6. Where a company which is a resident of a Contracting State derives profits or income from the other Contracting State that other State may not impose any tax on the dividends paid by the company, except insofar as such dividends are paid to a resident of that other State or insofar as the holding in respect of which the dividends are paid is effectively connected with a permanent establishment or a fixed base situated in that other State, nor subject the company's undistributed profits to a tax on undistributed profits, even if the dividends paid or the undistributed profits consist wholly or partly of profits or income arising in that other State.

Article 11 - Interest

1. Interest arising in a Contracting State which is derived by a resident of the other Contracting State may be taxed in that other State.
2. However, such interest may also be taxed in the Contracting State in which it arises, and according to the law of that State; but if the beneficial owner of the interest is a resident of the other Contracting State the tax so charged shall not exceed 10 percent of the gross amount of the interest.
3. Notwithstanding the provisions of paragraph 2) of this Article, interest arising in a Contracting State and derived by the Government of the other Contracting State, apolitical sub-division or local authority thereof, the Central Bank of that other Contracting State or any agency of that Government, or by any other resident of that other Contracting State with respect to debt-claims of that resident which are financed, guaranteed or insured by the Government of that other Contracting State, a political sub-division or local authority thereof, the Central Bank of that other Contracting State or any agency of that Government, shall be exempt from tax in the first-mentioned Contracting State.
4. The term "interest" as used in this Article means income from debt-claims of every kind, whether or not secured by mortgage, and whether or not carrying a righto participate in the debtor's profits, and in particular, income from government securities and income from bonds or debentures, including premiums and prizes attaching to such securities, bonds or debentures, but shall not include any item which is treated as a distribution under the provisions of Article 10 of this Agreement.
5. The provisions of paragraphs 1) and 2) of this Article shall not apply if the beneficial owner of the interest, being a resident of a Contracting State, carries on business in the other Contracting State in which the interest arises, through a permanent establishment situated therein, or performs in that other State independent personal services from a fixed base situated therein, and the debt-claim in respect of which the interest is paid is effectively connected with such permanent establishment or fixed base. In such case, the provisions of Article 7 or Article 15, as the case maybe, shall apply.
6. Interest shall be deemed to arise in a Contracting State when the payer is the Government of that State or a political sub-division thereof or a local authority or a resident of that State. Where, however, the person paying the interest, whether he is a resident of a Contracting State or not, has in a Contracting State a permanent establishment or a fixed base in connection with which the indebtedness on which the interest is paid was incurred, and such interest is borne by that permanent establishment or fixed base, then such interest shall be deemed to arise in the State in which the permanent establishment or fixed base is situated.
7. Where, by reason of a special relationship between the payer and the beneficial owner or between both of them and some other person, the amount of the interest paid exceeds, for whatever reason, the amount which would have been agreed upon be the payer and the beneficial owner in the absence of such relationship, the provisions of11this Article shall apply only to the last-mentioned amount. In such case, the excess part of the payments shall remain taxable according to the law of each Contracting State, due regard being had to the other provisions of this Agreement.

Article 12 - Royalties

1. Royalties arising in a Contracting State which are derived by a resident of the other Contracting State may be taxed in that other State.
2. However, such royalties may also be taxed in the Contracting State in which they arise and according to the law of that State; but if the beneficial owner of the royalties is a resident of the other Contracting State the tax so charged shall not exceed:

   a) in the case of royalties referred to in sub-paragraph a) of paragraph 3) of this Article, 10 per cent of the gross amount of the royalties; and

b) in the case of royalties referred to in sub-paragraph (b) of paragraph (3) of this Article, 10 per cent of the adjusted amount of the royalties. For the purpose of this subparagraph "the adjusted amount" means 70 per cent of the gross amount of the royalties.

3. The term "royalties" as used in this Article comprises:

a) payments of any kind received as a consideration for the use of, or the right to use, any copyright of literary, artistic or scientific work, including cinematograph films, and films or tapes for radio or television broadcasting, or any patent, know-how, trade-mark, design or model, plan, secret formula or process; and
b) payments of any kind received as a consideration for the use of, or the right to use, any industrial, commercial or scientific equipment.

4. The provisions of paragraphs 1) and 2) of this Article shall not apply if the beneficial owner of the royalties, being a resident of a Contracting State, carries on business in the other Contracting State in which the royalties arise, through a permanent establishment situated therein, or performs in that other State independent personal services from a fixed base situated therein, and the right or property in respect of which the royalties are paid is effectively connected with such permanent establishment or fixed base. In such case, the provisions of Article 7 or Article 15, as the case may be, shall apply.
5. Royalties shall be deemed to arise in a Contracting State when the payer is the Government of that State or a political subdivision thereof or a local authority or a resident of that State. Where, however, the person paying the royalties, whether he is a resident of a Contracting State or not, has in a Contracting State a permanent establishment or a fixed base in connection with which the obligation to pay the royalties was incurred, and such royalties are borne by that permanent establishment or fixed base, then such royalties shall be deemed to arise in the State in which the permanent establishment or fixed base is situated.
6. Where, by reason of a special relationship between the payer and the beneficial owner or between both of them and some other person, the amount of the royalties paid exceeds, for whatever reason, the amount which would have been agreed upon by the payer and the beneficial owner in the absence of such relationship, the provisions of this Article shall apply only to the last-mentioned amount. In such case, the excess part of the payments shall remain taxable according to the law of each Contracting State, due regard being had to the other provisions of this Agreement

Article 13 - Technical Fees

1. Technical fees arising in a Contracting State which are derived by a resident of the other Contracting State may be taxed in that other State.
2. However, such technical fees may also be taxed in the Contracting State in which they arise, and according to the law of that State; but if the beneficial owner of the technical fees is a resident of the other Contracting State the tax so charged shall not exceed 10 per cent of the adjusted amount of the technical fees. For the purpose of this paragraph, "the adjusted amount" means 70 per cent of the gross amount of the technical fees.
3. The term "technical fees" as used in this Article means payments of any kind to any person in consideration for any services of a technical, supervisory or consultancy nature, including the use of, or the right to use, information concerning industrial, commercial or scientific experience, but it does not include payments made to an employee of the person making the payments for dependent personal services mentioned in Article 16.
4. The provisions of paragraphs 1) and 2) of this Article shall not apply if the beneficial owner of the technical fees, being a resident of a Contracting State, carries on business in the other Contracting State in which the technical fees arise, through a permanent establishment situated therein, or performs in that other State independent personal

services from a fixed base situated therein, and the technical fees are effectively connected with such permanent establishment or fixed base. In such case, the provisions of Article 7 or Article 15, as the case may be, shall apply.

5. Technical fees shall be deemed to arise in a Contracting State when the payer is the Government of that State or a political subdivision thereof or a local authority or a resident of that State. Where, however, the person paying the technical fees, whether he is a resident of a Contracting State or not, has in a Contracting State a permanent establishment or a fixed base in connection with which the obligation to pay the technical fees was incurred, and such technical fees are borne by that permanent establishment or fixed base, then such technical fees shall be deemed to arise in the State in which the permanent establishment or fixed base is situated.
6. Where, by reason of a special relationship between the payer and the beneficial owner or between both of them and some other person, the amount of the technical fees paid exceeds, for whatever reason, the amount which would have been agreed upon by the payer and the beneficial owner in the absence of such relationship, the provisions of this Article shall apply only to the last-mentioned amount. In such case, the excess part of the payments shall remain taxable according to the law of each Contracting State, due regard being had to the other provisions of this Agreement.

Article 14 - Capital Gains

1. Subject to the provisions of paragraph 2) of this Article, capital gains which arise in a Contracting State may be taxed by that State in accordance with the provisions of its domestic law.
2. Gains from the alienation of ships or aircraft operated in international traffic and any property, other than immovable property, pertaining to the operation of such ships or aircraft shall be taxable only in the Contracting State in which the place of effective management of the business of the enterprise is situated.

Article 15 - Independent Personal Services

1. Subject to the provisions of Article 13, income derived by a resident of a Contracting State in respect of professional services or other activities of independent character shall be taxable only in that State except in the following circumstances, when such income may also be taxed in the other Contracting State:

   a) if he has a fixed base regularly available to him in the other Contracting State for the purpose of performing his activities; in that case so much of the income as is attributable to that fixed base may be taxed in that other State; or
   b) if his stay in the other Contracting State is for a period or periods amounting to or exceeding in the aggregate 183 days in the fiscal year concerned; in that case so much of the income as is derived from his activities performed in that other State may be taxed in that other State.

2. The term "professional services" includes especially independent scientific, literary, artistic, educational or teaching activities as well as the independent activities of physicians, lawyers, engineers, architects, dentists and accountants.

Article 16 - Dependent Personal Services

1. Subject to the provisions of Articles 17, 19, 20, 21 and 22 salaries, wages and other similar remuneration derived by a resident of a Contracting State in respect of an employment shall be taxable only in that State unless the employment is exercised in the other Contracting State. If the employment is so exercised, such remuneration as is derived therefrom may be taxed in that other State.
2. Notwithstanding the provisions of paragraph 1) of this Article, remuneration derived by a resident of a Contracting State in respect of an employment exercised in the other Contracting State shall be taxable only in the first-mentioned State if:

a) the recipient is present in the other State for a period or periods not exceeding in the aggregate 183 days in the fiscal year concerned; and
b) the remuneration is paid by, or on behalf of, an employer who is not a resident of the other State; and
c) the remuneration is not borne by a permanent establishment or a fixed base which the employer has in the other State.

3. Notwithstanding the provisions of paragraphs 1) and 2) of this Article, remuneration derived in respect of an employment exercised aboard a ship or aircraft operated in international traffic may be taxed in the Contracting State in which the place of effective management of the business of the enterprise is situated.
4. Notwithstanding the provisions of paragraphs 1) and 2) of this Article, salaries, wages and other remuneration earned by a national of a Contracting State in respect of services rendered to an enterprise of that Contracting State engaged in the operation of aircraft in international traffic as an officer or employee posted to the other Contracting State shall be taxable only in the first-mentioned Contracting State.

Article 17 - Directors' Fees

Directors' fees and other similar payments derived by a resident of a Contracting State in his capacity as a member of the board of directors of a company which is a resident of the other Contracting State may be taxed in that other State.

Article 18 - Entertainer And Athletes

1. Notwithstanding the provisions of Articles 15 and 16, income derived by a resident of a Contracting State as an entertainer, such as a theatre, motion picture, radio or television artiste, or a musician, or as an athlete, from his personal activities as such exercised in the other Contracting State, may be taxed in that other State.
2. Where income in respect of personal activities exercised by an entertainer or an athlete in his capacity as such accrues not to the entertainer or athlete himself but to another person, that income may, notwithstanding the provisions of Articles 7, 15 and16, be taxed in the Contracting State in which the activities of the entertainer or athlete are exercised.
3. Notwithstanding the provisions of paragraphs 1) and 2) of this Article, income derived from such activities as are referred to in paragraph 1) performed under a cultural agreement or arrangement between the Contracting States shall be exempt from tax in the Contracting State in which the activities are exercised if the visit to that State is wholly or substantially supported by public or government funds of either Contracting State.

Article 19 - Pensions

Subject to the provisions of paragraph 2) of Article 20, pensions and other similar remuneration paid to a resident of a Contracting State in consideration of past employment shall be taxable only in that State.

Article 20 - Government Service

1.

a) Remuneration, other than a pension, paid by the Government of a Contracting State or by a political subdivision or a local authority thereof to an individual in respect of services rendered to the Government of that State or subdivision or local authority shall be taxable only in that State.

b) However, such remuneration shall be taxable only in the other Contracting State if the services are rendered in that other State and the individual is a resident of that State who:

   i) is a national of that State; or
   ii) did not become a resident of that State solely for the purpose of performing the services.

2.

   a) Any pension paid by, or out of funds created by, the Government of a Contracting State or a political subdivision or a local authority thereof to an individual in respect of services rendered to the Government of that State or subdivision or authority shall be taxable only in that State.
   b) However, such pension shall be taxable only in the other Contracting State if the individual is a resident of, and a national of, that State.

3. The provisions of Articles 16, 17, 18 and 19 shall apply to remuneration and pensions in respect of services rendered in connection with a business carried on by a Contracting State or a political subdivision or a local authority thereof.

Article 21 - Teachers And Researchers

An individual who, immediately before visiting a Contracting State, was a resident of the other Contracting State and who is present in the first-mentioned State for a period not exceeding three years for the purpose of teaching, giving lectures or conducting research at a university, college, school or other recognized educational or scientific research institution in the first-mentioned State shall be exempt from tax in the first-mentioned State for a period not exceeding three years from the date of his first arrival in that State in respect of remuneration from such teaching, lectures or research.

Article 22 - Students, Apprentices And Trainees

1. A student, business apprentice or trainee who is or was immediately before visiting a Contracting State a resident of the other Contracting State and who is present in the first-mentioned State solely for the purpose of his education or training shall be exempt from tax in that State on:

   i) all remittances made from abroad for the purpose of his maintenance, education or training;
   ii) all scholarships, grants, allowances and awards from governmental, charitable, scientific, literary or educational organizations for the purposes of his maintenance, education or training; and
   iii) income from personal services performed in that Contracting State (other than any rendered by a business apprentice to the person or partnership to whom he is apprenticed, or, in the case of a trainee, other than services rendered to the person providing the training) in an amount not in excess of one thousand pounds sterling, or its equivalent in Chinese Yuan, for any year of assessment.

2. The exemptions under paragraph 1) of this Article shall only continue for such period of time as may reasonably or customarily be required to complete the education or training undertaken but in no event shall any individual have the benefit of paragraph 2) of this Article for more than 5 years from the commencement of such education or training.

Article 23 - Methods For Elimination Of Double Taxation

1. In China double taxation shall be eliminated as follows:

   a) Where a resident of China derives profits, income or capital gains from the United Kingdom, the amount of the United Kingdom tax payable in respect of such profits, income or capital gains in accordance with the provisions of this Agreement shall be allowed as a credit against the Chinese tax imposed on that resident. The amount of credit, however, shall not exceed the amount of the Chinese tax computed with respect to such profits, income or capital gains in accordance with the tax laws and regulations of China.
   b) Where the income derived from the United Kingdom is a dividend paid by a company which is a resident of the United Kingdom to a company which is a resident of China and which owns more than 10 per cent of the shares of the company paying the dividend, the credit shall take into account the United Kingdom tax payable by the company paying the dividend in respect of its income.

2. Subject to the provisions of the law of the United Kingdom regarding the allowance as a credit against United Kingdom tax of tax payable in a territory outside the United Kingdom (which shall not affect the general principle hereof):

   a) Chinese tax payable under the law of China and in accordance with this Agreement whether directly or by deduction, on profits, income or capital gains from sources within China (excluding, in the case of a dividend, tax payable in respect of the profits out of which the dividend is paid) shall be allowed as a credit against any United Kingdom tax computed by reference to the same profits, income or capital gains by reference to which the Chinese tax is computed:
   b) in the case of a dividend paid by a company which is a resident of China to a company which is a resident of the United Kingdom and which controls directly or indirectly at least 10 per cent of the voting power in the company paying the dividend, the credit shall take into account (in addition to any Chinese tax for which credit may be allowed under the provisions of sub-paragraph a) of this paragraph) the Chinese tax payable by the company in respect of the profits out of which such dividend is paid.

3. For the purpose of paragraph 2) of this Article, the term "Chinese tax payable" shall be deemed to include any amount which would have been payable as Chinese tax for any year but for an exemption from, or reduction of, tax granted for that year or any part thereof under any of the following provisions of Chinese law:

   a) i) Articles 5 and 6 of the Income Tax Law of the People's Republic of China Concerning Joint Ventures with Chinese and Foreign Investment and Article 3 of the Detailed Rules and Regulations for the Implementation of the Income Tax Law of the People's Republic of China Concerning Joint Ventures with Chinese and Foreign Investment;
      ii) Articles 4 and 5 of the Income Tax Law of the People's Republic of China Concerning Foreign Enterprises; so far as they were in force on, and have not been modified since, the date of signature of this Agreement, or have been modified only in minor respects so as not to affect their general character; or

   b) any other provision which may subsequently be made granting an exemption from or reduction of tax which is agreed by the competent authorities of the Contracting States to be of a substantially similar character, if it has not been modified thereafter or has been modified only in minor respects so as not to affect its general character.

Provided that relief from United Kingdom tax shall not be given by virtue of this paragraph in respect of income from any source if the income arises in a period starting more than ten years after the exemption from, or reduction of, Chinese tax was first granted in respect of that source.

4. For the purposes of paragraphs 1) and 2) of this Article profits, income and capital gains owned by a resident of a Contracting State which may be taxed in the other Contracting State in accordance with this Agreement shall be deemed to arise from sources in that other Contracting State.
5. Where profits on which an enterprise of a Contracting State has been charged to tax in that State are also included in the profits of an enterprise of the other State and the profits so included are profits which would have accrued to that enterprise of the other State if the conditions made between the enterprises had been those which would have been made between independent enterprises dealing at arm's length, the amount included in the profits of both enterprises shall be treated for the purposes of this Article as income from a source in the other State of the enterprise of the first-mentioned State and relief shall be given accordingly under the provisions of paragraph 1) or paragraph 2) of this Article.

Article 24 - Non-Discrimination

1. Nationals of a Contracting State shall not be subjected in the other Contracting State to any taxation or any requirement connected therewith which is other or more burdensome than the taxation and connected requirements to which nationals of that other State in the same circumstances are or may be subjected.
2. The taxation on a permanent establishment which an enterprise of a Contracting State has in the other Contracting State shall not be less favorably levied in that other State than the taxation levied on enterprises of that other State carrying on the same activities.
3. Enterprises of a Contracting State, the capital of which is wholly or partly owned or controlled, directly or indirectly, by one or more residents of the other Contracting State, shall not be subjected in the first-mentioned State to any taxation or any requirement connected therewith which is other or more burdensome than the taxation and connected requirements to which other similar enterprises of that first-mentioned State are or may be subjected.
4. Except where the provisions of Article 9, paragraph 7) of Article 11, paragraph6) of Article 12 or paragraph 6) of Article 13 apply, interest, royalties, technical fees and other disbursements paid by an enterprise of a Contracting State to a resident of the other Contracting State shall, for the purpose of determining the taxable profits of such enterprise, be deductible under the same conditions as if they had been paid to a resident of the first-mentioned State.
5. Nothing contained in this Article shall be construed as obliging either Contracting State to grant to individuals not resident in that State any of the personal allowances, reliefs and reductions for tax purposes which are granted to individuals so resident.

Article 25 - Mutual Agreement Procedure

1. Where a resident of a Contracting State considers that the actions of one or both of the Contracting States result or will result for him in taxation not in accordance with the provisions of this Agreement, he may, irrespective of the remedies provided by the domestic laws of those States, present his case to the competent authority of the Contracting State of which he is a resident.
2. The competent authority shall endeavor, if the objection appears to it to be justified and if it is not itself able to arrive at a satisfactory solution, to resolve the case by mutual agreement with the competent authority of the other Contracting State, with a view to the avoidance of taxation which is not in accordance with this Agreement.
3. The competent authorities of the Contracting States shall endeavor to resolve by mutual agreement any difficulties or doubts arising as to the interpretation or application of this Agreement.

4. The competent authorities of the Contracting States may communicate with each other directly for the purpose of reaching an agreement in the sense of paragraphs 2) and 3) of this Article.

Article 26 - Exchange Of Information

1. The competent authorities of the Contracting States shall exchange such information as is necessary for carrying out the provisions of this Agreement or of the domestic laws of the Contracting States concerning taxes covered by this Agreement insofar as the taxation thereunder is not contrary to the provisions of this Agreement, in particular for the prevention of fraud or fiscal evasion. The exchange of information shall not be restricted by Article 1. Any information so exchanged shall be treated as secret and shall be disclosed only to persons or authorities (including courts and administrative bodies) involved in the assessment or collection of, the enforcement or prosecution in respect of, or the determination of appeals in relation to, the taxes covered by the Agreement. Such persons or authorities shall use the information only for such purposes. They may disclose the information in public court proceedings or in judicial decisions.
2. In no case shall the provisions of paragraph 1) of this Article be construed so as to impose on the competent authority of either Contracting State the obligation:

   a) to carry out administrative measures at variance with the law and administrative practice prevailing in either Contracting State;
   b) to supply information which is not obtainable under the law or in the normal course of the administration of either Contracting State; or
   c) to supply information which would disclose any trade, business, industrial, commercial or professional secret or trade process, or information the disclosure of which would be contrary to public policy.

Article 27 - Diplomatic Agents And Consular Officials

1. Nothing in this Agreement shall affect the fiscal privileges of members of diplomatic or permanent missions or consular posts under the general rules of international law or under the provisions of special agreements.
2. Notwithstanding the provisions of paragraph 1) of Article 4, an individual who is a member of the diplomatic or permanent mission or consular post of a Contracting State or any third State which is situated in the other Contracting State and who is subject to tax in that other State only if he derives income from sources therein, shall not be deemed to be a resident of that other State.

Article 28 - Existing Agreement

Nothing in this Agreement shall affect the provisions of the Agreement between the Government of the United Kingdom of Great Britain and Northern Ireland and the Government of the People's Republic of China for the Reciprocal Avoidance of Double Taxation on Revenues arising from the Business of Air Transport, signed at Beijing on 10 March 1981, to the extent that they have effect as regards taxes to which this Agreement applies. However, where any greater relief for such taxes is afforded by any provision of this Agreement, that provision shall apply.

Article 29 - Entry Into Force

Each of the Contracting States shall notify to the other the completion of the procedures required by its law for the bringing into force of this Agreement. The Agreement shall enter into force on the thirtieth day following the date of the later of these notifications and shall thereupon have effect:

a) in China, in respect of profits, income and capital gains arising in any tax year beginning on or after the first day of January in the calendar year next following that in which this Agreement enters into force;

b) in the United Kingdom:

   i) in respect of income tax and capital gains tax, for any year of assessment beginning on or after 6 April in the calendar year next following that in which this Agreement enters into force;
   ii) in respect of corporation tax, for any financial year beginning on or after 1 April in the calendar year next following that in which this Agreement enters into force.

Article 30 - Termination

This Agreement shall continue in effect indefinitely but either of the Contracting States may, on or before the thirtieth day of June in any calendar year beginning after the expiration of a period of five years from the date of its entry into force, give to the other Contracting State, through the diplomatic channel, written notice of termination.

In such event this Agreement shall cease to have effect:

a) in China, as regards profits, income and capital gains derived during the tax year beginning on or after 1 January in the calendar year next following that in which the notice is given;
b) in the United Kingdom:

   i) in respect of income tax and capital gains tax, for any year of assessment beginning on or after 6 April in the calendar year next following that in which the notice is given;
   ii) in respect of corporation tax, for any financial year beginning on or after 1 April in the calendar year next following that in which the notice is given.

IN WITNESS WHEREOF the undersigned, duly authorized thereto by their respective Governments, have signed this Agreement. DONE in duplicate at Beijing this 26th day of July 1984 in the Chinese and English languages, both texts being equally authoritative.

Bibliography

Adams C, Park D (2009) Causes and consequences of global imbalances: perspective from developing Asia. ADB Economics Working Paper Series No. 157

Adams C, Jeong HY, Park C-Y (2010) Asia's contribution to global rebalancing. Asian Development Bank Working Papers on Regional Economic Integration Series, No. 58, September

ADB (2009) Enhancing ADB's response to the global economic crisis: establishing the counter-cyclical support facility. ADB Policy Paper, May

ADB (Asian Development Bank) (2007) Asian Development Outlook 2007: growth amid change. Asian Development Bank, Manila

ADBI Working Paper 343 China

Ahearne AG, Fernald JG, Loungani P, Schindler JW (2006) Flying geese or sitting ducks: China's impact on the trading fortunes of other Asian economies. Board of Governors of the Federal Reserve System International Finance Discussion Papers No. 887

Alesina A, Barro RJ (2002) Currency unions. Q J Econ 117(2):409–436

Arner D, Schou-Zibell L (2010) Responding to the global financial and economic crisis: meeting the challenges in Asia. Asian Development Bank Working Papers on Regional Economic Integration Series No. 60, October

Ashvin A, Lillian C, Han G, Nathan P, Zhang W (2010) Are housing prices rising too fast in China. IMF Working Paper

Asian Development Bank (ADB) (2005) Central Asia in 2015. CAREC Policy Brief No.1. http://www.adb.org/Carec/Policy-Briefs/CAREC-Policy-Brief-01-2005.pdf

Athukorala P (2008) China's integration into global production networks and its implications for export-led growth strategy in other countries in the region. Australian National University, Arndt-Corden Department of Economics Working Papers in Trade and Development No. 2008/04

Athukorala P (2010) Production networks and trade patterns in east Asia: regionalization or globalization? ADB Working Paper Series on Regional Economic Integration No. 56

Athukorala P, Yamashita N (2009) Global production sharing and Sino–US trade relations. China World Econ 17(3):39–56

Baidu B (2011) The U.S. subprime mortgage crisis. http://baike.baidu.com/view/1092871.htm. Accessed 19 Apr 2011

Baldwin RE (2008) The East Asian Noodle Bowl Syndrome. In: Hiratsuka D, Kimura F (eds) East Asia's economic integration: progress and benefit, IDE-JETRO Series. Palgrave Macmillan, Basingstoke, pp 45–81

Barro RJ, Lee J-W (2009) East Asian Currency Union. Paper presented at the Hong Kong Institute for Monetary Research and Asian Development Bank Workshop 'Quantifying the Costs and Benefits of Regional Economic Integration in Asia', Hong Kong, 19–20 January

L. Riccardi, *Chinese Tax Law and International Treaties*,
DOI 10.1007/978-3-319-00275-0,

Bery S (2010) Does Asia have common interests in global monetary system reforms? East Asia Q. October–December:38–39

Bhattacharyay B (2010) Institutions for Asian connectivity. ADBI Working Paper No. 220. Asian Development Bank Institute, Tokyo. http://www.adbi.org/working-paper/2010/06/25/3915.institutions.asian.connectivity/

BIMSTEC (2011) http://www.bimstec.org/about_bimstec.html. Accessed 24 Jan 2011

Bowles P (2002) Asia's post-crisis regionalism: bringing the state back in, keeping the (United) States out. Rev Int Polit Econ 9(2):230–256

Brazilian-Chinese Foreign Relations. Ministry of Foreign Relations. N.p., n.d. Web. http://www.itamaraty.gov.br/ingles

British Foreign & Commonwealth Office (FCO) Home. N.p., n.d. Web. http://www.fco.gov.uk/en/

Calder K, Min Y (2004) Regionalism and critical junctures: explaining the 'organization gap' in northeast Asia. J East Asian Stud (Spring):191–226

Cao F (2011) Corporate income tax law and practice in the People's Republic of China. Oxford University Press, Oxford

Capannelli G (2011) Institutions for economic and financial integration in Asia: trends and prospects. ADBI Working Paper No. 308. Asian Development Bank Institute, Tokyo

Capannelli G, Li J-W, Petri P (2009) Developing indicators for regional economic integration and cooperation. ADB Working Paper Series on Regional Economic Integration, No. 33, Manila

Central Bank of China (2011) The change of interest rate. Referenced 20 Apr 2011

Chen X (2006) The study of sustainable development of real estate market, 1st edn. Shanghai Tongji University Press, Shanghai

Chin G (2010) Remaking the architecture: the emerging powers, self-insuring and regional insulation. Int Aff 86(3):693–715

Chin G (2011) Mediating financial instability: China, the BRICs and continuing rise. In: Savona P, Kirton J, Oldani C (eds) Global financial crisis: global impact and solutions. Ashgate, Aldershot

Chin G, Helleiner E (2008) China as a creditor: rising financial power? J Int Aff 62(1):87–102

Chin G, Stubbs R (2011) China, regional institution-building, and the China-ASEAN free trade area. Rev Int Polit Econ 18(3):277–298

Chin G, Thakur R (2010) Will China change the rules of global order? Wash Q 33(2):125–127

Chin G, Wang Y (2010) Debating the international currency system: what's in a speech? China Secur 6(1):3–20

Taxation in modern China (2008) Routledge, New York

China Diplomatic Relations. Government of Canada. N.p., n.d. Web. http://www.canadainternational.gc.ca/china-chine/bilateral_relations_bilaterales/diplomatic_relations_diplomatiques.aspx?lang=eng

China Master Tax Guide (2011/2012) CCH Hong Kong, Hong Kong

China. Council on Foreign Relations. N.p., n.d. Web. http://www.cfr.org/china/us-relations-china-1949—present/p17698

Frontline Research on Chinese Tax Policy (2009) Zhong Guo Shui Wu Chu Ban She, Beijing

Ching MK (2009) CFO guide to doing business in China. Wiley, Singapore

Chu DL (2011) What if the China bubble bursts: China national wide property value/annual disposal income per urban household. http://www.marketoracle.co.uk/Article26687.html. Accessed 24 Apr 2011

Colorado State University (2011) The definition of validity and reliability. Referenced 20 Apr 2011

Cooper A, Subacchi P (2010) Overview: global economic governance in transition. Int Aff 86(3):607–618

Dent CM (2008) China, Japan and regional leadership in East Asia. Edward Elgar, Cheltenham

Devonshire-Ellis C, Scott A, Woollard S (2011) The China tax guide. Springer, Heidelberg

Drysdale P (2007) Deepening Asian integration and regional cooperation arrangements. Paper prepared for the study Emerging Asian Regionalism, Asian Development Bank

Drysdale P (2010) Asia's global responsibilities. East Asia Forum Q. October–December:26–28
Drysdale P, Armstrong S (2010) International and regional cooperation: Asia's role and responsibilities. Asian Econ Policy Rev 5(2):157–173
Fan G, Wang B, Huang Y (2010) Intraregional cross-holding of reserve currencies: a proposal for Asia to deal with the global reserve risks. Paper presented at the China Center for International Economic Exchanges (CCIEE) and Asian Development Bank Institute (ADBI) Conference 'Diversification of Reserve Currencies and Development of Regional Financial Markets in Asia', Beijing, 26 November
Finance and Taxation Law of the People's Republic of China (2011) Zhongguo Fa Zhi Chu Ban She, Beijing
China Tax and Financial Planning Briefing (2007) World Trade Executive, Concord
Foundation of China's Extraordinary Rise (2012) Wiley, Singapore
Franceâs Foreign Policy. French Diplomatie. N.p., n.d. Web. http://www.diplomatie.gouv.fr/en/france/france-in-the-world/france-s-foreign-policy/article/12588
Fulton T, Li J, Xu D (2010) China's tax reform options. World Scientific, Singapore
G20 Working Group 4 (2009) Final report: the world bank and other multilateral development banks
Gao X (2009) The foreign capital in Beijing real estate market. http://house.focus.cn/news/2009-03-10/92889.html. Accessed 20 Apr 2011
Garnaut R (2007) Making the international system work for the platinum age. Paper presented at 'World Economic Performance: Past, Present and Future – Long Term Performance and Prospects of Australia and Major Asian Economies' Seminar on the occasion of Angus Maddison's 80th birthday, University of Queensland, Brisbane, 5–6 December
Gensler H (2011) China tax & accounting manual. Asia Law & Practice, Hong Kong
Guangdong Statistical Yearbook (2008) Per capita disposable income of urban households (1978–2007). http://www.newsgd.com/specials/30yearsreform/data/content/2008-11/27/content_4735267.htm. Accessed 23 Apr 2011
Guo R (2012) Understanding the Chinese economies. Academic, Oxford
Hamanaka S (2010) Institutional parameters of a region-wide economic agreement in Asia: examination of trans-pacific partnership and ASEAN+ FTA Approaches. ADB Working Paper Series on Regional Economic Integration No. 67
Han S (2010) Value added tax (VAT) in China in the process of reform. Zhongguo Shui Wu Chu Ban She, Beijing
Hauptinhalt. Federal Foreign Office. N.p., n.d. Web. http://www.auswaertiges-amt.de/EN/Startseite_node.html
Helleiner E (2010) A Bretton Woods moment? The 2007-2008 crisis and the future of global finance. Int Aff 86(3):619–636
Henning R (2002) East Asian financial cooperation. Institute for International Economics, Washington
Henning CR (2011) Economic crises and institutions for regional economic cooperation. ADB Working Paper Series on Regional Economic Integration No. 81
Hu J (2009) China to further assist developing countries. Speech cited in China Daily, 24 September. http://www.chinadaily.com.cn/china/2009-09/24/content_8730395.htm
Hu R (2011) Hu Run Fortune Report in 2011. http://www.hurun.net/zhcn/NewsShow.aspx?nid=87. Accessed 22 Apr 2011
Hu J, Liangjun S, Sainan J, Wanjun J (2006) The rise in housing prices in China: bubbles or fundamentals? Econ Bull 3(7):1–8
Huang Y, Wang B (2011) Chinese outward direct investment: is there a China model? China World Econ 19(4):1–21 (Special Issue: China's Outward Direct Investment)
Pocket World in Figures 2012 (2011) Economist, London
Indian Foreign Policy and China. Institute for defence studies and analyses. http://www.idsa.in/strategicanalysis/IndianForeignPolicyandChina_hvpant_1006

Institutions for Asian Regional Integration: toward an Asian economic community. Asian Development Bank, Manila

International Bureau of Fiscal Documentation. N.p., n.d. Web. http://www.ibfd.org/

Ito T (2010) China as number one: how about the Renminbi? Asian Econ Policy Rev 5(2):249–276

Ji B (2010) The living situation of low-income people in America. Referenced 19 Apr 2011

Kawai M (2007) Emerging Asian regionalism: ten years after the crisis. Paper presented at the ADB–Thai Development Research Institute–Thai Ministry of Finance Joint Conference 'Integrating Asian Economies: Ten Years after the Crisis', Bangkok, 18 July

Kawai M, Wignaraja G (2011) Asian FTAs: trends, prospects and challenges. J Asian Econ 22 (1):1–22

Kreiser LA (2011) Environmental taxation in China and Asia-Pacific: achieving environmental sustainability through fiscal policy. Edward Elgar, Cheltenham

Krugman P (1994) The myth of Asia's miracle. Foreign Affairs 73(6):62–78

Kuroda H. and M. Kawai. 2002. Strengthening Regional Financial Cooperation in East Asia. Asia Pacific Economic Papers No. 332. Canberra, Australia: Australia-Japan Research Center, Australia National University. http://www.crawford.anu.edu.au/pdf/pep/pep-332.pdf

Lang X (2011) Real estate and China's economy. http://www.chinanews.com/estate/2011/03-27/3071993.shtml. Accessed 16 Apr 2011

Lang M, Liu J, Tang G (2010) European-Chinese tax treaties. Kluwer Law International, Alphen Aan Den Rijn

Li C (2009) China's new think tanks: where officials, entrepreneurs and scholars interact. China Leadership Monitor, Number 29

Li LC (2012) Rural tax reform in China: policy process and institutional change. Routledge, Milton Park

Li J, Paisey A (2007) Transfer pricing audits in China. Palgrave Macmillan, Basingstoke

Lie M (2011) Land price causes the high housing prices. http://365jia.cn/news/2011-03-26/454EB2F034BD5728.html. Accessed 26 Apr 2011

Lin RB, Wu JL (2009) Chin Tax. Shanghai: n.p.

Liu Z (2010) Taxation in China. Thomson Learning, Singapore

BIMSTEC Transport Infrastructure and Logistic Study (2008) ADB Technical Assistance Report, Project Number 38396. August 2008. Technical Assistance Completion Report, BIMSTEC Transport Infrastructure and Logistic Study, Project Number TA-6635 REG. http://www.adb.org/Documents/TACRs/REG/38396-01-reg-tcr.pdf

Lu G (2010) Achievements and challenges: 30 years of housing reforms in the People's Republic of China. Asian Development Bank

MacIntyre A, Pempel TJ, Ravenhill J (2008) Crisis as catalyst: Asia's dynamic political economy. Cornell University Press, Ithaca

Maddison A (2006) Asia in the world economy 1500–2030 AD. Asia Pac Econ Lit 20(2):1–37

Mark S, Philip L, Adrian T (2007) Research methods for business students, 4th edn. Pearson Education, England

McKibbin WJ, Chanthapun WP (2009) Exchange rate regimes in the Asia-Pacific region and the global financial crisis. ADB Working Paper Series on Regional Economic Integration No. 36

Ministry of foreign affairs of the People's Republic of China. N.p., n.d. Web. http://www.fmprc.gov.cn/eng/

Ministry of Foreign Affairs, Government of Japan (2006) Report of the India–Japan Joint Study Group. http://www.mofa.go.jp/region/asia-paci/india/report0606.pdf

Moser MJ, Zee WK (2011) Chinese tax guide. Oxford University Press, Oxford

National Bureau of Statistics of China (2010) Chinese real estate market in China in 2010. Referenced 26 Apr 2011

Nouel L (2011) OECD model tax convention on income and on capital: condensed version 2010; and key tax features of member countries 2011. IBFD, Amsterdam

Obama B (2010) Quoted in Obama Warns Nations Not to Rely on Exports to US. BBC News (Asia-Pacific). 13 November. http://www.bbc.co.uk/news/world-asia-pacific-11748433#story_continues_1

Ogawa E, Shimizu J (2005) A deviation measurement for coordinated exchange rate policies in East Asia. Research Institute of Economy, Trade & Industry, RIETI Discussion Paper No. 05-E-017

Ogawa E, Shimizu J (2006) AMU deviation indicator for coordinated exchange rate policies in East Asia and its relation with effective exchange rates. Research Institute of Economy, Trade & Industry, RIETI Discussion Paper No. 06-E-002

Park D, Estrada GB (2009) Developing Asia's sovereign wealth funds and outward foreign direct investment. ADB Economics Working Paper Series No. 169

Park D, Shin K (2009) Can trade with the People's Republic of China be an engine of growth for developing Asia? ADB Economics Working Paper Series No. 172

Park D, Shin K (2010) Can trade with the People's Republic of China be an engine of growth for developing Asia? Asian Dev Rev 27(1):160–181

Pervez G, Kjell G (2010) Research methods for business students, 4th edn. Pearson Education, England

Qu A (2008) The current situation of Chinese real estate market. http://house.focus.cn/newshtml/513460.html. Accessed 24 Apr 2011

Raj J, Dhal S (2008) Integration of India's stock market with global and major regional markets. BIS Paper No. 42

Rajamohan PG, Rahut DB, Jacob JT (2008) Changing paradigms of Indo-Japan relations: opportunities and challenges. ICRIER Working Paper No. 212

Rathus J (2009) The Chiang Mai initiative: China, Japan and Financial Regionalism. East Asia Forum. http://www.eastasiaforum.org/2009/05/11/the-chiang-mai-initiative-china-japan-and-financial-regionalism/

Ravenhill J (2001) APEC and the construction of Pacific rim regionalism. Cambridge University Press, Cambridge

Ravenhill J (2010) The "New East Asian Regionalism": a political domino effect. Rev Int Polit Econ 17(2):178–208

Sandler T (2010) Overcoming global and regional collective action impediments. Glob Policy 1 (1):40–50

Sharkey NC (2012) Taxation in ASEAN and China: local institutions, regionalism, global systems and economic development. Routledge, London

Sheng A (2010) The regulatory reform of global financial markets: an Asian regulator's perspective. Glob Policy 1(2):191–200

Singh M (2008) Cited in Indian PM confident of bigger roles India, China to play in world affairs. People's Daily. 15 January. http://english.people.com.cn/90001/90776/90883/6338755.html

Sinha C, Pradhan NC (2008) India's financial openness and integration with southeast Asian countries: an analytical perspective. BIS Paper No. 42

Song D (2010) The influence of interest rate to the real estate market. http://club.topsage.com/thread-1241238-1-1.html. Accessed 17 Apr 2011

Soo M-J (2010) Asia-Pacific tax and business fundamentals 2010. IBFD, Amsterdam

Summers L (2009) Quoted in lunch with the FT: larry summers. Financial Times. 9 July. http://www.ft.com/intl/cms/s/2/6ac06592-6ce0-11de-af56-00144feabdc0.html#axzz1fgAnKeEZ

Sutter RG (2012) Chinese foreign relations: power and policy since the cold war. Rowman & Littlefield, Lanham

Tax Planning for Expatriates in China (2010) Kluwer Law International, The Hague

The CAREC Program—development through cooperation in Central Asia. http://beta.adb.org/countries/subregional-programs/carec

The Developing Trends of China's Real Estate Market. http://www.360doc.com/content/11/0120/10/1959469_87780628.shtml. Accessed 2 Apr 2011

The emerging countries and China in the G20: reshaping global economic governance. Studia Diplomatica LXIII(2–3):105–124

The European Council on Foreign Relations. The European Council on Foreign Relations. N.p., n.d. Web. http://www.ecfr.eu/

UNCTAD (United Nations Conference on Trade and Development) (2008) World Investment Report 2008: transnational corporations, and the infrastructure challenge. United Nations Publications, New York

Walter CE, Howie FJT (2012) Red capitalism: the fragile financial foundation of China's extraordinary rise. Wiley, Singapore

Wang Q (2002) The study of real estate market in China, 1st edn. Peking University Press, Beijing

Wang X (2007) China as a net creditor: an indication of strength or weakness. China World Econ 15(6):22–36

Wang S (2010) The development of Chinese real estate market in the rapid urbanization. http://wenku.baidu.com/view/33fe8895dd88d0d233d46a12.html. Accessed 22 Apr 2011

Wang T (2011) The evaluation to China's real estate bubble. http://cn.wsj.com/gb/20110323/COL102249.asp?source=renren. Accessed 2 Apr 2011

Wang S, Hu A (2001) The Chinese economy in crisis: state capacity and tax reform. M.E. Sharpe, Armonk

Wong C, Heady CJ, Woo WT (2011) Fiscal management and economic reform in the People's Republic of China. Published for the Asian Development Bank by Oxford University Press, Hong Kong

World Bank (1993) The East Asian miracle: economic growth and public policy. World Bank Policy Research Report. Oxford University Press, Inc, New York

World Trade Organization. N.p., n.d. Web. http://www.wto.org/

Xiao S (2010) Is there a bubble in China's housing market. http://www.kth.se/polopoly_fs/1.57364!31.pdf. Accessed 22 Apr 2011

Xinhua Net (2007) The rapid urbanization in China. http://news.xinhuanet.com/newscenter/2007-09/27/content_6798582.htm. Accessed 22 Apr 2011

Xinhua Net (2009) China's Central Bank Governor says IMF needs improvement. 18 April. http://news.xinhuanet.com/english/2009-04/18/content_11210468.htm

Yang H (2000) The real estate economics, 2nd edn. Northeast Forestry University Press, Dalian

Yu Y (2007) The Asian financial crisis and the rise of Asian regionalism. Paper presented at the Asian Development Bank Conference, Kyoto

Zhai F (2010) The benefits of regional infrastructure investment in Asia: a quantitative exploration. ADBI Working Paper No. 223. Asian Development Bank Institute, Tokyo

Zhang JQ (2010) Cost accounting practices. Zhong Guo Lao Dong She Hui Bao Zhang Chu Ban She, Beijing

Zhang W-W (2012) The China wave: rise of a civilizational state. World Century, Hackensack

Zhao X (2010) Monetary and currency cooperation across emerging asia. Speech in Kunming, People's Republic of China. 27 July. http://www.adb.org/Documents/Speeches/2010/ms2010066.asp

Zheng X (2011a) The risk management of loose bank credit policy in China. http://www.brjr.com.cn/archiver/tid-52940.html. Accessed 25 Apr 2011

Zheng X (2011b) The influence of land policy in China to housing prices, 1st edn. Southwestern University of Finance and Economics Press, Chengdu

Zhou X (2009) Reflections on reforming the international monetary system. Speech given on 23 March. http://www.pbc.gov.cn/detail.asp?col=4200&ID=279 (Chinese); http://www.pbc.gov.cn/english/detail.asp?col=6500&id=178 (English)

MIX
Papier aus verantwortungsvollen Quellen
Paper from responsible sources
FSC® C105338
www.fsc.org

If you have any concerns about our products,
you can contact us on
ProductSafety@springernature.com

In case Publisher is established outside the EU,
the EU authorized representative is:
Springer Nature Customer Service Center GmbH
Europaplatz 3, 69115 Heidelberg, Germany

Printed by Libri Plureos GmbH
in Hamburg, Germany